Off The Beaten Track
AUSTRIA

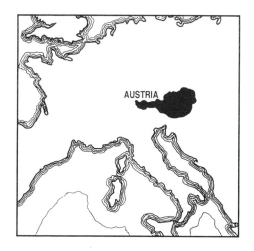

OFF
THE BEATEN TRACK
AUSTRIA

MPC

Published by:
Moorland Publishing Co Ltd,
Moor Farm Road,
Ashbourne,
Derbyshire
DE6 1HD
England

British Library Cataloguing in
Publication Data:
Austria. --- (Off the beaten track)
  1. Austria. - Visitor's guides
  I. Philpott, Don   II. Series
  914.36'0453

ISBN 0 86190 213 0 (paperback)
ISBN 0 86190 212 2 (hardback)

Colour origination by:
Scantrans, Singapore

Printed in the UK by:
Butler and Tanner Ltd, Frome,
Somerset

Cover photograph:
Town Hall, St Veit (*MPC Picture
Collection*).

Black and white illustrations have been
supplied as follows:

Austrian Tourist Board: pp 159, 235,
238, 239, 240, 245, 246, 254, 273, 275,
277, 281; MPC Picture Collection: pp
14, 17, 19, 20, 29, 30, 31, 32 (bottom), 34,
36, 42, 44, 45, 48, 58, 60, 61, 86, 95, 100,
104, 126, 129, 130, 132, 134, 136, 141,
143; D. Philpott: pp288, 295, 299, 301;
Photograph Mitteregger, Judenburg:
p167; A. Proctor: pp 10, 16, 23, 32 (top),
33, 35, 37, 38, 62, 63, 70, 71, 72, 73, 80,
81, 82, 83, 89, 111, 112, 117, 118, 119,
120, 128, 171, 173, 176; C. Speakman:
pp 190, 195, 197, 209; D. Speakman: pp
193, 199, 218; B. Spencer: pp 21, 47, 185.

Colour illustrations have been
supplied as follows:

MPC Picture Collection (*Zürs, Lech,
Leutasch valley, R. Isel, Kufstein, St
Johann, Jenbach, Pisweg, Maria Saal, St
Veit*); A. Proctor (*Rural chapel, Rog-
galspitze, Zug, Lachesee and Rote Spitze,
Coburger hut Ehrwald, Eng, St Peter am
Kamersberg*); D. Speakman (*Vorderer
Gosausee*); B. Spencer (*Brand, Klamm,
Seefelden Spitze, Neunerkopf Ridge,
Nesselwängle, Tauern valley*); P. Thorne
(*Waidhofen an der Ybbs*).

Acknowledgements

The authors and publishers wish to
acknowledge the assistance of the
Austrian Tourist Office and numerous
local and regional offices who
provided assistance. Patrick Thorne
would also like to thank Austrian
Airlines, Sally Brookes, Martha Wuitz,
Ingeborg Hirsh, Heinz Eppensteiner,
Helene Sengstbratl and family and the
many people in Austria who helped
with the research for his sections of the
book.

Contents

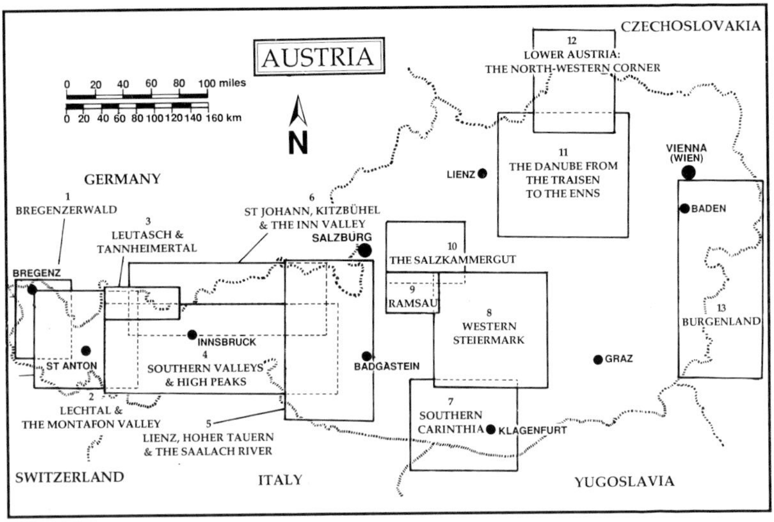
AUSTRIA
0 20 40 60 80 100 miles
0 20 40 60 80 100 120 140 160 km
N
CZECHOSLOVAKIA
12
LOWER AUSTRIA:
THE NORTH-WESTERN CORNER
GERMANY
1
BREGENZERWALD
3
LEUTASCH &
TANNHEIMERTAL
6
ST JOHANN, KITZBÜHEL
& THE INN VALLEY
SALZBURG
LIENZ
11
THE DANUBE FROM
THE TRAISEN
TO THE ENNS
VIENNA
(WIEN)
BADEN
10
THE SALZKAMMERGUT
9
RAMSAU
8
WESTERN
STEIERMARK
13
BURGENLAND
BREGENZ
INNSBRUCK
4
SOUTHERN VALLEYS
& HIGH PEAKS
ST ANTON
BADGASTEIN
GRAZ
2
LECHTAL &
THE MONTAFON VALLEY
5
LIENZ, HOHER TAUERN
& THE SAALACH RIVER
7
SOUTHERN
CARINTHIA
KLAGENFURT
SWITZERLAND
ITALY
YUGOSLAVIA

Note on Maps

The maps for each chapter, while comprehensive, are not designed to be used as route maps, but to locate the main towns, villages and places of interest.

Introduction

Western Europe is a continent of great diversity, well visited not just by travellers from other parts of the globe but by the inhabitants of its own member countries. Within the year-round processes of trade and commerce, but more particularly during the holiday season, there is a great surging interchange of nationalities as one country's familiar attractions are left behind for those of another.

It is true that frontiers are blurred by ever quicker travel and communications, and that the sharing of cultures, made possible by an increasingly sophisticated media network, brings us closer in all senses to our neighbours. Yet essential differences do exist, differences which lure us abroad on our annual migrations in search of new horizons, fresh sights, sounds and smells, discovery of unknown landscapes and people.

Countless resorts have evolved for those among us who simply crave sun, sea and the reassuring press of humanity. There are, too, established tourist 'sights' with which a country or region has become associated and to which clings, all too often, a suffocating shroud — the manifestations of mass tourism in the form of crowds and entrance charges, the destruction of authentic atmosphere, cynical exploitation. Whilst this is by no means typical of all well known tourist attractions, it is familiar enough to act as a disincentive for those of more independent spirit who value personal discovery above prescribed experience and who would rather avoid the human conveyor belt of queues, traffic jams and packed accommodation.

It is for such travellers that this guidebook has been written. In its pages, no more than passing mention is made of the famous, the well documented, the already glowingly described — other guidebooks will satisfy the appetite for such orthodox tourist information. Instead, the reader is taken if not to unknown then to relatively unvisited places — literally 'off the beaten track'. Through the specialist knowledge of the authors, visitors using this guidebook are assured of gaining insights into the country's heartland whose heritage lies largely untouched by the tourist industry. Occasionally the reader is urged simply to take a sideways step from a site of renowned tourist interest to discover a place perhaps less sensational, certainly less frequented but often of equivalent fascination.

From wild, scantily populated countryside whose footpaths and byways are best navigated by careful map reading, to negotiating the side streets of towns and cities, travelling 'off the beaten track' can be rather more demanding than following in the footsteps of countless thousands before you. The way may be less clear, more adventurous and individualistic, but opportunities do emerge for real discovery in an age of increasing dissatisfaction with the passive predictability of conventional holidaymaking. With greater emphasis on exploring 'off the beaten track', the essence of Austria is more likely to be unearthed and its true flavours relished to the full.

Martin Collins
Series Editor

1 • Bregenzerwald

B regenzerwald, the Bregenz Forest, is the northerly portion of Vorarlberg, Austria's most westerly and smallest province. It is part of that long narrow arm of Austria separating Germany, Switzerland and Italy. The Rhine is its only natural boundary and Bregenz, the major town in the sub-region, is on the shores of the Bodensee, or Lake Constance.

With the possible exception of Bregenz itself, only the southern part of the Vorarlberg is reasonably well known. Popular with skiers and mountaineers, the area is also visited, albeit fleetingly, by motorists travelling east to the Tyrol and other resorts farther east.

Bregenzerwald itself is often ignored simply because it does not have any mountains, or at least mountains which compete in height and grandeur with those of, say, the mighty Rhätikon and Silvretta ranges on the border between southern Vorarlberg and Italy, or the interesting limestone walls of Appenzell across the Rhine in eastern Switzerland. Bregenzerwald has few hills which can be termed peaks, if the normally accepted meaning is taken to be a sharp pointed craggy snow-covered mountain; certainly none of the hills can expect to have more than the odd tiny patch of permanent snow on their upper slopes in summer. But if the mountains of Bregenzerwald lack great height, they make up for it by their rolling tree-clad ridges guarding hidden valleys, where timber farmhouses on daintily flowered meadows are still owned by the descendants of the men and women who hacked clearings from the surrounding dense pine forests.

Folklore is not restricted to museums. The people of these valleys and mountain farms hold on to their traditional ways, incorporating and adapting them into modern use. A happy and hospitable people, the descendants of Alemannic tribes who settled in this area about the third century BC, they enjoy festivals and encourage visitors to take part in them. Coming from the same stock, they have an affinity with the people of eastern Switzerland and in 1919 the province

9

A typical Austrian old wooden farm with the traditional way of drying hay

began negotiations to become a semi-autonomous Swiss canton, or at least to exist independently like its neighbour Liechtenstein. However, the Peace Conference of St Germain after World War I decreed that Vorarlberg should remain part of Austria.

Colourful festivals and interesting customs are a major feature of this friendly region. Festivals come in varied forms; The annual Bregenz Music Festival is unique insofar as the stage, used by internationally famous orchestras and soloists, is on a beautifully flower bedecked raft moored on the Bodensee (Lake Constance)! Members of the audience sit on part of the attractive promenade lining the lakeshore. The best time to enjoy these concerts or light operas and ballets, is on a still evening when the setting sun silhouettes the floating stage and the distant view of the lake and Swiss mountains completes the magic of the setting. The festival is from mid-July to mid-August. In complete contrast, and on a different level not only geographically but in meaning, are the religious services held on the summits of mountains throughout the region. The one held on top of the Damülser Mittagspitze for example, is regularly attended by hundreds of worshippers. The local bishop in all his vestments conducts mass on the narrow summit of this steep-sided grassy mountain. Since mountains are windy places and bishops' robes are hardly the best clothing for mountaineering, visions of parachutes immediately spring to mind! There are no records of any bishop

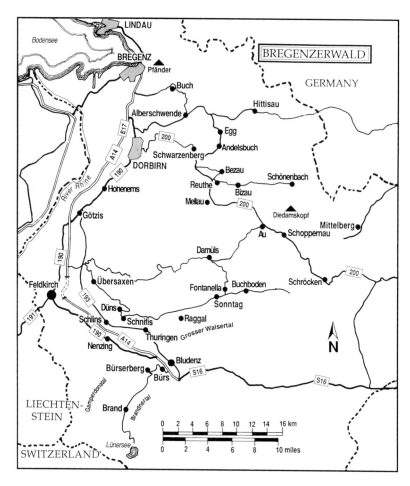

floating off into the sky, at least in post-biblical times, but his acolytes seem to spend most of the service holding on to him rather than helping to serve Mass!

The locals, both men and women, like to wear their regional version of Austrian national costume at any time, not only on official or festive occasions, but on birthdays, or simply for the fun of it. Austrian national dress has the advantage of being practical for everyday wear at the same time as being attractive. Although there are subtle regional styles (married women from the Bregenzerwald for instance, wear an elaborately folded scarf) most costumes are based on suede or waterproof loden cloth, spencer jackets for men and wide flounced skirts with embroidered bodices for women. During festivals many girls will be seen wearing small golden crowns. White is traditionally the colour of mourning.

The nearest motorists travelling into the Tyrol or points further east touch on Bregenzerwald, is if they enter Austria along the *autobahn* south from Germany and then travel eastwards across or under the Arlberg Pass. The main road into Austria from the west sweeps along the Rhine valley south from the Bodensee, then turns left at Feldkirch to reach the Arlberg. Bregenzerwald is the high land to the left of the road, but motorists intent on the delights further east will have only the slightest glimpse of this fascinating corner of a little known region. With the super efficiency of all modern roads, the *autobahn* bypasses all the Rhine valley towns and as a result there is only a hint of their attractions. Of Bregenz, the 'capital', only a backward glance will reveal part of the modern suburbs as the *autobahn* crosses the Bregenzer Ache, for the road tunnels deep beneath the Pfänder mountain at this point.

The only way to explore Bregenzerwald is to wander along its deep cut winding valleys through pine forests where sudden views of tiny farms and villages will reward the patience of a gentle exploratory drive. Sharp pointed as well as rounded peaks, buttressed by wandering grassy ridges, mark the skyline. This is not the country of the alpinist, but is still ideal country for hillwalkers who look for easier and lesser known summits.

The region is basically drained by one major river system, the Bregenzer. Its tributaries carve deep into the shaly mountains of the interior and have, along with the forest and the hand of man in building farmland, determined the geographical character of the Bregenzerwald. The remaining handful of west-flowing streams of the region, also draining into the Rhine, still retain the deeply cut almost 'V' shaped nature of their brethren. In the south, and marking the region's boundary, is the Grosser Walsertal, its river joining the valley used by the Arlberg section of the west-east trans-Austrian *autobahn*. Separated from the Grosser Walsertal by the Zitterklapfen range and the headwaters of the Bregenzer Ache, is the Kleiner (Little) Walsertal. This valley is the odd one out so to speak, part of Austria but completely within the geographical bounds of West Germany, and its river flows eventually into the Danube. The valley has no direct road contact with the rest of Austria, for its headwaters rise in a western arm of the steep Allgauer Alps. As a result of this inaccessibility, the Kleiner Walsertal has become a toll-free area, an anomaly still found in other parts of Europe similarly cut off from the rest of their country. Quick to take advantage of this concession, the inhabitants of the Kleiner Walsertal make a lucrative living from holidaymakers and trippers, mostly from nearby southern Bavaria who come to take advantage of the tax free goods on offer in local shops.

The easiest and most obvious motor route into the Bregenzerwald from western Europe is south along the Rhine valley *autobahn* to Basel in Switzerland then along the south shore of the Bodensee, or perhaps 'cut the corner' by way of a diversion through the Black Forest and either cross the Rhine at Schaffhausen where the dramatic Rhine Falls, scene of Sherlock Holmes' 'death', thunder their barrier to shipping. The other Black Forest route is to the north of the Rhine, then along the north shore of the Bodensee, through Ludwigshafen, Friedrichshafen and Lindau into Bregenz. Another route runs east across West Germany to Ulm then south to either Memmingen or Kempten into Lindau. For a more rural ride continue to Immenstadt or Sonthofen and follow one of the two valleys to the Austrian border by way of minor roads. From the east, there is a quiet road along the valley of the Lech from Reutte and over the Hochtannberg Pass into the Bregenzer valley.

Finally there is the main east-west route over or under the Arlberg Pass. If your destination is in one of the villages of south Bregenzerwald, leave the *autobahn* before the Feldkirch tunnel at Feldkirch-Ost and take the road to Rankweil and across the Furka Pass into Damüls. Alternatively continue along the *autobahn* as far as either Dornbirn (take the Dornbirn-Sud exit) or Bregenz. Rail travellers must use the trans-European Arlberg line either east or west to the station nearest their destination. There are no other railways inside Bregenzerwald, but most valleys and all major villages and many minor ones, are served by an efficient postbus service which despite the varied demands made by the postal deliveries, manages to run to a fairly reliable schedule.

The nearest international airports with rail connections are at Innsbruck, and Zürich in Switzerland.

Using Bregenz, the regional capital, as a jumping off point, the villages upstream along the Bregenzer Ache valley can be explored followed by the minor valleys and towns along the Rhine in a south to north order, on the return to Bregenz.

The pleasant holiday resort of **Bregenz** sits on a sunny ledge around the eastern extremity of the Bodensee (Lake Constance). It was the Romans who first 'discovered' the advantageous site on which Bregenz grew. They built a fortified trading post on their north-south highway between the Alps and what eventually became Germany, probably using the Rhine waterway for the movement of

Rankweil

heavy materials. They called their town *Brigantium*, a name which
has obviously been gradually changed throughout the intervening
centuries to modern Bregenz.

Sheltering the town from cold easterly winter winds are the
wooded slopes of the Pfänder mountain 1,063m (3,488ft) and the best
view of all is from its summit. Take the funicular railway to the top
(it is called a *Seilschwebebahn* in German). Try to choose a clear sunny
day for your trip. The Bodensee stretches westwards in a vast expanse of water over 64km (40 miles) long and up to 13km (8 miles)
wide in places. To your right the shoreline is German with the elegant
resort town of Lindau connected to the mainland by a narrow causeway. Gently indented bays, all with their formal bathing beaches,
stretch into the blue haze of a distant view backed by a hint of the
rolling hills of the Black Forest. On your left and across the canalised
Rhine, the border between Austria and Switzerland, is the busy little
Swiss town of Rorschach which looks north across the lake from a
wide bay. Further on is Romanshorn with its regular ferry services
to and from industrial Friedrichshafen in Germany. Finally Kon-
stanz marks both a frontier and also the outflow from the main lake
into the Untersee. Beyond the lesser lake the Rhine takes over again,
navigable with the exception of the Rhine Falls at Schaffhausen
(literally 'Boat Houses'), all the way to the North Sea.

Further round to the left the view is along the deep trough of the

Rhine valley southwards past Liechtenstein, a principality with close political links to Switzerland and yet geographically within Austria. On a really clear day the snow-clad peaks of the Swiss Alps mark the southern boundary of this wonderful view, said by many to be one of the finest in Europe. The view is complemented by the compact grouping of buildings in the oldest part of Bregenz. The attractive houses still partly within the remains of the thirteenth-century ramparts sit at the foot of the Pfänder mountain, blending well with the 'new town' which follows the lakeshore as far as the Bregenzer Ache, the main river of this region. Across the river and on low lying ground between it and the Rhine canal are the small industrial towns of Hard, Lauterach and Wolfurf, occupying the only space where modern expansion is possible.

Boats carrying the flags of West Germany and Switzerland, as well as Austria, regularly leave the busy harbour to the north of Bregenz Bahnhof, the main railway station, and visit towns all around the lake. Remember to take your passport and appropriate currency if embarking on a cruise along the Bodensee, it is not always convenient to change money at your port of call. .

Bregenz comes into its own in summer when the flowers decorating the beds of its spacious promenade are at their best. Regattas and informal sailing competitions are held on the lake throughout the summer season and the lakeside concerts enjoy one of the finest and most imaginative auditoriums possible.

Until recently there was a little railway which wound its way from Bregenz to Bezau, climbing about 253m (830ft) in the space of about 30km (18 miles). The line hugged the river for most of the way, mirroring its tight bends as it climbed through the narrow gorge. On either hand are pretty villages and neat farms within a colourful tapestry of meadows set against a backcloth of dark green forest. The village of **Buch** sits high above the valley and was a good half mile from its station, but neighbouring **Alberschwende** had no rail connections. What it does have is a useful chairlift to the top of the Brüggelekopf, a delightful pine-clad l,182m (3,878ft) mountain, the focal point of at least four easy-to-follow and clearly marked woodland paths. An enjoyable day could be spent by driving to Buch then taking the quiet lane which winds its way, more or less south to Alberschwende and its welcoming cafés and *Gasthöfe*. Take the chairlift to the top of the Brüggelekopf and descend to the east then south-east by way of the Gasthof Alpenrose where a winding hill road leads down to Egg. Since the closure of the railway, alternative means of return must be found from here.

The Stuttgartener hut, high in the mountains

The name **Egg** always amazes children. It has nothing to do with the products of hens, but is a local name probably connected with an old word for a ridge, the true meaning lost in the mists of time. There are several villages and hamlets with Egg somewhere in their title in the surrounding district. The village sits astride the main river, joined here by two minor streams both of which will reward a day's quiet exploration. By-roads follow the wooded high ground to remote villages like **Hittisau**, a scattered rural hamlet grouped around its white baroque onion-domed church. As with most alpine villages, the best time is early summer before haymaking when the meadow flowers are at their best. Another road from Egg leads to Grossdorf, and to **Ittensberg**, where there is a guest house and the delightful little Fatima chapel.

Continue south, upstream along the main river, where both the road and railway move away from the river in order to reach the area of habitation. At this point the farms and meadowland tend to be low lying and prone to flooding so all buildings are well away from any danger. **Andelsbuch** is the next station, a friendly little place where time seems to stand still. Again, the focal point is its white walled church with a tower capped by the ubiquitous onion dome.

Between Andelsbuch and Bezau a beautiful road goes off to the right, leading to **Schwarzenberg** and **Bödele** before twisting its way down to Dornbirn. Bödele is just a hamlet with a hotel, but Sch-

Typical Austrian mountain scenery in the Bregenzerwald

warzenberg is a proper little village.

After a temporary narrowing, the valley broadens and **Bezau** marks the terminus of the little train from Bregenz. From the eastern end of the village street a short cablecar ride reaches the Niedere ridge where the walking is ideal for all types of mountain lovers. To the east, the ridge is followed by a clear path marked by the standard red/white paint splashes to the Winterstade peak 1,877m (6,158ft), one of the highest points in this part of the Bregenzerwald. Easier paths, again well signposted and waymarked, wander down the forested ridge back to Bezau, although an extension can be made to the Gasthof Sonderlach close to the middle station of the cablecar. Especially on hot days, this option is likely to be the most popular part of an enjoyable day in the mountains.

A little further on, a road off to the left leads to Reuthe, Bizau and **Schönenbach**. The latter is about as far as the road is worth following, though it does go on to some farms. There are two guest houses at Schönenbach and some delightful walks in a lovely mix of woods and meadows.

The valley route now goes through a series of villages with 'Au' as part of their name. First comes **Mellau** where the lower crags of the Hangspitze rise steeply above the wooded valley sides and make the 1,746m (5,728ft) mountain appear to be higher than it actually is. South of the village a cablecar could take you to the Rosstelle Alm, a high corrie developed for winter skiing, but perfectly suitable for summer strolling, picnicking or enjoying the mountain flowers. A zigzag path leads to the Hofstätten Haus, an interesting alpine hut set just above the treeline beneath the rocky slopes of the Ranisfluh ridge.

Au marks the junction of two roads once more important than today. Beyond Au there is a fair spread of dwellings and several hamlets and this green and pleasant area tempts one to linger. However, continue along the valley route as far as **Schröcken**, a tiny village which makes a suitable base for high-level mountain rambling in the Allgäuer and Lechtaler Alps. Above the village, the road climbs in a series of tight hairpin bends to the Hochtannberg Pass at 1,679m (5,509ft) before dropping down into Lechtal and Warth where it divides, one road following the Lech downstream to Reutte and the German frontier and the other upstream to Lech and across the Flexenpass to join the Arlberg Pass road. A little way along the main road from Au is **Schoppernau**, a colourful place complete with all the amenities for a mountain holiday including a swimming pool, and also the bottom station of a chairlift to the summit of the Diedamskopf, 2,090m (6,857ft), the start of an exciting high-level walk well within the capabilities of anyone used to hillwalking. Several paths lead down from the mountain and the route should be chosen from the local map — Freytag and Bernt's 1:100,000 Bregenzerwald is ideal. A strong party could return by way of the Schwarzwasser Haus, an attractive alpine hut offering excellent refreshments, or if you want an easier walk, then try the footpath beneath the Falzerkopf to the Diedamsalm, again offering refreshment.

The other road from Au runs to the south-west above the left bank of the Argenbach stream to the Furka Pass, 1,760m (5,774ft), before dropping down to Rankweil in the Rhine valley. The steep road is narrow in places and sits on a rocky ledge, but the problem of passing other vehicles is avoided by the simple expedient of a tidal flow system. By this method vehicles run in one direction only during advertised times, the flow being reversed during alternate periods. The system works very well, but relies upon the patience of all road users — it only needs one thoughtless motorist to drive the wrong way along a particularly narrow part of the road to throw the whole operation into chaos.

The only village of any size on the Furka Pass road is **Damüls**, the highest in the Bregenzerwald. This is a popular ski resort in winter but far from being exploited as a mountain holiday village in summer, although it is a centre for mountaineering in the Vorarlberg.

Mellau

Two chairlifts take the effort out of climbing the steepest hillsides and strategically sited *Gästhofe* and alpine huts make Damüls an ideal centre for a real away-from-it-all mountain holiday. The shaly nature of the subsoil of the grassy mountains on either side of the Furka Pass have created an excellent growing media for a wide range of alpine flowers, their bright colours will tempt even the most blasé mountain walker to stop and admire their beauty. Hopefully he or she will only take photographs, because picking alpine flowers frequently kills the parent plant and in any case it is illegal to pick many of the species found growing in the Alps. The Damülser Mittagspitze is the venue for an annual Mass, held usually by the local bishop. Stand on the narrow grassy summit in a strong breeze and try to imagine the poor man's difficulty in keeping his feet on the ground when the wind fills his vestments like a parachute!

Damüls' church has long acted as a beacon for travellers on the Furka Pass road. It sits a little aloof from the modern hotels and *Gästhofe* of the village, high above a sharp right-hand bend in the road, the bright red onion-dome topping the slender tower which is visible for miles. Inside is the baroque splendour of its altar illuminated by the narrow, high-placed windows set in bare whitewashed walls. The old part of the village also has some interesting wooden houses.

By using either of the chairlifts, a whole new world of easy high-

Damüls

level walking opens across the hillsides and grassy ridges surrounding Damüls. Strategically placed alpine huts and *Gästhofe* wait to
provide sustenance for the inner man or woman and short, often
level tracks lead to neighbouring villages. **Fontanella** is such a spot,
sitting to the south on a sunny terrace high above the Grosser Walsertal. The track which links it to Damüls is flat and wooded, but to
reach it by car join the magnificent new road just below Damüls,
crossing the valley and climbing up to Faschina. The section across
the valley is in the form of a gallery, but below Faschina the road has
not yet been improved, and hairpin bends lead down beyond the
Faschina hotels to Fontanella. More hairpins lead down from Fontanella to the main valley, the Grosser Walsertal, which, despite its
narrowness, is worthy of a visit. The road is a cul-de-sac and so traffic
is rarely a problem. The valley gets its name from some of its early
inhabitants. In the thirteenth century the Montfort family became
vassals of Hugo of Tübingen. By the end of the century the Montforts
(Hugo had adopted the name) controlled what is now the Vorarlberg. They were responsible for opening up the country and
bringing in people from the Swiss canton of Wallis. Most of them
settled in what is now called after them, the Grosser Walsertal.

   Climbing up the valley there is the hamlet of **Buchboden** and a
few kilometres beyond is the head of the valley, with only one or two
farms. The last one is the Metzgertobel Alm, almost at the head wall.

Climbing the Damülser Horn

From the valley head paths lead upward into the foothills of the Lechtaler Alps to the south and the Zitterklapfen range to the north. The two main alpine huts are the Göppinger and Biberacher, but many of the small hill farms add to their income by selling refreshments. Lower down the valley is mostly forest, but farms and attractive hamlets line the road and side tracks. Going down the valley the first hamlet is **Sonntag**. This small village has a local museum and a cablecar climbing the south side of the valley. Two kilometres (just over a mile) down the valley there is a turning left to **Raggal**. There is a camp site at Plazera, just before Raggal is reached, and a turning left to Marul, a very small hamlet. Raggal is a pleasant little village with the local reservoir as an added attraction. The dam wall is 48m (157ft) tall. The parish church dates from the fourteenth century. There are plenty of footpaths and with the nearby villages of **Ludesch**, with an interesting church, and **Thüringen** which has two churches, the area can fill in quite a lot of time. The parish church at Thüringen has a silver monstrance and a rococo organ, the St Anna church dates from the sixteenth century. Nearby are two ruined castles — Jordan and Blumberg, dating from the thirteenth century.

The next little group of villages **Düns**, **Röns**, **Schnifis** and **Schlins** offer bathing at the Fallersee and cablecars up to the heights of the Dünserberg. Near Schlins there is yet another ruined castle, the Jagdberg, dating between the thirteenth and the sixteenth centuries.

Also for the odd wet day there is an indoor swimming pool. **Ubersaxen** is noted for the lovely walks round about the village.

At the other side of the Au to Schröcken road lies the Kleiner Walsertal, but this is completely inaccessible by road from Austria. A strong party could, however, easily walk over the Hochalp Pass from the top of the Hochtannberg Pass having reached the latter by postbus. The path leads round the dramatic western slopes of the rocky Widderstein, 2,533m (8,311ft) and reaches the Kleiner Walsertal road end at Baad. **Mittelberg** is about 3km (2 miles) further down the valley and depending on the time a profitable extension could be made to the duty free shops. But remember that anything you buy will have to be carried out and liquor weighs heavy after a while no matter how cheap it may be in the shops!

All the major towns of the region with the exception of **Bludenz** lie in the Rhine valley. This lovely old town is at the foot of the Arlberg Pass and its centre is closed to traffic which thankfully uses the bypass. The local band plays in the square on Saturday mornings. The town has four churches, two swimming pools, a museum, a castle and shops. Local legend has it that unicorns still roam in nearby woods, but none seem to have been sighted in living memory.

The Montafon railway runs between Bludenz and Schruns at hourly intervals throughout the day from 6am to 10pm, with occasional steam trains. This is a useful little railway if one wishes to leave the car behind for a change.

Continuing on the road towards Feldkirch, **Nenzing** dates back to AD850, and is an interesting village with two churches dating from the fifteenth century. The Red House is a wooden house from the seventeenth century, said to be impregnated with bull's blood to give it the colour. Nenzing also claims the most modern heated swimming pool in the Vorarlberg. There is a splendid walk taking in the ruined Schloss Ramschwag and giving a good view over the village.

Nenzing lies at the foot of the Gamperdonatal, a gloriously beautiful valley cutting deep into the Alps. Near the head of the valley lies **Nenzinger Himmel** (*Himmel* means heaven). Here, deep in the Rhätikon group of mountains, only a kilometre from the Liechtenstein border and just over two from the Swiss border, this lovely hamlet nestles in dramatically beautiful surroundings. Round about there is the tiny chapel of St Rochus, and an old watermill. Along the path to the Güfel Alm is the Stüberfall (waterfall) and not far from the village the Rotes Brünnele (Red Spring). Fortunately for this peaceful area, but unfortunately for the tourist, the road is closed to traffic.

Town band, Bludenz

Access is by way of a fleet of yellow and white minibuses from Nenzing, which are not cheap, or by foot along the 12km-long (7 mile-) valley.

The next valley, the Brandnertal, is just outside the Bregenzerwald, but can be reached on foot from Nenzinger Himmel, or by bus from the main valley. The last bus stop up the valley is right at the road head just about a kilometre (just over half a mile) from the Douglas hut but 400m (1,312ft) lower, so be prepared for a climb. However, the climb is worth the trouble. Surpassing the beauty of the Brandnertal and only reached by a cablecar is the Lünersee, 1,970m (6,460ft). The lake is about 2km (just over a mile) long and $1\frac{1}{2}$km (1 mile) wide. There is a good footpath all the way round. To work up an appetite for lunch one could walk round the west bank of the lake and go up to the Totalphütte, at 2,385m (7,822ft). Here the tiny Totalpsee sits like a jewel set in the alpine scenery. A little further west, the other side of the ridge, is the Brand glacier. Here another small lake is joined to the Totalpsee by a pipeline under the mountains. Another pipeline feeds water from the Lünersee down to the Montafon valley and the hydro-electric works at Latschau.

The road to the Brandnertal from the main valley is opposite Bludenz. **Bürs** is the first village, still quite low. Of interest is the late Gothic church and the Burser Schlucht (*Schlucht* means gorge), and the main river of the valley, the Ill, passes through a gorge at Bürs.

The village has a heated open-air pool. Nearby **Tschengla** is a quiet village sitting on a sun terrace up above the main valley.

Bürserberg is the next village up the valley and the first glimpse causes many people to stop and reach for a camera. **Brand** is the main tourist area of the valley. There is a daily programme of entertainments and lots of hotels, and there are chairlifts up to the western heights above the village.

Go on from Nenzing, via road 190, and on the edge of the ancient flood plain of the Rhine, close by the border with Liechtenstein, is **Feldkirch**, a romantic old town which boasts of all things a Museum of Hairdressing, tracing the fads and fashions throughout the centuries. The town dates from a first mention as *Veldkirchun* in the year AD830. Parts of the existing town are medieval, and in fact strategically placed Feldkirch once controlled movement from the Rhine into Austria proper. Powerful barons controlled this trade route from their Schloss Schattenburg, which is open to the public and which houses the local museum. There are no less than six interesting churches in the town, four towers dating from the thirteenth to the sixteenth century. There is also much more, so go to the information office in the Schosser Gasse where they have lots of leaflets giving fuller details. There is a nearby zoo and a camp site by the river to the north-west.

Travelling north, pass through the pleasant villages of Götzis and Hohenems to reach **Dornbirn**. This is an important little town, the centre of one of Austria's major textile regions. Each year a textile show is held when most of the top fashion designers vie with each other to produce the latest styles for the coming season. The show usually coincides with the Bregenz Music Festival. The old town centre is not spoilt, however, as industry is relegated to the outskirts. There are some good guest houses and restaurants, and a short cablecar ride to Karren from the south-eastern outskirts of Dornbirn will reach a series of gentle wooded ridges scattered with conveniently spaced mountain restaurants. There is ample scope across the broad ridges and hilltops for literally days of easy walking. The choice is almost unlimited, but as an example why not try the route which connects a series of paths, south-west from Karren by way of the Gasthof Schwarzenberg, then on to the Emser hut and eventually reach the main valley at Klaus? This is roughly 16km (10 miles) in length, but has easy forest and hilltop walking for most of its length.

To complete the circuit of the Bregenzerwald the series of south-west flowing valleys which drain into the Bregenzer river are well worth exploring. None of the broad intervening ridges are high or steep. Pretty farms make use of the sunny situation and many a happy hour can be spent wandering close to the German border along lanes and trackways rarely visited by anyone other than locals.

Further Information
— Bregenzerwald —

Accommodation

The region is well supplied by all grades of hotels and *Gasthöfe*. There are also several camp sites. For details apply to:
Verkehrsverband Bregenzerwald
A - 6863 Egg
☎ (05512) 2365
        or
Landesverkehrsampf Vorarlberg
Römerstrasse 77/1
A - 6901 - Bregenz
☎ (05574) 22525

Activities

Bezau
Swimming, tennis, fishing.

Bludenz
Swimming, tennis, riding, cycle hire, fishing, cablecar.

Bodensee (Lake Constance)
Lake cruises

Bregenz
Sailing, waterskiing, windsurfing, riding, fishing, cycle hire, cablecar, festival, open-air theatre. Funicular railway ascent of the Pfänder mountain.

Bürs
Swimming, cycle hire, tennis, riding.

Damüls
Swimming, tennis, fishing.

Dornbirn
Swimming, tennis, riding, cablecar.

Feldkirch
Swimming, tennis, riding, fishing, cycle hire, guided walks.

Maps

The following are recommended:
Kompass Wanderkarte 1:50,000,
Bregenzerwald — Westallgau
or Freytag and Berndt 1:100,000
sheet 36, Bregenzer Wald

Places to Visit in the Area

Bezau
Parish church, local museum, typical Bregenzerwald houses.

Bludenz
Parish church of St Laurentius, Dominican cloister church of St Peter, seventeenth-century hospital chapel, Holy Cross church, old town gate, local museum.

Bregenz
Benedictine abbey of St Gallus, Dominican cloister church, music festivals.

Vorarlberg Museum
Kornmarktplatz

Open: 9am-12noon and 2-5pm.
Closed Mondays.

Bürs
Late Gothic parish church, Burser
Schlucht (gorge).

Dämuls
Parish church, chairlifts.

Dornbirn
Parish church with fifteenth-
century tower, Markt Platz; Red
House, Markt Platz.

Vorarlberg Natural History
Museum
Marktstrasse
Open: 9am-12noon and 2-5pm.
Closed Mondays.

Feldkirch
Ancient town. Museum of Hair-
dressing; Schattenburg castle with
local museum; Chapel of Holy
Kreuz, Liechtensteiner Strasse;
Wasser Tower; Diebsturm; Churer
Turm; Frauenkirche; Johanne-
skirche; Stadtpfarrkirche of St
Nicholas; Theatre and concerts in
the town hall.

Kleiner Walsertal
Duty-free valley with only road
access through German territory.

Tourist Information Offices

Bezau
☎ (05514) 2295

Bludenz
42 Werdenberger Strasse
☎ (05552) 62170

Bregenz
15 Inselstrasse
☎ (05574) 23391

Bürs
☎ (055526) 2617

Damüls
☎ (05510) 253

Dornbirn
Dr Waibel Strasse
☎ (05572) 62188

Feldkirch
Schlosser Gasse
☎ (05522) 23467 or 23434

2 • Lechtal and the Montafon Valley

One approach to Austria is via Munich International Airport. Here all the major car hire firms are represented. A quick circuit of the town on the inner ring road and the A95 motorway will soon be found. This heads south towards Garmisch-Partenkirchen and the Austrian border. An alternative would be to come from Stuttgart by way of the A8 motorway to Ulm and the A7 to Kempten.

Either way, begin at **Heiterwang** on the 314 road between Ehrwald and Reutte. This tiny peaceful village provides a first opportunity to get off the beaten track by taking a stroll round the nearby lakes. It is a nice gentle walk, mostly level, and quiet and peaceful. It is possible to drive, following the signs to the lake, to the Hotel Fischer am See, but there is little traffic on the road so the walk can be relatively undisturbed. A round-the-lake boat service operates a regular timetable so it is possible to ride all, or part of, the way. Round both lakes, which are joined by a narrow channel spanned by a footbridge, is about 15km (9 miles), so be prepared.

At all three boat stops, the hotels Fischer, Seespitze and Forelle, there are camp sites, the last two being reached by a secondary road out of Reutte which eventually passes into Germany.

The route from Heiterwang goes by way of Reutte to the **Lechtal**. Soon after reaching the outskirts of Reutte only 7km (4 miles) from Heiterwang, take the road to Ehenbichl and **Rieden**. At Rieden there is an old watermill and a forest walk. Taking this road will be quieter than the 198 though they do join at Weissenbach am Lech.

This is about 8km (5 miles) into the Lechtal, which lies roughly south-westerly. Looking upstream, on the right are the Allgauer Alps forming the border with Germany, while on the left are the Lechtaler Alps. The river Lech rises in the Vorarlberg near the Rote Wand (Red Wall) which is 2,706m (8,875ft) high. Although here it is

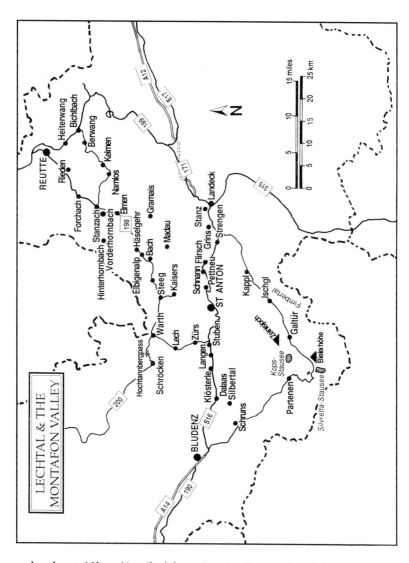

only about 10km (6 miles) long its size is awe-inspiring in spring when the snows are melting, and in the autumn judge by the size of the banks and the tumble of stones just how big it can get.

The villages of **Forchach** and **Stanzach** lie quietly off the main road and walks can be made from either of them. Just through Stanzach turn off the main road to Vorderhornbach and continue up to **Hinterhornbach**. Here, leave the car and take a walk up a mountain. From the end of the road it is just over 5km (3 miles) from

Elmen

Hinterhornbach to the Hornbachjoch (*joch* means pass). The pass is at 2,022m (6,632ft), 900m (2,952ft) above the village and it marks the border with Germany. The path follows a stream, the Jochbach, up the Jochbachtal almost to the pass. The Jochspitze is about 250m (820ft) south along the ridge and 200m (656ft) higher. Allow 3hrs from the village to the pass.

Between Stanzach and Bichlbach, back on the 314, there is a mountain road well worth the effort. It follows the Namloser Tal up to **Namlos**, a lovely little hamlet set in a junction of valleys in broad meadows. From Namlos the road undulates along through woods and meadows to Kelmen and Rinnen to Berwang, with a little side turning up to Brand and Mitteregg. There is no shortage of places to stay and it is a delightful backwater. A return could be made to Stanzach.

Back at the main valley the village of Elmen is passed and also a turning left which takes a secondary, though good, road over the Hahntennjoch and on down to Imst. The next village going up the valley is Häselgehr but just before the village is reached (if you cross the Lech that is too far), there is a turning left to **Gramais**. At the head of the road is the hamlet of Gramais and the valley leading up to it is the Gramaisertal. From the village, any of the footpaths will take the walker deep into a mountain paradise with very few people to disturb the peace. If you take path 626 and reach the Gufel hut the cowherds, who live up there for most of the summer, will do a deal for a jug of fresh cow's milk — and it is delicious. Path 624 leads up to the Kogelsee surrounded by giant peaks. Another path leads up to the Rosskarsee. All these paths have at least 700m (2,296ft) of climb so allow plenty of time.

Elbigenalp

From **Häselgehr** in the main valley to **Bach**, a distance of about 10km (6 miles), there is a path called the Grünauer Höhenweg (The High Green Footway) in the woods to the south of the river. By careful judging of the postbus times this could be made into a pleasant day out, with an interesting visit to one of the many *Pest Kapeller* in Austria. This one is dedicated to St Sebastian. A *Pest Kapelle* (Plague Chapel) was erected by a grateful populace to mark the limit of the plague's progress when the grim Black Death roamed Europe. Often armed guards manned strategic points to limit access when the plague was most rampant.

In between these two villages are Köglen, which is only a hamlet, and Elbigenalp which is a little larger and has a camping place. From Bach it is possible to drive up the Madautal to **Madau**, again a point from which paths branch off into the mountains. This valley is a little more accessible because cars are allowed higher up and from near the head of the road it is a relatively easy ascent to the Memminger hut. Allow 3hrs to reach this, which is one of the string of alpine huts. A favourite pastime at weekends is to walk up to an easily reachable hut for lunch or even for the weekend. For this reason some of them are very busy at these times.

An easier excursion into the mountains can be made from the next valley. From **Sulzbach** it is possible to drive up to the Sulzalpe, 1,466m (4,808ft) and from there follow the jeep track up to the goods

Warth

lift and on up to the Frederick Simms hut, 2,004m (6,573ft), $1^1/_2$hrs.

From Steeg, another 8km (5 miles) up the valley and passing Holzgau on the way, it is possible to turn left or south and follow the twisting mountain road up to **Kaisers**. This is 400m (1,312ft) above the main valley and it is a proper little alpine village. Here the road divides, and continues as jeep tracks up the two valleys going deep into the mountains.

At **Warth** the road divides. A right turn leads towards Schröcken and eventually goes to Dornbirn. This is the magnificent Hoch-tannberg Strasse, going through some of the most beautiful areas of the Vorarlberg. An area of high plateau, of bright green rolling meadows set against stark peaks. The summit of the pass is 1,679m (5,512ft) high. To the north is the peak of the Widderstein, and local tradition says that Noah's Ark scraped against it. Just below the summit of the pass is a turn left to the Korbersee, a landlocked lake which might be called a tarn, with its attendant lakeside hotel.

The left turn from Warth goes to **Lech**, a renowned winter sports resort. However, it is a genuine and pretty village. From Lech a minor road goes west towards **Zug**, a hamlet of chalets alongside the road, and the Upper Lechtal, which is an area of wild yet gentle beauty. The lower meadows and the riverside paths are peaceful and tranquil, yet all around are the gigantic towering peaks. Beyond Zug it is possible to drive up to the Formarin Alm and then walk to the

Chapel on the Hochtannberg Pass

The village of Lech

Freiburger hut for lunch overlooking the Formarinsee. Alternatively, drive up towards the Spullersee and take a walk round the lake (here, the Ravensburger hut is one of the few huts to be self-

A small rural chapel in the Bregenzerwald

The village of Brand in the Bregenzerwald

Mountain skiing at Zürs, in the Lechtal

The Spullersee

service) taking in the breathtaking views to the south and west down over the Klostertal to the peaks forming the Swiss border. Just beyond the Ravensburger hut and slightly below is an *alm*. This is a place where people live in summer when the cows are in the high pastures. They sell a delicious cheese.

Beyond Lech is **Zürs**, another winter sports resort, dominated by large hotels which close in summer, while beyond that is the Arlberg Pass. In fact this road over the Flexenpass, 1,774m (5,818ft), is an engineering triumph. It is the only north-south link over the Lechtaler Alps between Imst and Bludenz. On the descent side, which leads to the Arlberg Pass, much of the road seems to have been hewn out of the solid rock and left covered to protect it from the winter avalanches.

At the end of the Flexenpass, turn right to descend the Arlberg Pass, and reach the hamlet of **Stuben**, which sits uncomfortably below a series of hairpin bends, after which the road straightens out and the valley widens. It is a lovely run down the Klostertal to Bludenz. The rail tunnel starts, or ends depending on which way one travels, close to the road tunnel portal at **Langen**, a town which grew because of the railway. Then there is the hamlet of **Klösterle**, which has a pleasant woodland walk close to the river. **Dalass** is another pleasant little village on this scenic route.

On the outskirts of Bludenz, which is bypassed by the main road,

Zürs

be careful to take road 188 into the Montafon valley, to Vandans and Schruns. At Schruns take the minor road to Silbertal (Silver valley), no doubt named for the silver deposits. The works were taken over by the Fuggers of Augsberg but the seams were almost worked out. However, the influx of skilled craftsmen, who also worked for part of the year elsewhere, affected the outlook of the inhabitants of the area and the Montafon took the lead years later when tourism began. There is a guest house at the limit of the driveable road. Incidentally, the route is now in the Verwall group. There are many walks in the woods of this pleasant valley.

Schruns is a bustling little town, but with the main road taking the brunt of the traffic it is not too busy to be uncomfortable, and it caters well for tourists. There is an interesting church and a museum which shows much of the early way of life in the area. There are chairlifts and cablecars to whisk one to the higher regions for some magnificent views over the Verwall group of mountains to the north.

It is 18km (11 miles) from Schruns to **Partenen**. There the road becomes private, belonging to the electricity works. There is a toll — save the tickets for the return journey — and caravans are not allowed. However, it is a good road and although steep and winding (there are supposed to be thirty hairpin bends on the ascent) it is not difficult. Schruns is at 689m (2,260ft) and the summit of the pass at the Bielerhöhe is 2,036m (6,678ft). At the summit there is ample parking

A view from the Silvretta Pass

and an impressive panorama of giant snow-covered peaks. The walk along the dam of the Silvretta-Stausee is a must, it is 431m (1,414ft) long and 8m (26ft) high. Again it is used for hydro-electricity genera-tion and much of the power generated is exported to southern Germany. The peaks to the south over the lake are in the Silvretta group and form the border with Switzerland. The highest is Piz Buin, 3,312m (10,863ft).

On the descent towards Landeck there is a turning to the left about 7km (4 miles) down. That left turn leads up to the Kops-Stausee and a beautiful walk, nice and easy on a good lakeside path. Go right to the end of the road where there is a large car park and a snack kiosk nearby. Cross the dam and follow the lakeside path. The circuit will take about 1¹/₂hrs. It is quite as dramatic as the Bielerhöhe but more peaceful.

The Bielerhöhe also marks the border. The descent into the Paznauntal to Landeck is in the Tyrol. The Paznauntal is on the bus route from Landeck. It is a 2 hour ride from the town to Galtür where the public road ends and the toll road takes over.

This is an area of high altitude health resorts and winter skiing. Summer sees the influx of hardened mountaineers visiting the string of huts along the high-level footpaths in the Bläue Silvretta, so called because of the blue effect of the glaciers and the great peaks. **Galtür** is dominated by the Fluchthorn, 3,399m (11,148ft). There is sufficient

Landeck

gentler walking from any of the villages en route and one does not
have to be a hardened mountaineer to enjoy the feeling of rejuvena-
tion and contentment obtained from just being in the mountains.

To the north-west from Galtür a fascinating road leads up over the
Zeinisjoch, 1,842m (6,040ft), to the Kops-Stausee, which again helps
feed the hydro-electric works at Partenen, and gives some splendid
views of the surrounding mountains.

Rushing down the valley gaining strength and size as it goes is the
Trisanna river. It joins the Rosanna which comes down from the
Arlberg before they both lose their identity in the Inn at Landeck.

Beyond Galtür is the hamlet of Mathon before **Ischgl** is reached.
It is most attractive on its spur, and at the foot of its church. Ischgl is
a fairly popular resort but the reason for its mention here is for a good
walk crossing an international boundary. From Ischgl take the valley
south, the Fimbertal, drive or walk up to the Gasthof Bodenalpe,
1,842m (6,040ft) then walk up the good track to the Heidelberger hut,
2,264m (7,426ft). This is across the border in Switzerland and on that
side an eventual descent could be made down the Fenga valley to
Vria. Border formalities will be little, if any. Return the same way.

Below, the valley becomes deeper and the villages perch on spurs
to try to climb back up to the sun. **Kappl** is probably the prettiest.
There are chairlifts to whisk one quickly up the sunny side of the
valley. One goes to the Alpengasthaus Dias, a climb of about 600m

Kappl

(1,968ft) from where one can walk gently back down to the village again.

This is nearly at the end of this lovely valley. When a glimpse of the Schloss Wiesberg is obtained, park near the Trisanna Brucke Hotel and take in the view of the bridge. The castle is near the eastern end of this delicate looking bridge above the river, with the Parseierspitze, 3,036m (9,958ft), as a backdrop.

From the Trisanna Bridge it is only a short run down to the main Inn valley. Before going left along the 316, take a detour to **Landeck**, an industrial town which grew because of its situation at the junction of two important routes. It was founded in the thirteenth century when the castle was built by Meinhard II. Today it is the principal shopping centre for the surrounding area.

Back at the junction of the Paznauntal and the Stanzertal above Landeck there is a pleasant little road round to the north through the villages of Grins and Stanz which keeps off the main highway. **Grins** was the favourite spa of Margarete, the Margravin of Tyrol. In January 1363, having been widowed and also losing her son, she bequeathed her country to the Hapsburgs. A few months later she abdicated and spent the rest of her life in Vienna.

Go back now along the 316 to **Strengen**, a hamlet almost in a ravine, then as the valley broadens again there are **Flirsch**, **Schnann** and **Pettneu**, the last three lying on the sunny side of the valley. Be

Stanz bei Landeck

careful to take the old road, following signs for St Anton, or the new highway will whisk you swiftly to the Arlberg Tunnel. Pettneu is a charming little village which even the old highway bypassed. The centre has some quaint old houses and the village is on the northern side of the valley, so benefits from the sun. To the south wide meadows lie below the woods, beyond and higher are the peaks of the snowy Hohe Riffler. The church at Pettneu has a memorial to the men who lost their lives building the Arlberg Tunnel.

Going on up the valley **St Anton** is next. This has been a tourist village for a long time. Even the famous Arlberg Express stops here. As early as 1901 an Austrian called Hannes Schneider developed and taught 'alpine' skiing. In 1926 he made a film entitled *The Wonders of Skiing* which was a great success. In 1922 Arnold Lunn, who founded the British Kandahar Ski Club, introduced slalom gates to skiing. The two men met in 1927 and their collaboration resulted in the first Arlberg Kandahar Cup Race in 1928.

The ski runs are mostly above the treeline but there is plenty else to do. There are woodland and mountain walks and fishing in the mountain steams. A chairlift goes up to Gampen, where there is a mountain restaurant and a signposted walk back down. The top section of the chairlift goes up to the Kapall House at 2,333m (7,652ft). From here it is easy to reach the Lechtal High Level Footpath (Lechtaler Hohenweg) but that is for experienced walkers only.

From St Anton the road climbs again up to **St Christoph**, which lies just before the pass summit which is 1,771m (5,809ft). The original hospice was built in 1386 to aid travellers on the pass. Unfortunately it was burnt down in 1957 and the new building is the Hospice Hotel. Part of the original chapel remains and visitors may peer in through a viewing window. About a mile on the Bludenz side of the pass is the road, over the Flexenpass, back to Lech. Incidentally, it is now possible to take a round trip cablecar ride from St Anton to Zürs, or just to the Trittkopf and back, changing cablecars at the Vallugagrat.

Further Information
— Lechtal and the Montafon Valley —

Activities

Ischgl
Fishing, riding, swimming, cablecar.

Landeck
Cablecar.

Lech
Swimming, tennis, squash, fishing, cablecar.

Reutte
Swimming, sailing, riding, tennis, alpine flights.

Schruns
Swimming, tennis, riding, fishing, cablecar, chairlift.

Steeg
Swimming, fishing.

Warth
Swimming.

Places to Visit in the Area

Arlberg
Picturesque village.

Landeck
Market town. Parish church.

Lech
Parish church with fourteenth-century tower.

Lechtal
Small museums at Elbigenalp and Holzgau.

Partenen
Silvretta high alpine road; Kops Stausee (wonderful mountain views).

Reutte
Market town. Alpine Flower Garden reached by cablecar.

Schruns
Parish church, Montafon houses, local museum.

Silbertal
Parish church (neo-Gothic), St
Agath chapel, Litz waterfall.

Steeg
Seventeenth-century parish
church.

Tourist Information Offices

Arlberg
Pettneu am Arlberg
☎ (05448) 221

Ischgl
☎ (05444) 5318 or 5314
(also for the Paznauntal)

Landeck
☎ (05442) 2344

Lech
☎ (05583) 2161-0

Lechtal
Elbigenalp
☎ (05634) 6270 (for the area)

Partenen
☎ (05558) 8315
(also for Silvretta area).

Reutte
☎ (05672) 2336 or 2041

St Anton
☎ (05446) 2269-0

Schruns
Silvrettastrasse
☎ (05556) 2166

Silbertal
☎ (05556) 4112

Steeg
☎ (05633) 5308

Warth
☎ (05583) 3515

3 • Leutasch and Tannheimertal

Leutasch and its Valley

Every tourist entering Austria at Scharnitz on the road south from Munich and Garmisch-Partenkirchen to Innsbruck, will as they drive towards Seefeld, be aware of a countryside composed of low rolling pine-clad hills surrounded by sharp white limestone peaks. These low hills, to the right of the main road, fill the middle of a high sunny bowl perched about 695m (2,280ft) above the Inn valley. This area is known as Leutasch.

Winter visitors to Seefeld will have been introduced to the gentler eastern slopes if they are beginners to alpine skiing and the more proficient will have enjoyed the dramatic runs on the Seefelder Spitze. However, it is perhaps cross-country skiers who are best acquainted with the central area surrounded by the Leutasch forests. Winter trails lead for miles in all directions around the Leutasch valley and its tributaries.

This is certainly one of the most accessible mountain resorts in Austria. If you are travelling by road from northern or western Europe, the quickest route will be by way of Munich, then south along the E6 to Garmisch and south-east to Scharnitz. The alternative road for those with time to spare will be to cross the Black Forest diagonally south-eastwards and then pick up the *autobahn* system by entering Austria at Bregenz. This road, beneath or over the Arlberg Pass, is followed towards Innsbruck, with a left turn at Zirl for the short but steep climb to Seefeld. A side road through the hamlet of Neuleutasch leads into the main valley.

Air travellers are similarly fortunate; Munich is one of West Germany's major international airports and there is a frequent express train service into Austria from the main station — the *Hauptbahnhof*. And with the development of short take off and landing

41

Leutasch valley

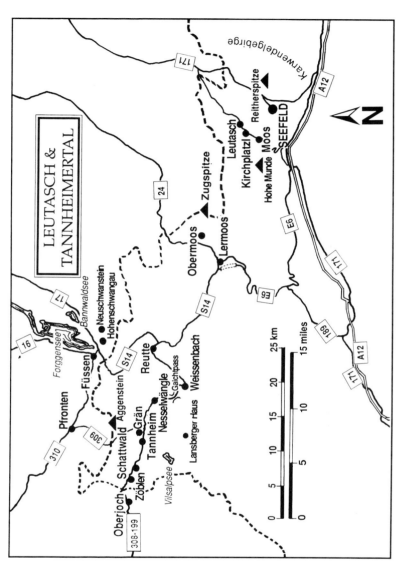

aircraft such as the Bae 146, the difficult approach to Innsbruck airport is no longer a problem and travellers can be in Leutasch within an hour of landing there. Although there are rail connections from Innsbruck along the main line into Seefeld, it is probably more convenient to use the postbus service as it will ensure direct access to Leutasch, often to your hotel door.

Rail travel is east across Europe either to Munich then south on the

Seefeld

Innsbruck line to Seefeld or by the Arlberg Express route to Innsbruck and north-west by postbus as described above.

Anyone with a young family who might feel intimidated by the prospect of a high alpine holiday could well consider Leutasch as an easy introduction to mountain walking. The scope is almost limitless. Armed with the footpath map of the area produced by Mayr of Innsbruck especially for the resort town of Seefeld, the walker can enjoy miles of secluded forest tracks or perhaps venture high on the limestone peaks and ridges surrounding this sun trap. As with most of the maps on offer throughout Austria, this map is lacking in many important details such as contour lines and the overall shape of forests and ridges. However, by carefully calculating height differences from the few spot heights quoted (remember they are in metres), some idea of the steepness of the slopes can be worked out. One useful feature on this map is the grading of paths with blue, red or black dots. Blue paths are mostly easy level tracks through forests and across meadowland; red routes tend to be steeper but are still easy to follow; whilst black are mountain paths where a good head for heights is necessary and boots are an indispensible aid to sure-footed walking.

Three mountain ranges lying to the north, east and west protect the Leutasch bowl from the harsh cold winds which sweep across central Europe in winter. Facing south and being at a moderate

The Seebach waterfall,
near Seefeld

altitude ensures the maximum hours of sunshine all the year round. The mountains to the east are the most accessible, these are the extremities of the Karwendelgebirge range. The Seefelder Joch — 2,074m (6,805ft) and Harmelekopf — 2,034m (6,673ft) can both be reached in comfort by using the funicular railway from Seefeld followed by cablecar rides. Anyone used to scrambling can reach the summit of the Reitherspitze — 2,374m (7,789ft) the highest peak in the Seefeld group.

North of the Leutasch valley, the towering peaks of the Wettersteingebirge mark the frontier with Germany; these are mainly out of bounds for anyone other than skilled rock climbers, but one or two detached satellites to the south of the main ridge are possible climbs for reasonably fit hill walkers. The Gehrenspitze — 2,367m (7,766ft) and Predigstein — 2,234m (7,329ft) are both accessible from the Gaistal above Oberleutasch. Both mountains are served by friendly farm house *Gasthöfe* where the proprietors are ready and willing to serve refreshments either before or after the ascent. Completing the barrier of high peaks is the Hohe Munde — 2,662m (8,734ft), the most easterly point in the Lechtaler Alps and the highest summit in the area accessible by footpath. This mountain dominates Leutasch, a focal point for all aspiring mountaineers.

To climb the Hohe Munde is a very serious undertaking. Even by gaining about 425m (1,394ft) on the Mundelift chairlift, the rocky path above the Rauthhütte is unrelentingly steep and the summit is one of those which always seems to be beyond that next rise. However, the summit will be eventually gained by anyone sound in wind and limb and the view is superb. All around it are giant peaks, to the north-west is the Zugspitze, Germany's highest point, while to the south across the Inn valley are ranged the snow-clad massifs of the Austrian Alps. **A word of caution to anyone climbing the Hohe Munde. The local map shows a path numbered 8A to the north-west of the summit. This is a climbing route and on no account should it be attempted by anyone other than skilled and well equipped mountaineers.**

Geologically the mountains in this part of Austria are similar to the Dolomites in the south, beyond the Austro-Italian border. Made from limestone they are, however, frequently inlaid with shales, with the low-level stratas to the east of Seefeld oil bearing. At one time, especially during World War II, an extensive oil industry grew in the area to process the valuable fuel locked within these rocks. With the coming of peace and cheaper oil from more traditional sources, the industry has disappeared and the only remaining links are a plastics factory at Maximilianshütte on the outskirts of Seefeld and one or two abandoned shale quarries on the hillside further north along the main road.

Leutasch is known as the longest village in Austria. The series of hamlets lining both sides of the Leutascher Ache, despite having separate identities and names, are all classed as Leutasch. The road into the valley from Seefeld first of all climbs a gently wooded rise dotted with the scattered farmsteads of Neuleutasch where gentle cattle graze the flowery meadows. Beyond Neuleutasch the road drops in a series of sharp bends to **Weidach**, the main village of the Leutasch group. The first feature on the left on entering the village is the Kreitlift, a chairlift climbing the gentle grassy lower slopes of the Katzenkopf. The lift can be used to ease the climb to the forested upper ridge where the possibilities of short or longer walks are almost unlimited. The other reason for using the Kreitlift is one which appeals to anyone who is young in heart, for the Katzenkopf is the start of a summer toboggan run. Small, single-seater self-operated toboggans race down the winding 1.2km ($^3/_4$ mile) concrete course and while first timers might feel they are running at speeds in excess of those on the famous Cresta Run near St Moritz, no one

Reitherspitze, the highest peak in the Seefeld group

seems to come to any harm! A hand brake is used to control the speed of descent and the driver is more or less in control. Weidach is the 'sophisticated' part of Leutasch, not quite as high class as Seefeld and certainly far less crowded but with all the best shops and a bank to provide for everyone's requirements. If your accommodation needs do not run to three or four star hotels, then you will be far better served by the family-run cosy establishments in the rest of the valley.

A short stroll to the west of Weidach will bring you to a complex of small lakes where for a moderate fee you can fish for beautiful fat trout. If you do not fancy your chances with a rod and line, even though the fish almost queue up to be caught, you can buy them at the Gasthof Forellenhof.

Across the main river is the oldest part of the valley, **Leutasch-Kirchplatzl**, which is the administrative centre of the area. Here you will find a most helpful tourist information office, the *Fremden-verkehrsverband*, together with a bank, the police, fire station and the post office all under one roof. Call in at the information office and ask for one of the local Guest Cards, it is free and will save money on such things as entry into Tirolen Abends, local evening entertainment in various hotels, or perhaps the nearby swimming pool. Walk over to the nearby delightful old church and go inside where the baroque splendour of the altar contrasts dramatically with the cool, gentle yet spartan nature of the nave.

Obern

Downstream along the Leutascher Ache the road leads towards the wooded frontier with Germany, a road which passes inns still retaining much of their old world charm hand in hand with modern comforts. Not so very long ago the river was used to power corn mills for local needs. One in particular is to the west of the Austrian Customs Post; gently sinking into old age it is a most attractive building, an ideal subject for camera enthusiasts. There is a good riverside camp site in the meadows between Ahrn and Puitbach.

Upstream from the Kirchplatzl are the hamlets of **Aue**, **Platzl** and **Klamm**, once simple farming communities, but now each has one or two quiet hotels or *Gasthöfe*. The main road swings round to the south at Obern, but an older road continues along the main valley through Klamm. Above the narrow rocky gorge a shrine to St Joseph looks down on hillwalkers just as it did on earlier travellers making their way west over the low col to Ehrwald and southern Germany. The rocky south side of this valley is too steep to be farmed and as a result the forested lower slopes of Hohe Munde, the valley's most prominent peak, are mostly unchanged by the hand of man. To the north easier hillsides climb towards the bare walls of a jagged frontier range. This is the Wettersteingebirge and on the lower slopes pleasant farmsteads offer a welcome to mountain walkers following the high paths connecting alpine meadows and pine forests. Satellite peaks such as the Gehrenspitze or Predigstein should be well within the capabilities of most hillwalkers. Long, high-level tracks above the main valley connect the farms and the Wetterstein hut. Here is a place where anyone can enjoy a mountain environment close to high limestone ridges and summits without having to set foot on them.

From Obern the road follows the forests and broad meadows of the upper Leutasch valley south as far as Buchen before descending in a series of steep but easily negotiable zigzags to the Inn valley which it joins at Telfs.

About 1.2km ($^3/_4$ mile) south of Obern and along a side road from Moos, is the bottom station of the Mundelift, a steeply climbing chairlift to the Rauthhütte and the usual start of the exhaustingly steep climb of the Hohe Munde. If your inclination or energies will not allow you to climb this mountain, a trip to the Rauthhütte is still highly recommended if only for the views from its sunny terrace, or perhaps to enjoy the short stroll north-west along the easier middle section of the Hohe Munde path. Here it leads to a spectacular view of Germany's highest mountain, the Zugspitze. Its shining snow-covered summit stands above the upper reaches of the Leutascher Ache and is the western terminus of the Wetterstein range.

At **Buchen** a small but interesting collection of old farm implements will naturally delay the start of a walk around the southern rim of the sunny Leutasch bowl. If you do not want to use your car and, say, walk to Seefeld or perhaps climb through the Hochmoos Forest, then use the local bus service — it is friendly and cheap. Low-level paths wander eastwards through the 18-hole Seefeld golf course, past lakes which only appear after heavy rain and where side paths lead to hilltops marked by bench seats where you can get your breath back whilst admiring the view.

The possibilities of enjoying a quiet mountain holiday around Leutasch are almost limitless. The beauty of the place lies mostly in the fact that while it readily conveys the true atmosphere of an away-from-it-all resort, it is conveniently close to Seefeld and access to busy Innsbruck is only a matter of a short drive, either by car or bus, or even by train. Steep, but easily climbed peaks to the east of Seefeld contrast with the gentle pine-clad slopes of the rounded lesser hills of the central basin. Above all it is a place for relaxation and the true ambiance of a mountain resort without the demands of the higher ranges.

Tannheimertal

There is an almost 'hidden' valley tucked away in the north-west corner of Austria. This is the Tannheimertal, a sunny glen high above the valley of the Lech and surrounded on two sides by Germany. It lies about 6km (4 miles) as the crow flies over the mountains west of Reutte and is approached by a road from Weissenbach am Lech zigzagging above the deep wooded ravines of the Gaicht Pass. Two roads lead out of the valley into Germany; the first, from the middle of the valley, climbs from the village of Grän through the forests of the Engetal and then down to Pfronten. Further west and surprisingly downstream is the Oberjoch Pass and the entry into Hindelang and Sonthofen, one of the popular ski areas of western Germany.

On entering the Tannheimertal from the Gaicht Pass and following it north-westwards, the impression one gets beyond the lake at Haldensee, is that the river is flowing the wrong way. The truth of the matter is that you must look carefully to realise that there are two river systems draining the valley. The outflow of the Haldensee is to the south-east and down into the Lech by way of the Gaicht Pass. Beyond the lake the broad col, if one can give it such a grand title, is imperceptible, but streams flowing north or south into the valley beyond this point, eventually turn north-west to become the Vils river which travels by way of Pfronten to join the Lech near the German border to the south of Füssen. In this way, waters which were separated at Grän do not have far to travel before joining forces and gaining strength, flowing northwards through the Bavarian plain eventually to join the Danube.

Anyone who is familiar with photographs of the fairytale castle of Neuschwanstein, the grand folly of mad King Ludwig of Bavaria, will, even if they do not know about the Tannheim, be familiar with the northern aspect of the Tanheimer group of mountains. These are the shapely peaks which appear beyond the lake and on the top right of aerial photographs of the castle.

Translated, Tannheimertal means 'the valley of the pine trees'. It is a long time since pine forests completely filled the broad, fertile trench created by a side or hanging glacier above the main ice flow which created the Lech valley. The first people who settled in the valley began to colonise it by cutting out sections of what was then dense forest and burning it in order to create fields for their summer grazing. These people probably had their main farms in the lower valleys, but later, realising the advantage of the sheltered and sunny environment provided by the valley's direction (at right angles to the prevailing winds), gradually thinned out the trees, using the timber for building, fuel, and later as the basic raw material to provide charcoal for the growing metal industries. The shape of the farmsteads has changed little over the last century or so; perhaps the only obvious change to any reincarnated farmer of yesteryear would be the number of farmhouses which over the years have become hospitable *Gasthöfe* and small hotels. Villages still surround their all-embracing churches, without doubt the least changed buildings in the valley. Most have the traditional onion-domed towers and many are quite imposing. All still follow the ornate styles of the baroque traditions in their interior décor.

Mountains dominate both sides of the Tannheimertal; those to the north are mostly limestone and as a result are steeper and more dramatic. Those to the south are the shaley foothills of the Lechtaler Alps. The rock wears more easily than limestone and so the summits and ridges tend to be gentler, but their hillsides, even though tree-covered, are fairly steep. The main summit of the area is the limestone peak of Rote Fluh, 2,111m (6,926ft) not the highest, but because of its position masking its taller neighbour the Kellespitze 2,240m (7,349ft). Reminiscent of the dolomitic peaks further south and in fact made from similar limestones, the Rote Fluh and its neighbours rear up in a series of vertical crags above the wooded slopes above Nesselwängle at the eastern end of the valley. The Rote Fluh and Kellespitze, together with the attendant summits of Gimpel and the Schneidspitze, make an almost impenetrable wall of white limestone which turns to rosy pink in the reflected rays of the setting sun on cloudless evenings.

North-west from these giants, the ridge eases slightly, still the domain of the experienced mountaineer, all the way to the Aggenstein, 1,987m (6,519ft) a mountain which marks the frontier between Austria and Germany. There is a cosy little hut, the Pfrontner, about 90m (300ft) below the summit on the Austrian side which can be reached by a fairly strenuous walk, but without any technical difficulties, from the Füssener Joch chairlift. The last 90m to the top of the Aggenstein are not without their problems, but a fixed wire rope is handy on the most exposed section of this popular mountain climb. The view from the narrow summit ridge makes the effort worthwhile: to the north the land falls dramatically into the haze of the Bavarian plain and to the south, east and west the Alps stretch in an awesome wall of shining black rock and white snow.

The main valley has one lake, the Haldensee, a popular lake for both bathers and sailors, especially sailboard enthusiasts. In common with most Austrian bathing lakes, the Haldensee has a bathing beach provided with changing cabins and a small café. You must therefore be prepared to pay an entrance fee for this facility. The lake is well stocked with trout and if the stuffed specimens in the bar of the Alte Poste Hotel in Haller are anything to go by, several monster pike. There are no records of any attacking swimmers, but one did unwittingly allow itself to get caught by the mother of the late President Roosevelt who once spent a holiday nearby; the pike's head now holds pride of place in the Alte Poste. The lake is also the winter venue for curling competitions, a sport which began in Scotland, but has been taken up by many European winter sport resorts.

Reached by a short road south along the Vilstal from the central village of Tannheim, is, almost unexpectedly, another lake. This is the Vilsalpsee, which lies in a perfect bowl beneath the Geisshorn, part of a massive wall separating the two countries, and is the first of three lakes which decrease in size with their altitude one above the other. To the south-east and only reached by a tiringly steep and rocky track is the partly dammed Traualpsee, then by climbing yet again, what is possibly the finest setting of the three lakes is reached. Nestling at the foot of the Lachenspitze, the Lachesee, which one must call a pool even though there is no equivalent word in German, has the advantage of being overlooked by a pleasant and most hospitable mountain hut. The pool and hut can be reached by an easy high-level traverse from the Neunerkopf which will be described later.

People living in Bavaria can reach the Tannheimertal in the space of a couple of hours and it is not surprising that many discerning Germans have bought holiday homes in the valley along with those who regularly come for holidays and weekends, for this is an ideal family holiday centre. The walking is as easy or as hard as you wish to make it. There are plenty of low-level and forest paths as well as high-level mountaineering expeditions. Using the valley as a base, it is possible to explore southern Bavaria and follow the footsteps of King Ludwig by visiting his fabulous castles. He imagined himself to be a latter-day Lohengrin and in fact was a personal friend of Wagner whose music was often played in the specially built ornate concert hall of Neuschwanstein castle. A little further afield but still within easy access, one can visit Garmisch-Partenkirchen and also Oberammergau, scene of the wonderful Passion Play. Innsbruck with its shops and ornate arcades is only an hour or so's drive to the south-east. The Zugspitze, Germany's highest mountain 2,963m (9,721ft) is an easy climb if you take the cablecar from Ehrwald. The mountain has not always been part of Germany and was in fact a goodwill gift made by Austria.

Drive up the road from Weissenbach above the deep ravine

marking the Gaicht Pass and the first habitation is centred around the original water mills which once ground corn grown further along the valley. On the right of the road are the scattered farmsteads and the one tiny *Gasthof* of **Gaicht**; then about three-quarters of a mile further on and reached by a side road on the left marked by an attractive hillside chapel, is **Rauth**. This hamlet is the only habitation in the wild Weissenbach valley, and has one very friendly *Gasthof* where the bar is a regular meeting place for woodsmen, farmers and forest rangers. The inn is a place of character; the German word to describe the atmosphere is *Gemütlichkeit*. An evening visit will be a night to remember in later years.

The road upstream beside the south-east flowing Ache levels, and in the widening valley is the village of **Nesselwängle**, where there are several excellent and reasonably priced hotels and a camp site. The Berghof Hotel is highly recommended. Run by one family, visitors are made very comfortable. The village is at the base of a long and steep path to the Gimpelhaus hut, a useful resting place for the Rote Fluh climb, but propably the easiest approach to this limestone tower is by the cablecar from Höfen in the Lech valley, then traversing around the Hahnenkamm mountain and beneath the steep middle slopes of Schneidspitze and Kellespitze to the hut.

Across the valley from Nesselwängle, the steep but easier Krinnespitz — 2,002m (6,568ft) — can be climbed from the top of a convenient chairlift. By following paths downhill to the west, the Ödenalpe hut makes a convenient lunch stop before reaching an easier track through the forest to Haldensee.

Before leaving Nesselwängle, take a look at the rather macabre war memorial in Nesselwängle's churchyard. Unusual in its design, it portrays a waxwork diorama of World War I in the Austrian Alps. The church by contrast is gentle and full of light and colour.

Continuing along the road **Haller**, above the eastern shore of the Haldensee, is the oldest village in Tannheimertal, with its Alte Poste Hotel a delightful mixture of ancient timber and mounted trophies of rod and gun. **Haldensee** village has the best class hotels: the Rote Fluh is probably the best in the area and is certainly the most expensive, with facilities for both indoor and outdoor tennis and a heated swimming pool. The night life of its *Keller* can be expensive, even for those who might only take soft drinks! Despite the influx of modern hotels and second homes, the older buildings still retain their timeless character; the tiny church in the middle of the road still evokes the rural charm of the area.

Beyond Haldensee the road forks. To the right is **Grän** with its fortified tower which still commands, but now peacefully, the road into Germany. There are several shops and restaurants as well as holiday apartments and a camp site. The Lumbergerhof at Enge about a mile further along the road, sells exotic ice creams and excellent coffee, an ideal place to end the high-level walk which starts by way of the chairlift from Grän to the Füssener Pass. A path known as the Tannheimer Höhenweg keeps above the treeline and is easy to follow, to the north-west as far as the Pfrontner hut, where if energies allow, the Aggenstein can be climbed before descending steeply through the forest to Enge.

From Grän a side road to the west, probably following the line of the original valley road, serves a group of rural villages. Behind them easy footpaths across the south-facing hillside can be followed for enjoyable low-level walks.

Following the left-hand fork after Haldensee, **Tannheim**, the central village in the valley, is thankfully bypassed by the main road and the criss-crossing narrow streets can still follow the patterns laid down on either side of the church in more leisurely times. This is the best village for shopping for food, clothing and gifts. There are also banks and the main tourist office for the area. Closer to the main road a woodcarver's shop will tempt many *Schillings* from your wallet. His skilful craft has been handed down through several generations and when the author was last there, the woodcarver's little daughter was busy whittling away at a childish drawing on a piece of wood. Obviously the skills are safe for yet another generation.

There is a long two-stage chairlift from Tannheim to a few feet below the summit of the Neunerkopf — 1,864m (6,116ft).

Follow the side road south and you will reach the **Vilsalpsee**, a lovely tree-shrouded lake ideal for bathing or rambling. The two lakeside restaurants offer lake-bred trout as well as other traditional Austrian fare. Easy paths follow the lakeshore and can be used to climb through the forest to the south to reach a dramatic waterfall which cascades in lacy spray below a series of high impenetrable crags.

An easy, more or less level path runs south from the top of the Neunerkopf to the first of three descending lakes; the first is marked by a small but very hospitable alpine hut, the Landsberger. The walk is easy to this point, but beware of the sting in its tail, for you must lose something like 602m (1,978ft) down a rocky path in a little over three-quarters of a mile, to reach the valley and the lake at Vilsalpsee.

Back on the main road, the last two villages in the Tannheimertal before reaching the German border are **Zöblen** and **Schattwald**.

Zöblen is quieter, even though it lines the busy main road. The village makes a good starting point for a series of walks, both high- and low-level, through woods on either side of the road. Schattwald is a little brash as is the case of many frontier villages; its shops offer duty free Austrian rum, a drink which regretfully seems to lose its character when taken out of the country. The customs post is about 2km (just over a mile) on the Austrian side of the frontier below the rarely closed Oberjoch Pass. Pedestrians can follow a much better route into Germany by following the Vils valley northwards, still in Austria to Gasthof Rehbach before crossing the sparsely wooded semi-moorland border to reach the pretty German village of Unter- joch. The border crosses open fields and is marked by small, often overgrown concrete blocks, but once into Germany the houses have undergone an imperceptible change and for people who live away from mainland Europe the walk can make an exciting culmination to their holiday.

Further Information
— Leutasch and Tannheimertal —

Leutasch and its Valley

Accommodation

Details of hotels, *Gasthöfe* and camp sites can be obtained from local tourist information offices:
Fremdenverkersverband Leutasch
A – 6105 Leutasch – Tirol
☎ (95214) 6207
    or
Fremdenverkersverband Seefeld
A – 6100 Seefeld – Tirol
☎ (05212) 2313

Places of Interest in the Area

Innsbruck
Major centre for the Tyrol. Rail and bus links, shops, restaurants. Famous architecture, museums, events. Cablecar ascent of the Karwendel range.

Leutascher Klamm
Deep gorge made by the Leutasch river and only accessible by a planked footpath which penetrates deep into the shady recess of the narrow defile. May be viewed on the walk to Mittenwald.

Mittenwald
(Germany)
Attractively decorated buildings. Violin centre (museum in old part of town). Rail link. NB: It is pos- sible to reach Mittenwald on foot by following the Leutasch river downstream to the border and using the forest paths as far as the town. Return by public transport via Seefeld.

Oberammergau
(Germany)
Old town famous for its Passion

Play. Access by road or rail and/or bus from Seefeld.

Seefeld

Shops, restaurants, play area, swimming pool, horse riding, golf, funicular railway and cablecar ascents of nearby mountains.

Recommended Map

Mayr Wanderkarte 1:30,000 Seefeld (NB: If you have any difficulty finding a supplier of this map outside Austria, it is available through the Seefeld Fremenverkersverband.)

Tannheimertal

Accommodation

Hotels range from the four-star Rote Fluh to inexpensive *Gasthöfe*. Rented apartments, camp sites. For details apply to
Fremdenverkehrsverband
A – 6675 Tannheim
☎ (05675) 6220 or 6303

Places of Interest in the Area

Füssen
(Germany)
Smart busy town on the south shore of the Forggensee. Shops, banks, lake cruises. Conveniently near King Ludwig of Bavaria's Neuschwanstein and Hohenschwangau castles.

Hahnenkamm Alpenblumengarten
Alpine garden with plants growing in their true environment. Access by cablecar from Höfen near Reutte.

Hindelang
(Germany)
Ski and holiday resort below the Oberjoch Pass. Shops, swimming pool (spa) and chairlifts.

Jungholz
Curious diamond-shaped portion of Austria to the north of the Oberjoch Pass and completely surrounded by Germany. Access from the road between Oberjoch and Wertach.

Kleiner Walsertal
Austrian toll-free area, only accessible through Germany by way of Immenstadt.

Pfronten
(Germany)
North of the Tannheim mountains. Shops. Nearest railway station to Tannheim. Useful for special deliveries of luggage before or during the holiday. Bus connections.

Reutte
Busy but pleasant town at the junction of the Lech and Grundbach valleys. Shops, restaurants, camp site, cablecar (Höfen). Nearest Austrian railway station for the Tannheim area — good bus service. Road and rail connections via Ehrwald for the cablecar ascent of the Zugspitze, Germany's highest mountain.

Recommended Map

Kompass Wanderkarte 1:50,000 Sheet 2
Füssen — Ausserfern

4 • Southern Valleys and High Peaks

The main Inn valley goes south-west from Prutz to cross the border into Switzerland just beyond Pfunds, or beyond Nauders and the Reschenpass into Italy. However, the valley now has a motorway. At Prutz there is a choice of routes. On the western side of the valley there are three delightful villages — Ladis, Fiss and Serfaus. They all give fast access to the peaks of the Samnaun group by either chairlift or cablecars from where peaks of over 2,500m (8,200ft) can be relatively easily reached by good walkers. At **Ladis** the castle ruins and the little white bell tower on the church are worth a visit, while **Serfaus** has a fourteenth-century baroque church and some pretty painted houses. Across the valley and reached from Prutz is the hamlet of **Fendels**, a typical small Tyrolean village — a collection of houses in an area of meadows with woods and mountains as a background.

Descending from Fendels to Prutz turn right up the Kaunertal. It is 25km (15$^1/_2$ miles) up to the Stausee Gepatsch. From the lake the new road runs on to the Gepatsch House, from where all year round skiing takes place on the nearby glacier. Probably missed by the midsummer skiers on the way up, or down, the Kaunertal, are the delights of Kaunerberg. This is the collective name given to the area just east of Prutz and occupying a sunny terrace on the south facing side of the valley. Three villages make up the Kaunerberg: **Prantach**, **Kaltenbrunn** and **Kauns**. All these villages near Prutz are off the beaten track, are unbelievably photogenic and are set on sunny terraces above the main valley rivers.

Above Pfunds the road divides. The 315 goes over the Reschenpass into Italy, the right fork, now the 184, goes into Switzerland and the Engadine valley. By going up the 184 into Switzerland at Martina, via a narrow cleft in the mountains, a minor road can be

Nauders

used to cut back, steeply uphill, to Nauders.

Nauders lies in a basin where, it is claimed, the sun shines more brightly and for longer than anywhere else. Even at this altitude, (1,400m, 4,592ft) crops are grown. The village has facilities for swimming, tennis, riding and, of course, walking. The castle began life as the administrative centre for the upper Inn valley, gaining strategic importance during the Swiss Wars of Independence. However, the real strategic spot is Old Finstermünz. The old road crossed the river at the Innbrücke and a tower was built to straddle the road. This was backed up by a secondary tower and natural caves were used as another back up. Successive enlargements have left nothing earlier than the fifteenth century.

Pfunds is really two villages divided by the river, Pfunds Stuben and Pfunds Dorf. In the village there are a number of fine old inns, typical of the area. Express horsedrawn coaches used to run this way and Pfunds was one of the post stations. In a village of this importance there would have been anything up to fifty horses.

On the way down the main valley again pause at the Pontlatzer Bridge. On the left bank there is a memorial commemorating the battles in which the Tyroleans held the Bavarians in 1703, and also in 1809 a French force marching to Finstermünz. Lower down a turning to the right twists its way up to **Fliess**, another beautiful village sitting high on a terrace to catch the sun. It is the gateway to the

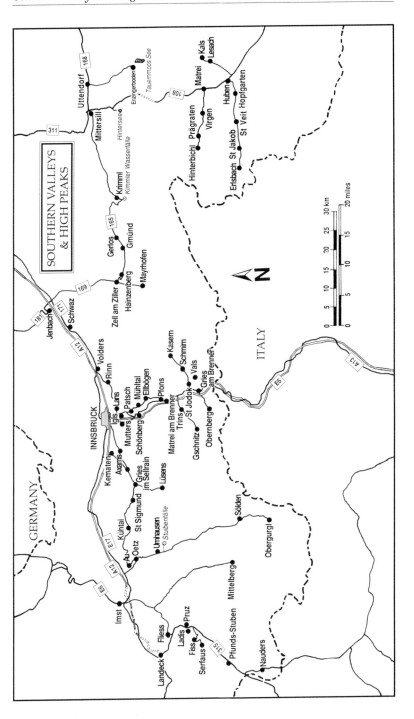

SOUTHERN VALLEYS
& HIGH PEAKS

Pfunds

Pillerwald and the hamlet of Piller. This beautiful byway climbs from about 800m (2,624ft) at the river Inn, to 1,073m (3,519ft) at Fliess, then to 1,558m (5,110ft) at the Pillerhöhe Gasthaus, all within 6km (3½ miles), then descends gradually into the next valley, the Pitztal. Close to the Alpenblick Gasthaus the road divides. To the left is Wenns and to the right Jerzens and the Pitztal.

There are five villages in the Pitztal and the highest at the head of the valley is Mittelberg, at 1,734m (5,688ft). Nearby the Riffelsee can be reached by cablecar taking the sting out of the climb up to this fantastic region of peace and quiet among the glaciers of the Ötztaler Alps. The valley begins around **Imst** and ends abruptly, after 25km (15½ miles), at **Mittelberg** and the steely blue ice wall of a glacier. The villages cater for mountain holidays, with frequent guided walks in the valleys and guides available for rock or ice climbing parties.

The Ötztal is the next valley to the east. It is famous for being the place with the village of **Obergurgl**, at 1,927m (6,321ft), the highest village in Austria with a church. As such it attracts visitors and is a visiting point for coach tours. For some, the best part of the village is the statue of the old fashioned mountain guide, hand outstretched

The hamlet of Au

pointing to the mountains. The Ötztal Glacier Road, which is one of the highest in the Alps (2,822m, 9,256ft at the highest point) enables the less active to visit and see the glories of the high mountains and glaciers. The objective in building the roads was to open up the Rettenbach glacier to all year round skiing. The opening of the Tiefenbach tunnel enabled the adjacent valley glacier to be used. There is a large parking area here beside the restaurant Tiefenbach. The road from Sölden is a toll road, and a very exciting drive. At **Umhausen,** the oldest village, the large Gasthaus Krone is typical of the district. Customers may still ask to see a room furnished in seventeenth-century style. From the tourist office a signposted path leads to the Stuibenfälle, a picturesque cascade where the torrent tumbles down a rocky ravine.

On the way back down the deep cut and often narrow valley (it was closed in August for 2 days a few years ago after rain and snow caused an avalanche) stop at **Ötz** for a diversion over the Kühtai.

The original Schloss Kühtai was a hunting lodge of Emperor Maximillian I. It has now been converted into a hotel. The road from Ötz soon passes the hamlet of Au and then climbs up to the hamlet of Wald. Another steep climb follows which leads up to the Kühtai plateau. There are walks round the larger lakes in this entrancing area and views over the many smaller lakes dotted around like jewels. The summit of the pass is just beyond the village. Beyond is the weekend playground for the people of Innsbruck, the Sellraintal.

Near the summit of the Brenner Pass

Almost as if they want to keep this for themselves, and who could blame them, this area hardly gets a mention in any guide books. A lovely circular walk is possible from just below the pass summit. Take the path to the Hirscheben See, from there to the Plenderles See. Actually there are three Plenderles lakes — the Unteren, the Mittleren and the Oberen Plenderles See. At this altitude go easy unless you are used to it. The air starts to thin at 2,000m (6,560ft), so anyone gasping is not necessarily unfit. Because the air is thin the sun is less filtered so a good sun cream is advisable, and a hat to shade the back of one's neck. The return route joins path 146 down to the village. A chairlift can whisk the less agile from just below the pass summit to the middle lake. Allow 4 hours if the whole walk is to be accomplished.

On the descent side of the pass towards Innsbruck the villages of Haggen, St Sigmund and Gries im Sellrain follow in that order, all of which are worth investigating. From Gries a valley goes south for about 15km (9 miles). Passing the hamlet of Juifenau, the next village, Praxmar, is off up the west side of the valley, while near the valley head is Lüsens. Appropriately named the Lüsenstal, there are opportunities from either village for circular walks. From **Praxmar** experienced hillwalkers could attempt the Zischgeles peak, 3,004m (9,853ft). Climb by path 1 and allow 4 hours to the peak, which is a splendid viewpoint. The return goes easterly at first before swinging

The Brenner motorway

north back to the village. A slightly easier walk goes from Lüsens to the Westfalen Haus, 2,276m (7,465ft), a mountain hut. There is also an alternative return route.

From Gries down the Sellrain is about 8km (5 miles). Here a decision must be made. Directly down the valley is Kematen, the main Inn valley, and Innsbruck, within an hours drive. However, at Sellrain look for the minor road going to **Axams** and Axamer Lizum. It is 22km (13$^{1}/_{2}$ miles) from Innsbruck and the area has been host to the Winter Olympics. A choice of chairlifts or a funicular railway can quickly take visitors to an area which boasts of its unspoilt mountain scenery.

From Mutters the road leading up to the Brenner Pass is soon reached. Avoid the motorway but stop at the viewpoint for the Europa Bridge and wonder at the construction.

Schönberg marks the turning point to the Stubaital. Summer skiing is possible on the glaciers at the head of the valley so there is always some traffic. The main valley is famous as the Brenner Pass but the valley itself is the Wipptal. It is not one of the most beautiful valleys in the Tyrol, but the ease of access makes it popular. Above the Stubai is the Gschnitztal, and there are two hamlets decorating this romantic valley, Trins and Gschnitz. If visiting this valley do take the footpath 126 from **Gschnitz** to the little church of St Magdalena. The view from the church back down the valley is enchanting. Allow $2^1/_2$ hours for the ascent. An alternative descends by footpath 102 to the bus stop below the village. This is a perfect example of an unspoilt high alpine valley, as is the next one off the main valley, which is even higher. The Obernberg Tal is reached from **Gries am Brenner** via the hamlet of Vinaders. The village of Obernberg is strung out along the valley. At the end of the public road is the Gasthaus Waldesruh.

This pearl among so many alpine jewels is easily reached in 45 minutes from the car park, up the private road to the Gasthaus Orbernberger See at the northern end of the lake. The lake itself is in two parts and on the eastern shore, on a hillock, is the tiny Seekapelle or Lake Chapel.

Between Gries and Steinach is **St Jodok**. It is just off the main valley road (the junction is at the hamlet of Stafflach) and gives access to the Valsertal and the hamlet of Vals. The railway makes a great loop round St Jodok and although some of it is in a tunnel, it is fascinating to mark the passage of a train and follow the easiest contour for the ascent of the line. On some maps the road is shown as ending at Vals, but in fact it continues up to a castle ruin. The southern branch of the valley from St Jodok, though not much longer, has the hamlets of Rohrach, Schmirn and Kasern, which is the last one. These are the ones shown on road maps, though there are other hamlets. The road goes on beyond Kasern to the road head, where there is a modern chapel and a parking space.

The next valley to the right on the way down the Wipptal is the Navistal which is reached almost at Matrei am Brenner. The road ends just beyond the village as far as traffic is concerned, though two private roads go higher and it is perfectly in order to walk these roads.

On the return to the main valley be sure to take the minor road to Pfons, Innerellbögen, Mühltal and then, missing Igls, take the right fork towards Lans and Sistrans. This is the Ellbögen road and it was once a salt road. Just south of **Patsch** there is a good viewpoint of the Sill Valley. **Igls** is a popular point for visitors from Innsbruck and there are frequent buses to and from the city and a tram car. Visitors to the area often prefer to stay at Igls and visit the city from there.

It would be a shame to be so close and not visit **Schloss Ambras**, one of the best preserved castles in Austria. Take the road from Lans to Aldrans. The first record of a castle was in the eleventh century, built for the dukes of Andechs. Archduke Ferdinand had the place

The Roggalspitze above Spullersee, Vorarlberg

The winter sports resort of Lech

Zug, Vorarlberg

completely rebuilt and in 1576 the family moved in, but building went on for some years afterwards. Much of the archduke's personal collection has been removed to Vienna but an impressive display of weapons and armour remain along with many other displays in various rooms. The grounds are extensive and contain the original jousting area. A guided tour of the house takes $1\frac{1}{4}$ hours, and with a tour of the grounds and lunch a good part of a day can easily be spent at Ambras.

Leave Ambras on the minor road to Rinn and Tulfes via Aldrans. Beyond Tulfes take care not to miss the turn to **Volders**. The Servites' church (Servitenkirche) is a fine example of baroque art, completed in 1654 with the clock tower added in 1740. There is a good view of the church from the river bridge. Linked to the church by a passageway is the monastery which is now a seminary for the Servites.

Volders has a camp site, as have Weer and Pill, which are all on this road leading to **Schwaz**. This is a very interesting place, as it was hereabouts that rich finds of silver were made, making the moving of the mint from Meran a sensible proposition. The mines were in full production in the fifteenth and sixteenth centuries. It had a higher population at that time than any Tyrolean town except Innsbruck, and remains an important town today. On the outskirts, sitting boldly on the castle mound, is Schloss Freundsberg, now the town museum. The town dates from the twelfth century and there are exhibits reflecting this, and the mining industry. The local council care for 50km (31 miles) of footpaths. This is a custom in Austria, and especially in the Tyrol. With an eye to the tourist industry, towns and villages care for the footpaths to ensure the safety and comfort of guests.

From Schwaz take the road across the river, across the valley and across the motorway heading for Stans. Continue towards Jenbach and prepare to be entranced, amazed and awed. A jewel among so many jewels, anyone interested to the slightest degree in historical buildings will be delighted with **Tratzberg**. Its beginnings lie almost in the realms of legend, early records are few but its first mention was in 1149. Two brothers of the Rottenburg line were squires to the counts of Andechs but disputed about which house to follow, Hapsburg or Bavaria. One took over Rottenburg, across the valley and now a ruin, the other brother started to build Tratzberg, out of spite it is said, and the name is derived from *trotzen* meaning 'to defy'. The castle's present state of good repair is due to the owners, the counts of Enzenberg, who inherited in 1847. They halted decay and did much restorative work.

Not all of the castle is open to view, but even so, it is impossible to describe fully here. The family rooms are open, along with the Hapsburg Hall, the armoury and the queen's bedchamber which shows the culmination of the splendours of the Renaissance period. In the castle chapel, dedicated to St Catherine and consecrated in 1508, the altar painting shows the beheading of the saint. It has been said of the castle that 'It ideally imparts a picture of sixteenth century culture'.

Carry on through Jenbach to the Zillertal and Mayrhofen. The Zillertal is well known to many British visitors, so only the splendid high alpine road built up the Zemmtal to the large lake of Schlegeis-Speicher, passing the village of Dornauberg on the way, will be mentioned here. There is a car park near the lake beside the Dominikus Hütte, from where moderately level walks can be made to look at the views. The whole road gives magnificent views of some of the highest peaks of the Zillertal Alps. There are some tunnels above Dornauberg, the first of which is 3km (nearly 2 miles) long, and there are a number of hairpin bends.

Return to the main valley at Zell am Ziller and take road 165 towards the Gerlos Pass, a toll road, passing through the hamlets of Hainzenberg and Gmünd with a series of hairpin bends on the first assault up to Hainzenberg. **Gerlos** itself is in a hanging valley, a winter and summer resort in a secluded combe. The route over the Gerlos Pass is classed as a scenic route, and this in an area of spectacular scenery.

The road winds through an area of pinewoods and pastures, and many visitors travel this romantic route. There are comfortable low-level walks through the woods and meadows to the welcoming *alms*, and chairlifts to whisk the more adventurous up to the higher levels. To the north of the village are the Kitzbüheler Alps and a chairlift goes up to the Ebenfelder Aste, 1,820m (5,970ft), from where a path, D2, goes to the Kreuzjoch, which is the highest peak in the range. The path is not too difficult for experienced hillwalkers and the start is over wonderful alpine pastures, full of flowers in their season. Allow 6 hours for the round trip. There are some wonderful quiet side valleys worth exploring from Gerlos.

A wide sweep of road round the Durlassboden Dam starts the climb to the pass, with a second sweep climbing higher with a good view over the lake. The old road to the original Gerlos Pass has been left in favour of a newer road which goes even higher. The route left the Tyrol just by the Durlassboden Dam and is now in the province of Salzburg. From the car park at the pass summit the descent is fast and winding. Do not stop on the road to admire the view, there are car parks at the best viewpoints. The first view is the Pinzgau valley, running to the east, and the **Krimml Falls**. Next is a view of the Burgwandkere Lake with its hillock the Trattenköpfl. Just as the road sweeps round to enter a tunnel there is another car park and a closer view of the falls.

The falls are the highest in Europe descending 383m (1,256ft) in a series of giant falls and cascades. The best time to view the falls is at midday when the sun is behind them. The biggest of the sections are the higher falls and it is worth the effort to see them. Allow 3-4 hours altogether, as the path from Krimml twists and turns up through the wood with many side turnings to viewing points. There is the Tauernhaus at the top of the falls and the Schönangerl on the lower section for that welcome refreshment. If the falls are in spate a raincoat is a good idea, as there is a lot of spray. There is a car park convenient for visiting the falls. Also visit the church in **Krimml**, where the Madonna in the parish church is notable.

This is the Upper Pinzgau valley. To the south lies the Hohe Tauern range which contains the highest peaks in Austria. This is an area of folklore and romantic fable. Stories of mountain caves lined with crystal abound. They are true, in essence. A local historian, Josef Lahnsteiner, was amazed when he shone his torch into a crevice on the Knappenwand near Neunkirchen and saw 'a profusion ... shining and sparkling ... glowing with unimaginable grandeur'. Aquamarines and garnets of a high quality used to be found.

On the road down the valley below Rosenthal is the Rasthaus Venedigerblick. As the name implies there is a view, south up the Untersulzbachtal, to the Gross Venediger. Stop in the village of **Habach** and visit the Habachtal, the one place in Europe where emeralds could be found. There are emeralds from here in the British Crown Jewels. Sadly, stones of comparative purity were always rare and attempts in recent years to revive the emerald mines have failed. However, stones are still found, even if of a poorer quality.

It is now just over 12km (7¹/₂ miles) to Mittersill past the villages of Bramberg, Mühlbach and Hollersbach, and the run down the widening valley is delightful and relaxing after the Gerlos Pass. **Mittersill** is a bustling little town just off the main 108 road going south to the East Tyrol. There are a number of shops, as befits a winter and summer resort. There is no shortage of accommodation, and in the main street there is a delightful *Konditorei* (cake shop). Here the customer chooses at the cake counter and then proceeds to the café where the waitress serves the chosen cake — a delightful custom.

From Mittersill take road 108 south towards Lienz and the East Tyrol. When, in 1918, the South Tyrol was given to Italy the East Tyrol became a backwater. Cut off from the North Tyrol it was isolated for most of the winter as the Grossglockner Strasse is closed for a few months. The inhabitants had to deal with serious economic problems. The Felber Tauern Tunnel changed all that. The tunnel, 5km (3 miles) long, joins the Pinzgau, by way of the Amertal, with the Iseltal. This gave the East Tyrol an all weather road to the north. Many of the tunnels and high passes in Austria are toll roads. This is because many have been improved, and some even had to be built, just to cater for through traffic. The Austrian authorities decided that the traffic should help bear the cost.

On the way up from Mittersill, after about 6km (3½ miles) there is the hamlet of Amerthal and the chance to branch off to the right up to the Hintersee. To the left of the road there is a huge area dedicated as a nature reserve (*naturschutzpark*). Access can be gained to the other side of this reserve via Uttendorf 8km (5 miles) east of Mittersill. Here there is another side valley climbing deep into the mountains. At its head is **Enzingerboden**, a small hamlet with a mountain inn, a car park, an electricity works and a cablecar. The cablecar goes in two stages up to the Rudolfshütte, 2,315m (7,593ft) which is open all year round, quite a feat at this altitude, and is classed as an alpine centre. This is a fantastic area. There are four lakes, the highest of which is the Weisssee (White Lake), and the largest the Tauernmoossee. The cablecar ride gives extensive views over the lakes and mountains. These high mountain lakes have been extended by dams and, of course, are associated with the hydro-electric schemes.

Experienced walkers might like to try walking back down (buy a one-way ticket). It is only 5 or 6km (3-4 miles) but it does descend over 800m (2,624ft). Walking down is easier on the lungs, but it really bites the knees. The less energetic could go to the halfway station at the Tauernmoossee and walk along the dam.

Along the valley ascent from Uttendorf are the hamlets of Fellern and Schneiderau. A quiet walk up the side valley south-west from **Schneiderau** may be rewarding to bird watchers. Eagles are reasonably common, and there are supposed to be vultures in this area.

All this has been in Salzburg province. The tunnel takes the road through to the East Tyrol. Climbing upwards, the main road reaches the head of the Amertal. On the final stretches the vegetation gets sparse and snow lingers in the crevices longer. Finally the tunnel is entered.

On emerging from the tunnel look for the car park. There is a good viewpoint to the west to the Grossvenediger. Just a little way down the valley there is a turning to the right and the chance for a walk from near the Matreir Tauern House to visit a beautiful valley and an unusual chapel at Aussergschloss. It is part of a huge rock. At the Matreir Tauern House drive on between the inn and the chapel and a little way on is a narrow gap which leads through to a large car park close to a chairlift, enabling people to reach the higher walks. There is a restaurant at the top of the chairlift at 2,000m (6,560ft), and a little higher is the Grünsee, in a splendid mountain setting. The main valley road, however, also provides entrancing views.

The main valley track is wide and the going is easy. There is a refreshment stop at the top of the first rise. The chapel in the rock is a little way further; it must have been hollowed out of the solid rock and the front built on. The track passes, at **Aussergschloss**, a small group of what by now must be historic farm buildings. Pass the Felsen chapel (the chapel in the rock), and then on, almost level, to **Innergschloss**, another ancient hamlet. The valley is beautiful and the view ahead of the Grossvenediger is dramatic. A brilliant white peak set against a blue sky dominates the head of the valley. The ascent of the peak takes 9 hours and is only for skilled mountain walkers.

Return to the main road and continue down the valley. The route has crossed another major European watershed: the river down this valley is the Tauern, which loses its identity at Matrei to the Isel, which comes down the Virgental. The Isel in turn loses its identity to the Drau at Lienz. The Drau actually starts in Italy and comes down the Pustertal. When the river reaches Yugoslavia it is called the Drava. However, it will be some time before Lienz and the Drau are reached, as there are some interesting side valleys to explore.

Pause at **Matrei**, which could be used as a base for the exploration of the area. There is an information office in town which has many leaflets on things to do and places to visit. A single sheet newspaper type leaflet also offers comprehensive information about what is available in the town. The list includes the open air pool, hotel pools open to the public, tennis — both indoors and out — riding, bicycle hire, fishing, hunting and even wild-water raft touring trips on the Isel. If all this sounds exhausting there are still the quiet, gentle footpaths with convenient seats under shady trees where the views may be enjoyed in solitary contemplation.

One of the attractions of Matrei is the Prosseggklamm (gorge), which is close to the hamlet of Prossegg and about 2km (just over a mile) north of Matrei on a byroad. Another attraction is the Zedla-

Schloss Weissenstein, Matrei

cher Paradies, where the larchwoods are the main attraction. Another circular walk starts from the nearby hamlet of Zedlach, 4km

Virgen

(2$^1/_2$ miles) west of Matrei into the Virgental. Both walks take about 2$^1/_2$ hours and are easy going.

Back in Matrei there is a late baroque church attributed to Hagenauer and the Nikolauskirche with some early thirteenth-century frescoes, some of the oldest in Austria. The nearby castle of Weissenstein is unfortunately not open to the public, but a convenient layby on the main road just north of the town gives a good view. Matrei also has a small museum, quite a number of shops, and is the local centre for climbing in the area. It lies at the junction of the Virgental, and this fine, unspoilt valley is well worth visiting. On this south side of the massive Tauern range, which contains the highest mountains in Austria, the climate begins to change, and down in Lienz there are even palm trees. From Matrei, go into the Virgental. It is 23km (14 miles) long and has three main villages, Virgen, Prägraten, and, at the head of the valley, Hinterbichl. This is a very pretty and unspoilt valley, quiet, as there is no through traffic, and a splendid walking area. A lovely place for a peaceful holiday.

Huben stands guard at the next valley junction and here there are two side valleys to explore. To the east is the Kalsertal, with quite an easy drive up to the New Lucknerhaus beyond Kals. Here there is a

Mariahilf in the Defereggental

large car park and a glimpse of the peak of the Grossglockner. The path to the Luckner hut, or even the Studl hut (2,801m, 9,187ft) is quite safe and from the Studl hut there are some good views to the glaciers round the higher peaks. Indeed this can be a start point for an ascent of the Grossglockner itself — but only for experienced mountaineers.

From **Lesach**, the hamlet below Kals, walk up the beautiful unspoilt valley to the Lesacheralm hut, a climb of 500m (1,640ft). The road can be followed up, and after refreshments at the hut, the path by the stream can be followed down.

On the opposite side of the main valley, through Huben, is the Defereggental, cutting deep into the Defereggen mountains. **Hopfgarten** is the first village, with a chairlift going up to the north which gives access to the higher ridge and splendid views. St Veit and St Jakob follow, both fine unspoilt villages. In the parish church at **St Veit** there are some fourteenth-century frescoes. **St Jakob** is a lovely little tourist village and would make a good centre for a stay. There are tours to other areas, shops, banks, hotels, a swimming pool, sports hall and some lovely short walks.

Until recent years the last village, Erlsbach, marked the end of the road but it is now possible to drive over the Staller Pass, 2,055m (6,740ft) and so into Italy. The descent side into Italy is one of the most

St Veit in Defereggental

dramatic roads it is possible to drive on. It is narrow, twisting, steep and definitely not for nervous drivers. However, it is possible to drive down into Italy and return via Toblach and the Pustertal to Lienz. On the last approach to the Staller Pass pause and walk round the lake and the nearby area. It will only take an hour. Even if you do not intend to drive down into Italy it is possible to stand with one foot on each side of the border and look down the steep slope onto the Italian side. The view is worth the effort.

Back in the main valley, towards Lienz, it is worth stopping off the main road to visit St Johann, Görlach or Schlaiten, all lying quietly off the main road between Huben and Lienz. During the seventeenth and eighteenth centuries **Schlaiten** was a place of pilgrimage, to the parish church, which is dedicated to St Paul.

Further Information
— Southern Valleys and High Peaks —

Activities

Finkenberg
Swimming.

Fugen
Swimming.

Gerlos
Sailing, fishing, swimming.

Gmünd
Swimming.

Hintertux
All year round skiing, easy walking, cablecars, chairlifts.

Hochgurgl
Swimming, summer skiing.

Igls
Patscherkofel cablecar, swimming, bathing lake, safe, high-level walks.

Jenbach
Zillertal railway, Jenbach to Mayrhofen. Occasionally in steam. Also rack and pinion railway to Achensee.

Kalsertal
Chairlift, walking from Lesach.

Kaprun
Skiing (summer), cablecar, chairlift.

Langenfield
Swimming, fishing, riding, cycle hire.

Matrei
Swimming, riding, chairlift.

Matrier Tauern House
Walk up the valley, chairlift, splendid views.

Mayrhofen
Tennis, riding, swimming.

Nauders
Swimming, tennis, fishing, summer skiing in Kauntertal.

Obergurgl
Chairlift, swimming, tennis.

Obernberg
Lakeside walk.

Schlitters
Swimming.

Ötz
Fishing.

Schwaz
Chairlift, swimming, riding, tennis.

Sölden
Cablecar, swimming, summer skiing, fishing, riding.

Stubaital
Summer skiing, swimming.

Virgental
Unspoilt, high alpine valley.

Zell am Ziller
Cycle hire, fishing, swimming, tennis.

Places to Visit in the Area

Ambras
Superb castle between Lans and Aldrans
Collections of armour, paintings and rare objects from medieval times. Original jousting area and attractive gardens.
Open: May to September daily (except Tuesdays) 10am-4pm.

Axams
Funicular railway.

Defereggental
Charming, unspoilt mountain villages.

Imst
Parish church and old town.

Kalsertal
Kalser Tauern House.

Krimml
Krimml Falls. Parish church.

Langenfeld
Museum, plague chapel, larch-woods.

Lannersbach
Watermill.

Maria Luggau
Pilgrimage church.

Matrei
Small town, shops, small museum.

Mittersill
Lovely little town at a useful junction of roads.

Nauders
Old castles. Picturesque villages of Pfunds and Reid im Oberinntal.

Obernberg
Seekapelle.

Schlegeis-Speicher
Large lake at 1,780m (5,838ft) with magnificent views, reached by high alpine road.

Schwaz
Fifteenth-century parish church; Franciscan church; cloisters.

Museum (Schloss Freundsberg)
On the south-eastern outskirts of the town.
Open: mid-April to mid-September daily 9am-5pm.

Tratzberg
Superb castle on a minor road between Jenbach and Stans
☎ (05242) 3566 (castle) or (05242) 2284 (estate office) for details of guided tours
Open: summer months.
Fantastic collection of arms, furniture and paintings, set out as a home.

Umhausen
Stuiben Falls, seventeenth-century
inn.

Wald
Gothic churchyard.

Tourist Information Offices

Bruck
☎ (06545) 295

Gerlos
☎ (05284) 5244

Gries am Brenner
☎ (05274) 254

Gries im Sellrain
☎ (05236) 224

Hintertux
☎ (05287) 308

Hopfgarten in Defereggental
☎ (04872) 5356

Huben
☎ (04872) 5238

Igls
☎ (05222) 25715

Kals
☎ (04876) 211

Krimml
☎ (06564) 239

Matrei
☎ (04875) 6527

Matrei am Brenner
☎ (05273) 6278

Mayrhofen
☎ (05285) 2305

Mittersill
7 Poststrasse
☎ (06562) 369

Nauders
☎ (05473) 220

Neukirchen
☎ (06565) 6550

Obernberg am Brenner
☎ (05274) 532

Ötz
☎ (05252) 6669

Prägraten
☎ (04877) 5217

Reid im Zillertal
☎ (05283) 2307

St Jakob im Defereggental
☎ (04873) 5228

St Leonhard
☎ (05413) 8216

Schlitters
☎ (05288) 2847

Schwaz
☎ (05242) 3240

Uttendorf
☎ (06563) 585

Wenns
☎ (05414) 263

Zell am Ziller
☎ (05282) 2281

5 • Lienz, Hohe Tauern and the Saalach River

L ienz is the focal point of the East Tyrol. It lies at an important junction: the Isel valley to the north, the Pustertal going up to the Italian border to the west, the Drava valley going south-east and the route east then north over the Iselberg and then the Grossglockner road. At one time this was a strategic crossroads. The counts of Görz chose to live at Lienz and built Schloss Bruck, probably on the site of a Roman citadel which had previously guarded the valleys.

Schloss Bruck lies just outside the town and is now the town museum (Ost Tiroler Heimatmuseum). Exhibits include finds from the nearby Roman excavations, local antiquities, handiwork, folklore and paintings by Tyrolean painters. The castle dates from the thirteenth century, was partially restored in the sixteenth century and is very well preserved. Among the outstanding features are the tower, the Rittersaal (Knights Hall) showing how the castle must have looked in medieval times, and the Romanesque chapel which has frescoes painted in the fifteenth century by Simon Van Taisten who worked on a number of churches in the Pustertal. The frescoes were commissioned by Count Leonhard and his wife Paula. Count Leonhard was the last of his line, the House of Görz. On his death the province passed to Emperor Maximillian I and became part of the Tyrol.

Lienz is very old, but unfortunately has suffered six great fires in its history. The first was in 1444 and the last in 1825. However, the town is delightful. The parish church survived the fires and there are the tombstones of Count Leonhard and his wife in Salzburg marble. A large gallery in the town gives a comprehensive view of the works of Albin Egger-Lienz (1868-1926) whose work was often inspired by the peoples and landscapes of the Tyrol. There are many shops, banks and interesting buildings round the old Hauptplatz and the

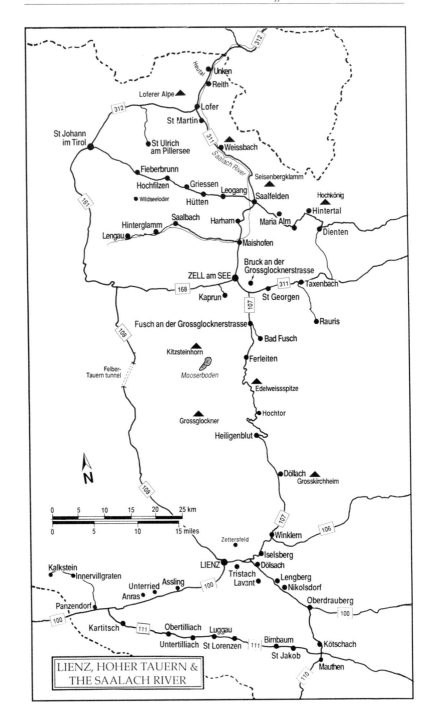

LIENZ, HOHER TAUERN &
THE SAALACH RIVER

nearby Johannesplatz and, of course, there are several lovely and fascinating churches.

A cablecar to the north-east ascends the slopes of the Zettersfeld. Good footpaths and the mountain inns make walking these areas delightfully comfortable. To the west a chairlift goes up to the Restaurant Sternalm, in two stages with a break at Schlossberg. From here one can follow the ski piste higher, or if a car is available drive up to the Bannsberger Alm. Ten minutes will then bring one up to the Hochstein hut. From there it is an hour of easy going to the peak of the Böses Weibele, 2,521m (8,269ft). Return the same way. The ridge has the Pustertal on one side and the Iseltal on the other. To the south-east the Lienzer Dolomites dominate the view.

Very close to Lienz, in fact less than 3km (2 miles) along route 100 south-east towards Spittal or Oberdrauburg is the Roman city of *Aguntum*. This is a splendid dig, the only one in the world going ahead with the aid of an original map. This map is in the form of a sheet of lead, presumed to have been part of a roof. It gives the distinction that at least here the archaeologists know where to dig. The layout of the streets and buildings can be seen in this fantastic relic of the past. At one time the ancient city had far more inhabitants than present day Lienz. However, in the fifth century the Avars and the Slavs laid waste to the city and the nearby temple. Details are still being discovered, but the ancient bishopric of *Aguntum* was last heard of in the year AD604.

The nearby temple is at **Lavant** and the outline of the ancient place of worship can be traced. There are also two more modern churches nearby; until recent years this was a place of pilgrimage.

Another fine, and dramatic, walk from Lienz is via **Tristach**. Drive up the good road to the Lienzer Dolomiten hut, then walk up to the Lasersee and the Karlsbader hut on a good, safe and easy footpath. This path cuts deep into the heart of the Lienzer Dolomites and gives closer views of the surrounding peaks. The time to the lake is 2¹/₂ hours. It was reputedly an Englishman who first recognised, in these mountains, the likeness to the larger, and more famous, Dolomites. Tristach has a small lake, the Tristacher See, which is pretty and has facilities for swimming. There is also a path all the way round the lakeside.

West from Lienz road 100 goes up the Pustertal, following the course of the river Drau. The road is good and the valley broad. To the south are the Lienzer Dolomites while to the north are the Defereggen mountains. On the south slope of the Defereggens there are a number of villages on a 'sun terrace', higher than the main valley,

The Roman temple at Lavant

and reached by a minor road. Bannberg, Assling, Unterried and Anras must be sought out on a good road map and the turning to them carefully spotted. However, they are worth the effort as they are typical unspoilt villages.

At the hamlet of Panzendorf, not far from the border, turn right for yet another of these romantic valleys. This one is the longest off the Pustertal, about 12km (7½ miles) to the top. Pass through Ausservillgraten and take the right turn through Tilliach to the Sillianer Haus, which is a mountain inn at the head of this branch. The other branch of the valley is just about as long and has the hamlets of **Innervillgraten** and **Kalkstein**, which is at the head of this branch and is in a loop of the Italian border. These small villages, almost hidden from the rest of the world, are absolutely beautiful and almost entirely unspoilt.

Retracing ones steps towards the border, **Sillian** is the highest village and is almost at the frontier. Nearby is Heinfels castle, which is slowly decaying, though a wander round the walls and courtyards is rewarding. It belonged to the counts of Görz and dates from the thirteenth century.

Yet another dramatic valley lies within reach. Just beyond Panzendorf, on the way back down the valley towards Lienz, there is a

Roadside shrine at Sillian in the Pustertal

turning on the right. It leads up to Kartitsch and this remote valley, the Lesach. To the north, though not in evidence, are the Lienzer Dolomites and to the south the Karnische (Carnic) Alps. The road is number 111 and leads eventually to Villach.

Beyond Kartitsch is the highest point of the valley and by the time Leiten is reached the river Gail is running in the same direction as the road, almost south-east. The river is well below the road, deep cut in the bottom of the valley, and there are reputed to be seventy-two ravines on its course. However, the road is high on the northern, or sunny, side and the ravines are far below. This means that there are some very fine views of the valley from the road itself. These are best seen by driving down the valley on the route described. There is a

The old bridge at Panzendorf in the Pustertal

splendid double waterwheel near **Untertilliach** and a mill museum at **Luggau**.

Altogether there are six villages in this beautiful valley, which are certainly off the beaten track. Below Leiten and in order of appearance are Obertilliach, Luggau, St Lorenzen, Kornet and St Jakob. From the pass summit it is 53km (33 miles) to Kötschach. In the course of this run the route leaves the East Tyrol and enters Carinthia.

The border is hardly notable but the next village, **Luggau**, is. Here is the pilgrimage church of St Maria Luggau. Testimonials from satisfied supplicants are on display, currently dated. On either side of the village, on the approach, the stations of the cross line the road. The story started in 1513 when a young woman had a dream, various miracles followed and the story began. It is told in full on a series of picture boards in the cloisters. The stations of the cross are repeated at St Jakob, but this time leading up a grassy ridge to a chapel on a hill.

Just outside the hamlet of **Birnbaum** is a small layby from where there is a good view south to the hamlets of Woodmaier and Nostra, across the river. Even more remote is the hamlet of **Tuffbad**, which can be reached by a very minor road turning left just as the outskirts of St Lorenzen are reached. It is claimed that in this remote corner of Carinthia more of the local colour and original costumes survive than anywhere else. The local summer festivals attract a wide local

The double waterwheel near Untertilliach

audience, and Carinthian cooking specialities are renowned. It is also an area where the walking and climbing are superb. This valley has a happy and contented feel to it, giving a sense of wellbeing and calm.

At the twin resorts of Kötschach and Mauthen, once the last hairpin bends have been negotiated (not bad ones) there is a cross-roads. East is the Gailtal and Villach. South is the Plöcken Pass and Italy, and north is the Gailbergsattel, leading back to the Drau valley and on towards Lienz. In Kötschach there is a sixteenth-century Gothic church, and in its doorways and buttresses the local red sandstone has been used in the complicated vaulting and groining typical of the late Gothic.

The main valley is reached once more at Oberdrauburg. Those with time to spare should not rush headlong back to Lienz but, soon after re-entering the East Tyrol, branch off to the right to Nikolsdorf and Lengberg to escape the traffic. Soon after being forced to rejoin the main road a decision must be made. A turn left leads to Lavant, and Tristach where the locals from Lienz spend summer weekends by the lakeside. On the other side of the main road is the straggling hamlet of Dölsach and a short cut through to main roads 106 and 107.

The road now starts to climb the Iselsberg Pass, and just above the hairpin bends, which present no problem on this wide main road, is the village of Iselsberg. This little village has two hotels and many smaller establishments, and a shop. It is convenient for Lienz if used as a base and it is a quiet backwater from which to explore the area. There is a fair amount of self-catering accommodation available, ask at the tiny local information office which is close to the shop. There is also a holiday village higher up the pass.

Beyond the pass the road descends to Winklern where the 106 leaves, going east. This route goes north on the 107 into the Heiligenblut basin. This is the Mölltal, from the river Möll, which springs from the foot of the mighty glacier higher up beyond Heiligenblut. Incidentally the Iselsberg Pass crossed back into Carinthia for a short distance. The approach to Heiligenblut is easy and gentle, there are no steep gradients and the valley is broad and green.

Between Winklern and Heiligenblut there are five villages of different sizes, all of which cater for tourists. There are also three official camp sites. **Döllach** is one of the large villages and is a winter and summer resort, with facilities for riding as well as mountaineering, and a zoo.

In the village of **Grosskirchheim**, a few kilometres south of Heiligenblut, the proprietor of the Schlosswirt Hotel leads groups on horseback excursions into the surrounding area using the ancient mule tracks. The tracks go back to the time of the Celts and the Romans, when mule trains carried goods over the mountains. Later tracks were developed by the gold miners of the area.

Heiligenblut is a must as a stopping place, even if almost everyone else seems to think so too. The main road does bypass the village. The first sight of this dramatically sited village, dominated, as are most of the mountain villages, by its church, must bring a desire to stop. The tall slender spire reaching up to the sky and the mountains make a picture which cause many to reach for the camera. The church dates from the fifteenth century when the monks of Admont started it to perpetuate prayers in the name of the Relic of Holy Blood (Heiligenblut). This relic was said to have been brought to the site in the tenth century by Briccius, an officer of the court of Byzantium. His tomb lies in the crypt. An awe-inspiring sight, which is one of the great treasures of this church, is the triptych altar screen reputed to be one of the finest in Austria. In the churchyard there is a 'book' with metal pages on which are recorded the names of the victims of 'our mountains'. The village has one of the finest mountaineering schools in Austria. In the summer months it transfers to the Franz Josephs Haus.

To get away from the press of tourists take the minor road to Winkl-Heiligenblut about 2km (just over a mile) away. Really it is just an area of houses and farms, there is not even a central hamlet, but it is certainly off the beaten track and must be carefully sought out by the discerning. There are some splendid walks from here.

Clear of Heiligenblut, but before the river is recrossed, is a small collection of houses. From here path 915 goes on the south side of the river Möll up to the Wirtsbaueralm, a mountain guest house. The path does go beyond, for those who want a longer walk. It is 5km (3 miles) and 500m (1,640ft) up to the *alm*. Another interesting walk, just a little longer, is to branch off onto path 919 then branch right again at the next main fork to cross the Leiterbach and the valley of the Möll to visit the Briccius chapel from where a return can be made along long distance path 702B. A direct walk to the Briccius chapel can be made from the tiny car park at Hinterzelen. A good broad path goes up past the Sattlealpe to the chapel and requires about an hour. There is a view up to the Franz Josephs Höhe and a lovely view back over Heiligenblut and the Mölltal. Also on this path there is a fascinating little garden of alpine plants, most with a name plate which, of course, adds to the interest.

The harder and more experienced walkers could even follow the 702B from the hamlet up to the Glocknerhaus, 2,132m (6,993ft) (surely the correct way to arrive at a mountain inn, even if it is full of car-borne tourists). From there descend to the Stauzer Margaritze, 2,002m (6,567ft). Cross the dam and soon take a left fork to eventually rejoin path 915 back to the village.

If anyone has doubts about driving over the Grossglockner High Alpine Road, then relax. The drive presents no great difficulty. It is a broad highway. The car needs to be fit, of course, for there is a great amount of climbing, much of it in low gear, but the bends are wide sweeps and the edges well guarded. The Romans kept a route open all year round over this range, by a slightly different route, but the feat has never been equalled since. The present road is open from mid-May to mid-November, but early or late snowfall can always close the road temporarily. Snow can fall on the higher reaches at any time of year but it is never much of a problem in the summer months. It is quite an experience to start off in a rainy valley and gradually drive up to where 3in of snow settle on the car roof while one is absent for lunch, but the air does not feel cold and the roads remain clear. The highest point of the pass, the Hochtor, which is a short tunnel, is at 2,505m (8,216ft). Viewing areas are provided with parking, but stopping on the road is forbidden.

Motoring up the Grossglockner road one soon arrives at the toll booths. The first available stopping place is at the Kasereck where there is a good view back over the Heiligenblut basin. Soon the fork

Heiligenblut

is reached where the turn is made to visit the Franz Josephs Höhe. In busy times attendants direct the parking.

There is a path beyond all the buildings, which actually starts off through the car park exit. It is a ledge on the side of the mountain but it is quite safe. Stroll along for a while with a magnificent view over the Pasterze glacier which has a flow of 10km (6 miles). This path goes to the Hofnanns hut which is only 2km (just over a mile) away. There is a funicular railway which enables visitors to get down to the glacier itself. Plenty of people do walk out on the glacier, it is probably safe, but do have shoes with a good slip-resistant sole if you do so. Plenty of refreshments are available, but to continue the climb you must first descend to the fork.

The tunnel at the Hochtor marks the summit of the road (at 2,503m, 8,210ft) and also the border between Salzburg and Carinthia. If there is little traffic about, it is surprising how a big mountain soaks up people. It would be quite possible to imagine one was on the moon. At this altitude there are only sparse grasses, mosses and lichens growing, and a few tiny alpine flowers, far too small to be seen from the car. In the area between the Hochtor and Mittertor tunnels it is worth stopping and searching one of the grassy areas for the brilliant blue gentians — there are a few about. There are also recognisable remains of gold mining. The Hochtor area is where a small Roman statue of Hercules and a small clay lamp were found.

In just over 2km (1 mile), with the Brennkogel, 3,016m (9,892ft), on the left, the Mittertörl is passed. The next point, after a short straight section, is the small Fuscher Lacke. A short climb follows then a descent to the Fuscher Törl where there is a parking area and a mountain inn. It is also possible to visit the so called Edelweissspitze, 2,580m (8,462ft). Though your chances of spotting an edelweiss are pretty slim the views are dramatic.

It is now possible to drive up to the Edelweissspitze where there is a guest house and a pictorial story of the mountain flora and fauna in a small tower, the top of which provides a panoramic viewpoint. Apart from the official car park there are many small places where it is possible to park and leave the car for a while to test out the snow and the air.

Now the descent begins and though the engine can relax a little the driver will still need to take care. There are plenty of hairpin bends and remember to stay in low gear.

Down in the river valley when the hairpins and the gradient have eased, look for the turning to **Ferleiten**. This tiny hamlet can easily be missed by the headlong rush down to the valley. There is a pretty little church and the Hotel Tauern House, also the chance to relax on a quiet riverside walk. A narrow mountain road actually goes about 6km (3$\frac{1}{2}$ miles) back up the valley, there is little traffic and it stays round about the 1,200m (3,936ft) line.

Further down the valley, which now continues a gentler descent, there are a few hamlets, any of which are worthy of inspection. They all contain a mixture of old and new buildings. **Fusch-an-der-Grossglocknerstrasse** is the first place of some little size. A right turn here takes a road back up to **Bad Fusch**, only 6km (3$\frac{1}{2}$ miles) off the main road. Bad means bath and, of course, it is a spa. Small but pretty, it also claims to be a health resort. From Fusch to Bruck, both 'on the Grossglocknerstrasse', is only 7km (4 miles). **Bruck** is in the Pinzgau valley, a winter as well as a summer resort. It is a pretty, though touristy village. There is a camp site and a famous view of the nearby Fischorn castle. The town is saved from being overwhelmed by tourists by the fact that it is quite close to Zell-am-See which is well known to many British holidaymakers. After a tiring day in the mountains Bruck, or one of the nearby hamlets, could be a good choice to stay for a few days. There is a camp site, and there are three nearby valleys to explore.

Kaprun is the first, to the west, and is a place worthy of a visit. The sight of the dams of the Kaprun-combine is impressive. The waters thundering down from the Glockner glaciers have been harnessed and channelled into a hydro-electric scheme which is one of the most outstanding contemporary engineering feats of this country. The machine rooms are open to visitors. The town of Kaprun stands where the valley finally begins to broaden out. There is a view of the Kitzsteinhorn (3,203m, 10,506ft). It is possible to go to the summit of the mountain either by cablecar or by a funicular railway, which is mostly underground. On both it is necessary to change at the Alpine Centre Kaprun, and on the cablecar there is another change at the Salzburger hut.

This can be a spectacular and unforgettable day out. The Alpine Centre, at 2,446m (8,023ft), has one of the largest skiing areas in Austria where all year round skiing is possible. From the cablecar summit (3,029m, 9,935ft) and just below the actual Kitzsteinhorn summit the panorama of glistening snowcapped peaks is breathtaking. There is a 300m (984ft) tunnel which gives access to a panoramic gallery opening up the views to the south of the mountain and the Glockner range. To the north the views include the Berchtesgaden Alps, the Dachstein, the Karwendel, Kaisergebirge and the Wetterstein ranges.

Should you not desire to go up the mountain then there is a bus shuttle service from the Kesselfall Alpenhaus to the valley station of the Lärchwald funicular. The journey provides a view of the valley and Kaprun as well as the lakes. The engineering feats and the scenery combine to hold one in awe of the strength and beauty combined in this area. A gallery, 12km (7½ miles) long, brings water from the Pasterze glacier to the Mooserboden Lake. The Margaritze Dam, at the foot of the Grossglockner, and the Mooserboden are joined by this pipeline. A bus continues from the lower lake, the Wasserfallboden, to the upper, the Mooserboden. It is possible to walk along the dams and enjoy the views.

The next excursion into side valleys is into the Rauris valley and a change from modern to medieval. From Bruck-am-der-Grossglocknerstrasse go east on road 311 past **St Georgen**, with its Gothic church, and Gries to Taxenbach. Here take the road south into the Rauristal.

The main sight in the valley is the 100m (328ft) Kitzloch waterfall, and the gorges cut by the stream, the Rauriser Ache. Further into the valley is the town of **Rauris**, the largest in the valley and the medieval mining centre. Rauris was famous for its gold mines in Roman times. Though there was no gold rush an amazing amount of ore was removed from 100km (62 miles) of shafts and tunnels. An estimation of a million tons of ore was moved by 2,000 workers, before the

The Grossglockner

invention of gunpowder. The heyday of the mining only lasted from 1460 to 1558, and at the end of the sixteenth century a rapid decline set in which was to affect the whole social history of the Land Salzburg. Apart from mining, gold was washed down in the streams and panning for gold was known in the earliest times. One authority states that some farms in the Longau district had to pay a portion of their rent in gold. Like other areas there was also a considerable trade in precious and semi-precious stones and rock crystal; some samples weighed as much as fifty pounds. Among more than seventy types of mineral are yellow and green titamite, clear and smoky topaz and, the most precious of all, rock crystal laced with threads of gold.

Back in the main valley go east again on the 311 to Eschenau (the village is off the main road) and the turning to Dienten is almost 2km (just over a mile) on. Under the railway and over the river the road twists and turns as it climbs gently, following the Dientenbach for about 14km ($8^1/_2$ miles), to the village. Just about 4km ($2^1/_2$ miles) beyond the village the Filzensattel (saddle) is reached, at 1,291m (4,234ft).

At this point the big mountain to the north-east is the Hochkönig, 2,941m (9,646ft), but as the road turns west and starts to descend, the big range to the north marks the southern tip where Berchtesgaden lies. The south-western side of this great wall has the name Steinernes Meer, which means stony sea, and some of the villages adopt 'on the stony sea' as part of the name. When local people do this sort of thing, it can be extremely helpful. For example, there are many villages in Austria called St Peter, and even to distinguish the region does not help as there are many in one region. To identify the valley or river where the village is situated can greatly clarify the situation.

Early Austrian history is interesting, and superficially it parallels British history. Celts moving in, Roman invasion, the breakdown of the Roman Empire and subsequent withdrawal followed by invasion of warring tribes. In Austria's case it was Attila's Huns, and also the Goths. However, the Celts built a capital and called it *Noreia* and the Celtic Kingdom was known as *Noricum*. Noric horses are still bred and well liked in this area of Austria.

Turn westward to reach Hintertal, a hamlet just north of the road, and next is Hintermoos, an even smaller hamlet to the south of the road. Next again is **Maria Alm** where the pilgrimage church must be visited. Most of the village is off the main road so it is quiet, and there is a network of marked paths making strolling easy and safe.

Beyond Maria Alm by about 4km ($2^1/_2$ miles) take the minor road southwards towards Gerling. There are many hamlets and small roads down this way but why worry, let time take care of itself. Sooner or later emerge back at the main road after a sojourn in this lovely and peaceful area. Make your way eventually to Maishofen.

Across the main road here lies the Glemmtal. The valley carries the river Saalach, and along its length are four villages. In ascending order they are, Viehofen, Saalbach, Hinterglemm and Lengau which is at the road head. This is an area known as the Mitter Pinzgau (Middle Pinzgau), an area of great scenic beauty. Not the stark beauty of the high mountains and glaciers, but a gentler green beauty of bright green meadows and darker green tree covered hills. The area is a winter sports area but is also frequented very much in summer. The chairlifts go up to viewpoints from where walks are possible, or it is possible to walk at lower levels along the river valley, as the mood dictates. The river Saalach rises from the mountains round the head of this valley and runs east then north. Near Salzburg it runs into the Salzach which was seen crashing down the Krimmler waterfalls. Continuing its run through Germany the Salzach runs into the Inn near Burghausen then the Inn runs into the Danube at Passau.

Having explored the peaceful Glemmtal, drive down the valley of the Saalach to the German border. The hamlet of Harham is about halfway, once the main valley is reached, to **Saalfelden-am-der-Steinernen Meer**. This is a lively market town in the basin formed by the Leoganger Steinberg to the north, which are cut through by the river gorge. Round about the town some of the interesting sights are the parish church with a late Gothic altar, the Christmas Crib Museum in the Ritzen castle just outside town, and the Farmach castle which dates from the fourteenth century.

From Saalfelden the road goes north to **Brandlhof**, which is almost at the mouth of the gorge. The village has a chapel, built into rock, which contains a winged altar and the cell of a hermit who lived there. There are magnificent views along here southwards towards the higher mountains through the gap at Zell-am-See to the Grossglockner.

In a country with a strong folklore tradition this area has more than most. The area was one of the first of the mountain regions to be colonized in the Middle Ages, and the first in the Pinzgau. According to one source *Brettlrutschen* was in use until comparatively recently, as a euphemism for death. *Brettl* was a plank on which the corpse was carried and slid — *rutschen* — into the grave. The plank then served as a memorial when it was fixed to the side of the late owner's barn with the dates of birth and death engraved on it. This custom survived for over 1,000 years in this one small area round Saalfelden.

Between Saalfelden and Weissbach the road and river are almost on the same level at times. The steeply rising forests contain a mixture of conifers and deciduous trees which, in the autumn, give a most amazing mix of shades and is most beautiful. Between Weiss-bach and Brandlhof are the Diesbachfall, a series of cascades to the north of the road.

At **Weissbach** pause and take the marked road to a car park to visit the Seisenbergklamm. Stairways and galleries enable visitors to walk under the foliage in this fissure in the rocks where the Weiss-bach roars its way down to the main valley (for the energetic the hamlet of Stocklaus lies higher up the valley). There is a small church, and the Gast Haus Lohfeyer for refreshments. Also at Weissbach there is a road going over the border into Germany, crossing a pass, and leading to Ramsau and Berchtesgaden. The pass is the Hirschbi-chl and in the Napoleonic Wars it was a strategic route and the scene of several battles.

A stone's throw beyond the village are the Lamprechtshöle (caves), a series of illuminated galleries and great domed chambers with waterfalls and cataracts. Continuing along this road the next hamlet is **St Martin bei Lofer.** From here a detour up to the pilgrim-age church of Maria Kirchental is a pleasant diversion. The church contains votive tablets from the seventeenth and nineteenth centu-ries. The village of **Lofer** itself is a little larger; its twisting old main street contains houses more reminiscent of Bavarian architecture, in some contrast to the older peasant houses on the outskirts. From here an outing on foot can be made to the Loferer Alpe, 1,747m (5,730ft), in about 2½ hours. The trip can also be made by car, or even cablecar.

A trip can also be made to the Auerwiesen (Au meadows), a beautiful place which makes a popular outing. **Au** is a very pretty hamlet lying quietly off the main road on the other side of the river from Lofer and about 3km (2 miles) away. There is a nice walk behind the village to the east, up to **Haggen** with its inn and chapel, just beyond the meadows in fact, and a return can be made by way of Mayrberg.

The route is now heading towards the German border, past Reith. Beyond the hamlets of Hallenstein, which is on the main road, and Reith, which is not, the Kniepass lends a touch of excitement. The Saalach again foams beside the road, and an old castle guards the pass. After a few metres, cross the bridge into **Oberrain**, where another castle guards the road.

Soon, turn left into **Unken.** This little corner is not unknown to Austrians and Bavarians, but it is little known further afield. Unken marks the entrance to the Heutal, which could easily be missed. This valley is wide and leads to a number of ravines and side valleys. By following the main river, the Unkenbach, both the Eiblklamm and the Swarzbergklamm (gorges) are visited. The latter was once described as 'the most magnificent gorge in the German Alps'. Quite a claim for this area. However, a word of warning. According to legend the area is the haunt of the *Tatzelwürmer*. In the year 1779 one Hans Fuchs died of fright after being chased by one. At **Fuchs**, one of the hamlets in the valley, there is a memorial tablet recording the event. The worms are said to have a poisonous bite and to be very swift. The best way to escape is to run a zig-zag course.

This is a marvellous area for some gentle strolling in beautiful woods and meadows. But do get a local footpath map from the tourist office in Unken.

Going back via Lofer, follow road 312 towards St Johann in Tyrol. This is a moderately busy main road, but fortunately it will soon be possible to leave it. Pass Strub is quite low by alpine standards and it is only 2km (just over a mile) from Lofer. About 4km ($2\frac{1}{2}$ miles) beyond the pass turn left into the hamlet of **Strub** which has a chapel and Gast Haus Strub. Pass Strub marked the border, and the route has left Land Salzburg and is once more in the Tyrol.

The road west from Strub wanders along for about 6km ($3\frac{1}{2}$ miles) to Unterwasser, Waidring, and Winkl. Between Waidring and Winkl there is a swimming pool and camp site, but there is much more too. However, first inspect **Waidring**. The central group of houses round the square is very picturesque. Some of the old houses nearby still have the old fashioned shingle roofs, held down against the winter storms by large stones. Strub was in the Strubtal, and at Waidring there is a turning to the Inner Strubbachtal, a fairytale area of beauty not to be missed.

St Ulrich am Pillersee is a tiny village set beside a lake in meadows surrounded by green hills. For such a small village it offers a remarkable programme for holidaymakers. Marked footpaths of course, with fishing, boating and swimming. The lake is just about 2km (just over a mile) long and it is possible to walk all the way round quite easily. With an extra kilometre up to the chapel dedicated to St Adolari, and the diversion up the Teufelsklamm (Devils Gorge) where there is a lovely waterfall, the walk will take about 3 hours.

Another walk, starting at the Gast Haus Adolari, goes up quite easily to the Talsen Alm, where refreshments are available. Time required for this walk is about 2 hours. St Ulrich's own claim, to being a haven of peace, is quite true. The only reason to travel this road is to reach one of the hamlets along it. The main routes pass by.

Beyond St Ulrich are the hamlets of Strass and Flecken. At Flecken, just past the lake, turn right through the hamlet on the back road to Hochfilzen.

It is worth backtracking to Saalfelden again to explore this quiet valley. Road 164 goes west from Saalfelden, and within 2km (just over a mile) there is a turning north to **Lenzing**. This tiny village is on the river meadows and is the starting point for some surprisingly level walks. There is a side road leading along in a westerly direction through the hamlets of Ecking and Otting. After passing through Rosental it emerges onto the 164 again at Leogang, a wonderful diversion. There is a record, in **Leogang**, of a family being in possession of one of the outlying farms since the twelfth century. A good walk from Leogang follows the Swarzbach on footpath 2. Beyond the Matzalm it becomes No 26, crosses the river and swings round north-easterly. Just across the next stream, the Klammbach, turn north to follow the stream. Go towards the Gast Haus Streckau on path 27 which returns to Leogang.

Beyond Leogang is Hütten which is just off the main road, and there is also a quiet side valley to explore. Footpath 32 follows the Schwarzleobach and footpath 38 then 34 will return one almost to the start point. On the other side of the main road footpath 16 goes up to the Maurer Alm, from near the station, from where one has a choice of return paths.

The next village is Griessen, though there is not much of it, and just beyond is the Griessen Pass. This marks the boundary between Land Salzburg and the Tyrol and there is an interesting story that bears upon the character of these proud mountain peoples. Not so many years ago there were military manoeuvres in the area. The 'opposing' army on the Salzburg side began to press back the army on the Tyrol side. Becoming aware of what was happening farmers on the Tyrol side rushed home for weapons and hastened to the aid of 'their' army, to the astonishment of witnesses. This was on the old road which is to the north of the new one and in fact slightly lower.

Passing through Hochfilzen the next hamlet is Feistenau, where a minor road leads off to the twin hamlets of **Hofenberg**, both Ober and Unter. A nice quiet corner to stay awhile and walk in the woods and meadows. Pfaffenschwendt, across the valley, is also off the main road. Near **Walchau** is a good base from which an ascent of the nearby Wildseeloder peak (2,117m, 6,944ft), can be made. Take the chairlifts to the top (Bergstation) at 1,580m (5,182ft) and proceed south to the Wildalm where fresh cool milk can be obtained. Path 711 goes up to the Wildseeloder hut which stands beside the Wild See. Easy going and about $1\frac{1}{2}$ hours time required. An easy scramble leads up to the summit. On the return from the Wildalm take the path

Fieberbrunn

to the Lärchfilzhochalm hut, then descend the Jägersteig to rejoin path 711 at the middle station, where one can either take the chairlift back the rest of the way, or walk the remaining 2km (just over a mile) and 400m (1,312ft) down through the meadows, almost alongside the chairlift.

Going on down the valley Fieberbrunn, Hütte and Rosenegg could almost all be one place. Just south of Fieberbrunn is the hamlet of **Lauch** and the tiny Lauchsee gives one the opportunity of swimming in a lake which is warm enough once summer has advanced sufficiently. There are both indoor and outdoor pools not far away at **Hütte**.

Fieberbrunn translates as Fever Spring, and the village has a short history as a spa with visitors coming to 'take the waters'. Some claim is also made that Fieberbrunn is the prettiest of the surrounding villages, but that is surely a matter of opinion. In this picture postcard country one could be gasping for breath all day long as one beautiful view unfolds after the other.

From nearby **St Jakob in Haus** on the road to St Ulrich, there is a chairlift which can whisk one up to 1,455m (4,772ft) where the Kammbergalm is open for refreshments, on the way down to Flecken. A more direct return is possible from the Berghof, a mountain inn at the top of the chairlift, by way of footpath 4 through meadows and forest to St Jakob.

Further Information
— Lienz, Hohe Tauern and the Saalach River —

Activities

Döllach
Riding, trips on old packhorse trails.

Dorf Dienten
Chairlift.

Fieberbrunn
Walks, swimming, tennis.

Hinterglemm
Chairlifts.

Lienz
Tennis, riding, fishing, cycle path, cablecar, chairlift.

Saalbach
Walks, cablecar, chairlift.

St Ulrich am Pillersee
Boating, fishing, swimming, quiet walks.

Strub
Quiet walks

Tristach
Bathing in lovely lake, walks on the Lienzer Dolomites.

Places to Visit in the Area

Aguntum
Ongoing excavation of a Roman town.

Brandlhof
Hermit's cave.

Heiligenblut
Gateway to the Glocknerstrasse

high alpine road. Walk up to the Briccius chapel.

Kaprun
Ruined castle; Kessel waterfall; Kaprun power station.

Lavant
Temple ruins.

Lienz
Old town centre; Bruck Castle museum, open Easter to October; Albin Egger-Lienz gallery; Parish church; Lieburg Palace, now the municipal offices.

Lofer
Old market town.

Maria Alm
Pilgrimage church.

Pustertal
'Sun terrace'. Peaceful villages off the main road (Assling, Anras). Romantic side valleys to Innervillgraten etc.

Saalfelden
Large market town. Gothic parish church; fourteenth-century Farmach Castle; Christmas Crib Museum in Ritzen Castle (times change, enquire at Saalfelden tourist office).

St Martin bei Lofer
Pilgrimage church with votive tablets from the seventeenth century.

St Ulrich am Pillersee
Tiny village in lakeside setting, quiet and beautiful.

The Leutasch valley, near Seefeld

The narrow rocky gorge near Klamm in the Leutasch valley

*Walking on the Seefelden Spitze, Leutasch (above)
and on the Neunerkopf Ridge, Tannheimertal (below)*

Unken
Entry point to lovely side valleys
of the Unkenbach.

Waidring
Old houses.

Weissbach
Seisenberg gorge, Hirschbichl Pass,
Lamprectsofenloch caves.

Tourist Information Offices

Ausservillgraten
☎ (04843) 5333

Fieberbrunn
☎ (05354) 6304

Heiligenblut
☎ (04824) 2001

Heinfels
☎ (04842) 6262

Hochfilzen
☎ (05359) 363

Iselsberg
☎ (04852) 4117

Kaprun
☎ (06547) 644

Kartitsch
☎ (04848) 5216

Lavant
☎ (04852) 8216

Lienz
At junction of Iseltaler Strasse and
Pustertaler Strasse
☎ (04852) 4747

Maria Alm
☎ (06584) 316

Obertilliach
☎ (04847) 5255

Saalbach-Hinterglemm
☎ (06541) 7272

Saalfelden
☎ (06582) 2513

Sillian
☎ (04842) 6280

St Martin-Lofer
☎ (06588) 520

St Ulrich am Pillersee
☎ (05354) 8192

Tristach
☎ (04852) 2094

Unken
☎ (06589) 245

Waidring
☎ (05353) 5242

Zell am See
☎ (06542) 2600

6 • St Johann, Kitzbühel and the Inn Valley

S t Johann is the largest town in this area, second only to Kitzbühel as a winter sports centre. The facilities are just as good, but a little cheaper as it is not quite so fashionable. It is a market town and the holiday centre for this corner. Lying in a large flat area at the junction of two valleys means that the town has the advantage of good modest walks, indeed the town lays claim to 100km (62 miles) of promenades and gentle paths. There is a climbing school and a school for ramblers — mountain walking needs some expertise. The town also lays on a programme of guided walks and there is a special programme matched to the steadier pace of senior citizens. To the south a funicular railway and a cablecar climb the slopes of the Kitzbüheler Horn with a choice of return paths.

Just 5km (3 miles) north lies **Kirchdorf**. The main part of the village is off the main road, in a broad valley with glorious views of the east face of the Wilder Kaiser. The almost separate ridge, ending quite close to Kirchdorf, is the Nieder Kaiser and on the eastern end are two places worth visiting. Local footpath No 9, which starts near the Gast Haus Hüttschaden at Litzfelden, climbs up through the woods to visit Lourdes Grotte, which is claimed as the site of some miraculous cures some years ago. Close by is the tiny Gmail-Kapelle built onto the cliff face.

The main road between St Johann and Kirchdorf is the 312 or the European route E17 carrying traffic from Salzburg to the Inn valley. However, one can thankfully soon get away from the bustle by taking the 171 to the north, following the river, down the Kössener Tal which eventually leads to Kössen. Just before the turn is made for the Kössener Tal the village of **Erpfendorf** lies off to the right, happily bypassed by the main road. The church is modern, it was finished in 1957 and was the work of Clemens Holzmeister, a master

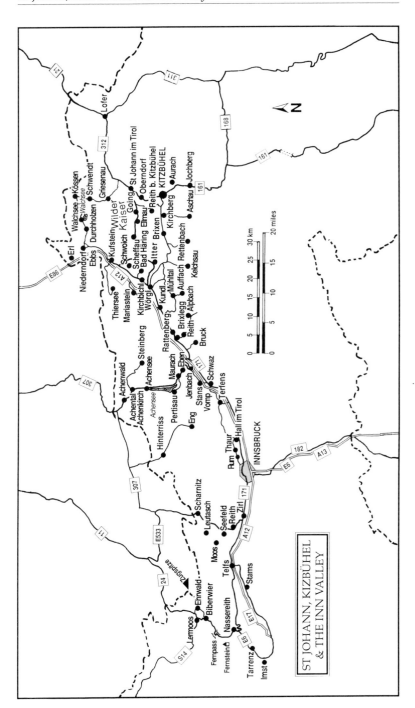

ST JOHANN, KIZBÜHEL
& THE INN VALLEY

St Johann

of contemporary religious architecture. Both Kirchdorf and Erpfendorf are in the Leukental. The best view is from the east where the
village church towers stand out in the valley with the Wilder Kaiser
mountains as a dramatic backdrop.

Within 1km (just over half a mile) of turning, the road crosses the
river. There are paths down each side of the river, and as there is a
bridge at Laufer a return can be made on the other side of the water,
the whole distance being about 4km (2$\frac{1}{2}$ miles). But at the hamlet of
Wöhlmuting, by the bus stop, there is a turning left to Pfeifer. This is
the opening to the Eisental, a short and not very steep valley, which
carries the Taxa-Bach down through the houses to join the main
river. The stream runs through the Taxaklamm (gorge) and crashes
down a waterfall. The Taxa has also been spelt as Daxa on some
maps.

By a careful study of bus times and the local map it is possible to
make an interesting excursion and visit a mountain inn. From near
the Gast Haus Lauferau, close to **Kössen**, footpath 27 climbs gently
up the Lauferberg. On emerging into meadows there is a right turn
leading on and upwards towards the Straubinger Hütte, a mountain
inn at 1,598m (5,241ft). The total climb is 1,000m (3,280ft) so allow 3
hours. A descent can be made past the Kreuzanger Alm and the
Hasenau Alm to the road near the bus stop for a return journey. This
walk goes very close to the German border which is just to the left on

the ascent.

On the other side of the valley is the Unterberghorn, the approach to which is through **Hütte**. Near the Gast Haus Oberach there is the valley station for the two stage chairlift to whisk the less energetic up to 1,690m (5,543ft) at the mountain station. From here there are some splendid and popular views, obviously the easier ascent will tend to make it more popular. The descent goes via the Lack Alm, 1,312m (4,303ft), then down a steep and zigzag path to the Niederhauser Tal where the going becomes gentler as the river is followed back to the start point.

Kössen, Hütte and Waidach share a level area at the junction of three valleys. This corner, so near the border, is relatively peaceful and calm. Though popular with locals and Germans it does not have the bustle of the more famous areas which attract the tour companies. Outside 'high season' (which itself is not crowded), there is a serenity that only comes to places bypassed by through routes. There are the usual facilities offered by the villages both for sport and evening entertainments; there is even a hang gliding school and there are band concerts and a folk theatre.

The river this route has been following is called the Grosse Ache in Austria and the Tiroler Ache after it passes into Germany. This it does to the north of Kössen after passing through a most beautiful and colourful gorge where a light and modern metal footbridge, part of a lovely walk, crosses the river and makes a splendid vantage point. South of Kössen, road 176 runs back up to St Johann. However, there is an interesting excursion from here that can easily be made. Beyond the hamlet of Schwendt, and about 12km (7½ miles) from Kössen, is Griesenau, where there is a turning right to the Griesener-alm, a mountain inn where the road ends. 2km (just over a mile) on and 500m (1,640ft) up is the Stripsenjoch Haus. To the north of this is the Stripsenkopf, 1,807m (5,927ft) where there are spectacular views, but none better than the north wall of the Kaiser mountains.

For the more experienced mountain walker there is an exciting walk. Just below the Stripsenjoch Haus path 812 leaves the main path and goes off to the south. Soon this path is clinging perilously to the wall of the mountain as it goes along before turning to the south and climbing up the Steinerne Rinne. It is protected in placed by fixed ropes, but is not a place for the nervous. On the local maps it is shown dotted as a 'climbers path'. However, older people do use the path, and once up at the Ellmauer Tor, 1,995m (6,544ft), the descent is not too bad. Directly ahead down the valley is the large car park at the Wochenbrunner Alm. An exciting walk if transport can be arranged, but busy at weekends.

To the west of Kössen, on road 172, is Walchsee, a warm water lake which claims a temperature of 20-25 °C (68-77 °F) after the summer sun has warmed it up, but not in June or July. It is a most beautiful and serene area, with swimming in the lake, level walks round about the lake and all the usual facilities, and the old town. Here the old houses round the square and the water troughs make a most pretty picture. To the south of the lake footpath 51A goes up the Habersauer Tal to the previously mentioned Stripsenjoch Haus, only getting steep on the last stretch. A return can be made on footpath 51B which arrives back at the western end of the lake.

The next hamlet is **Durchholzen**. A chairlift goes up from here to the Gast Haus Zahmer Kaiser, named after the range of mountains to the south of the road. A network of footpaths spreads through the meadows and woods which climb the slopes. As the valley widens and prepares for the descent to the main Inn valley the hamlets on either side of the main road increase in number. Soon road 175 is joined, coming down from Germany to Kufstein, and it is time for yet another decision, which is best made at Neiderndorf. Communication from here is good, north, south or west. West by 2km (just over a mile) is an access point to the motorway, across the river Inn and the German border. If staying, take a walk up the Höhenberg, visiting the shrines on the way and the church on the summit. Again, if staying here then Erl is within walking distance to the north via meadow paths or by the road if driving. Erl is the home of one of the lesser known passion plays, but also one of the oldest. It originated in 1613. Not as well known as Oberammergau it is mainly patronised by Austrians and Bavarians. The play is performed every 6 years. A new theatre was built in 1958 on the edge of the village, and performances include folk music, orchestral concerts and the world famous Vienna Boys Choir. Also take a walk out to visit the quite spectacular Trockenbach waterfall which lies to the north-east.

Two kilometres (just over a mile) south of Niederndorf is **Ebbs**. The village is set in relatively flat meadows which, when viewed from the north-west, emphasize the dramatic slopes of the mountain range which appears as a backdrop. Ebbs, apart from being very picturesque, is home to the Fohlenhof Ebbs. This is the largest Haflinger stud in Europe. There is a small, sturdy four wheel drive vehicle named after the Haflinger, made by Steyr-Puch. The village claims 105km (65 miles) of safe footpaths and a 21km (13 mile) cycleway.

Continuing south, the village of **Obernberg** is the last before Kufstein. This small village is ignored by guide books, tourist office brochures and tours, so it is a pleasant place to stay awhile and perhaps use as a centre to explore the area. Just south of the village the road, river, and railway get squeezed between the rocky thrust of the Kaiser Gebirge, and the Schanzer Wande (*wande* means wall) rises almost 500m (1,640ft) from the roadside. On the other side of the river the Brandenberger Alps are much gentler and greener.

Kufstein is a medieval town dominated by the massive fortress. The Geroldsech Fortress (Festung) was built in the twelfth century by the dukes of Bavaria to guard the entrance to the Inn valley. In 1703, when the fort was under siege by a Bavarian force, the garrison commander had the town burnt to give him a good field of fire. Many sieges have been fought off and some of the guns and cannon are on show. It is now a museum and English speaking guides are available. The tour includes part of the large central tower, the Emperor's Tower, with walls 4.5m (15ft) thick and built round a central column. It is encircled by a vaulted gallery. On one level are the cannon, while on another higher level are cells used by political prisoners, now a part of the museum, with mementoes of some of the more famous. A feature of the fortress is the famous well, over 68m (223ft) deep. An ingenious way of raising water was arranged, with prisoners operating a treadmill winch. Also a part of the fortress, in the Burghers Tower, is the Heldenorgel (Heroes Organ), which is controlled from the gallery for the audience at the foot of the rock. It is claimed that on a clear still day it can be heard from a distance of 8km (5 miles). It was built as a memorial to the Austrian and German dead of World War I and was first played in 1931. An approach can be made to the fortress from near the church in the Unterer Stadplatz, from where a covered stairway goes beneath the Burghers Tower. An easier approach is by the lift from the riverside promenade. It is also possible to stroll round the walls where there are some magnificent views, or to take refreshments in the courtyard café.

Kufstein has a smart modern shopping centre and a romantic old street, the Römerhofgasse, which contains the oldest winehouse in the Tyrol, the Batzenhäusl. There are free guided tours of the town which take in the Heldenhügel (Hero's Hill), where there is a statue of Andreas Hofer who fought the French and Bavarians here in 1809. There is a good view of the fortress from the hill. Numerous footpaths and four chairlifts make for easy walking into the approaches to the Kaiser Gebirge.

Just south of Kufstein road 173 goes south-east and starts to climb, not dramatically but steadily and easily. About 2km (just over a mile) from the main junction there is a turning for the village of **Schwoich**.

Kufstein

Being on an almost dead-end road (there is a very minor road going on), and above the river valley, it has no through traffic. It is not on any tourist route, and is absolutely beautifully peaceful. There is a network of quiet minor roads and footpaths over the meadows, and there is an open-air swimming pool. There is a part-time tourist office and the village is a peaceful base from which to explore the surrounding area. It is about 180m (590ft) above the main river valley, on a plateau protected from the north and east by high ground. The main roads and the motorway are about 4km (2¹/₂ miles) away so communication is easy, and buses run into Kufstein.

Back on road 173, continue to climb. It is quite busy but the end result is worth the effort. **Scheffau-am-Wilden Kaiser** is off the main road to the left, 3km (2 miles) after joining the 312, on the road to St Johann. The road through the village is a dead-end, so there is no traffic except the odd car or two, going on to the Hintersteiner See. One of the claims of the village is that it has very pure air. A most peaceful and easy walk is round the lake, which has facilities for swimming, and a pool near the eastern end. The Gast Haus Wildauer marks the turn-back point so whichever way one chooses to go refreshments are available halfway. At the very foothills of the Wilder Kaiser but on the southern slopes, this particular area, along to Stangl, is well protected.

The next two villages, Ellmau and Going, fortunately bypassed, are typically Tyrolean. **Ellmau** has wooden fronted houses on the main street and a charming little chapel in the meadows. **Going** has a beautiful little bathing lake, though it is 1.5km (1 mile) from the village, and a lovely old domed church. There is a network of good safe paths to the south of these two villages through meadows and woods and never going higher than 1,500m (4,920ft).

Ellmau marked the high point of the road and from there it descends gently to St Johann. However, just beyond the turning to the lake at Going, and close by the Gast Haus Stangl, there is a minor road to the right which cuts off a few kilometres and leads to **Oberndorf** which is a village typical of the area. There is an outdoor pool, heated, as are most of them, and a huge sunbathing area, plus the usual facilities.

Retrace the road back to the Gast Haus Reinachen and turn left, going south, to **Reith-by-Kitzbühel**. This is a beautiful broad green valley and the decorative buildings enhance the scene. The usual facilities are available. Reith-by-Kitzbühel is in fact about 6km ($3\frac{1}{2}$ miles) outside the famous old town. On the way into town the Schwarzsee is on the left, a popular spot, but sometimes a little noisy. Waterskiing is allowed on the lake but the bathing area is fenced off from the boats.

Kitzbühel is over 1,000 years old. The old town walls were over 4m (13ft) thick, but hollow, as they contained rooms, some of which are now the town museum. The town owed much of its early prosperity to silver mining and a cross-section model of one of the deepest mines is on show. Fortunately the Vorderstadt and Hinterstadt are now pedestrian precincts and the town has been bypassed by the main road. There is a lot to do and see in the town whether your taste is for churches, old houses or museums. Local walks are assisted by a huge network of cablecars, both up to the Kitzbüheler Horn to the east or the Hahnenkamm to the west. The latter is, of course, well known as a ski run. There is also a variety of evening entertainment varying from band concerts to a casino.

Road 161 south of the town would eventually lead to Mittersill in the Pinzgau. However, there are two villages on the Kitzbühel side of the pass. The highest is Jochberg. Set in the green slopes, in almost parklike surroundings, there are tennis courts and a heated pool with a sunbathing lawn. Of course, there are splendid walks as well.

Aurach is the other village and here there is a wildlife park (Natur und Wildpark Aurach) which is 4km ($2\frac{1}{2}$ miles) along a side valley. The animals have large enclosures in a beautiful setting. Local information offices will be able to supply current opening times.

West of Kitzbühel is road 170 going towards Wörgl along the Brixental. **Kirchberg** is the first village and is very picturesque. There is a bathing lake and a heated swimming pool. The main part of the village is off the main road making it quiet, and pleasant for a stroll. South from the village there is the beautiful and quiet Spertental leading about 8km (5 miles) into the Kitzbüheler Alps to the hamlet of Aschau. The valley has chairlifts leading off to the sides.

Going on up the main valley the next village is **Brixen im Thale**, which caters for tourists a little more than Kirchberg. There are supposed to be twenty-three tennis courts and two swimming pools, a programme of free guided walks and a tiny fishing lake. A chairlift goes up the north side of the valley to Hochbrixen and footpath 5 passes an old mill on the way back down.

Westendorf lies off the main road, and a little higher on a sunny plateau. There is a variety of gentle walks on the meadows southwest of the village, which has an active programme of evening entertainments. There is another very pleasant and peaceful valley cutting south into the mountains with the hamlets of Rettenbach and Windau along the way. It is signposted from the junction near the church at the centre of Westendorf.

Four kilometres (2¹/₂ miles) beyond Westendorf there is a turning left to **Kelchsau**. This is a delightful small village with some traditional wooden houses. One or two still have the traditional stones on top to hold the roof on in the winter gales, something more often seen in the higher regions. At the end of the surfaced road, a little way past the village, the road divides and the valley with it. To the west is the Langer Grund and the eastern arm is the Kurzer Grund. The river up the Langer (long) Grund is the Kelchsauer Ache. It rises high up near the Kreuzjoch, 2,558m (8,390ft) which is over 15km (9 miles) from the fork. The river grows to quite a size by that time and is used by whitewater canoeists.

The turning to Kelchsau is just outside Hopfgarten. Once the main valley road is regained, turn left and soon, just after going under the railway bridge, **Hopfgarten** is reached. This is 'the stately market town of the farmers'. The town prides itself on the profusion of flowers and, though of modest size, there are sufficient facilities. There is evening entertainment available and riding, tennis and swimming. In the town centre is the lovely twin-towered parish church of St Jakob and St Leonhard, the 'Cathedral of the Farmers'. A three stage chairlift goes up to the Hohe Salve, 1,827m (5,993ft), with refreshments available at all the stations. The views from each succeeding station widen as height is gained until distant snowcapped peaks can be seen.

Kirchdörfl, 3km (2 miles) from Hopfgarten, is a hamlet with a history going back 1,000 years. The castle at Itter was started in AD902. Originally it was in the Regensburg See until 1380 when it was taken over by the archbishop of Salzburg. The restored castle is now a luxury hotel and a tourist attraction. The village street leading towards it is full of *pensions* and guest houses but manages to retain some of its charm. There is a camp site and swimming pool nearby.

Before descending to the main Inn valley, which is now quite close again, go from Hopfgarten to Niederau on a minor road, not even marked on many maps. This leads along to an area of green hills, woods and delightful meadows with a network of paths, generally known as Wildschönau. There are four named hamlets — **Niederau, Oberau, Dorf** and **Auffach**, in this beautiful valley. Between them there are a surprising number of facilities including a rural life museum, two chairlifts and a small bathing lake.

From Mühltal, between Dorf and Auffach, there is a traffic free road leading down to Kundl, which is in the main Inn valley. This road leads down beside the Wildschönauer Ache, which is crossed and recrossed, to follow the deep cut Kundler Klamm (gorge) passing the Gast Haus Klamm and a ruined castle on the way. Do go on down far enough to see the decorated wooden bridge, just before the ruin. The really energetic could walk down the valley to turn by the Gast Hauser Köfler and Zauberwinkl and so on up to Oberau. **Oberau** is a lovely little village with a delightful church and main street. Nearby are some interesting old wooden farmhouses.

A road leads from Niederau to **Wörgl**, which is a thriving market town well situated in the main Inn valley with a main line railway station and a motorway access point. There is not only a programme of guided walks but guided cycle rides as well. There are various exhibitions and galleries in the town. The best source of up to the minute information about these changing events is the local information office. The staff in information offices are always friendly and helpful.

Just to the north along the 171 are Kirchbichl and **Bad Häring**. Bad, of course, means bath or spa and there is a *Kurhaus*, though not on a grand scale. Across the river there is a real gem. Cross the river Inn and the motorway by way of Angath to the hamlet of **Mariastein**. In the fourteenth century the massive defensive tower was built on a huge rock. The Lady Chapel became a place of pilgrimage which gradually changed the purpose of the tower from its military beginnings. The Knights Hall contains the treasures of the castle, the crown and sceptre of the counts of the Tyrol. There are two chapels above and nothing is later than sixteenth century, though some redecoration has been done.

From the next hamlet, **Niederbreitenbach**, there is a good walk, starting just south of the village, up to the Höhlenstein hut. This goes on a forest-type road through beech and spruce trees to the guest house, with its nearby Andachtskapelle. Beyond the Gast Haus Bärenbad the road soon ends and the path zigzags upward. The total time needed for this walk is 3 hours.

The outskirts of Kufstein must be used to obtain access to the next objective which is the miniature 'Lake District' nearby. The area round the Hecht See, Egelsee, Längsee, Pfrillsee and Thiersee is idyllic. There are level walks round the lakes, quiet paths through the woods, bathing facilities at Thiersee, Hecht See and Pfrillsee, and there are three indoor pools, three tennis courts, band concerts and a folk theatre. Thiersee is also known for its passion play. Performances began in the seventeenth century and it is re-enacted every 6 years. There is a fairly modern theatre which seats 900 people. The actors are a village amateur group and non-villagers are not allowed to take part.

Go now up the Inn valley. By far the best route is by the minor road to the north of the river, back through Mariastein to **Breitenbach** which is a pleasant little village. Stay on the north bank of the river following the minor road to Kramsach. Before reaching the village some of the lakes are passed quite close by. Three of the lower level lakes have bathing facilities. **Kramsach** boasts 60km (37 miles) of low level paths and 90km (56 miles) of mountain paths. There is a chairlift just on the edge of the village, the Roskogel lift, going up from 600m (1,968ft) to almost 1,800m (5,904ft) near the Roskogel hut. Many people also walk along the pretty little Zireiner See. This high alpine lake sits in a hollow at the eastern fringe of the Rofan mountains, and it has a dramatic backdrop as the higher peaks of the Rofan group come into view on the approach.

On a lower level there is a good walk from Kramsach, past the Frauen See and up the side valley to Brandenberg, (one could take the bus to Brandenberg). Go down to the river and cross by a bridge to turn downstream following the river all the way back to Kramsach. In its upper reaches the walk goes through the Tiefenbach-Klamm (gorge) which is quite spectacular.

The whole area of the Brandenberg valley is very pretty and quite peaceful. It is a no-through-road with only forest tracks beyond the Kaiserhaus, an inn popular in the area for its food, with trout as a speciality. There is also a lovely walk from the Kaiserhaus, through another gorge. This one is the Kaiserklamm, and as the area has deciduous trees it is particularly lovely in autumn. Of course, there is a refreshment stop, and the walking time to the Erzherzog-Johann-Klause, another mountain-style inn, is $2^1/_2$ hours.

Back at Kramsach there are still things to do and see. In the village there is a famous school, teaching the art of etching, engraving or painting on glass. Nearby is the seventeenth-century Schloss Achen-rain and an open-air museum of farm buildings, the Tiroler Bau-ernhöf, with the old rebuilt farm buildings placed in natural sur-roundings.

Just across the river Inn lies **Rattenberg**, which claims to be 'the smallest town in the Tyrol'. Rattenberg was once a rich and famous silver mining town, but its fortunes were short lived as the mining only lasted from 1500 to 1560. When the mining collapsed the town became quite poor, so it missed the heyday of baroque building. That left an almost unspoilt medieval town to enjoy. The town was saved because it is at a point where the river Inn narrows. By exerting control over river traffic the town was able to survive. The well preserved ruined castle may be visited and there are occasional concerts in the castle grounds (Schlossberg-spiele). The parish church, alongside the bluff on which the castle stands, is well worth visiting, built in 1473 of pink marble, and in Gothic style. Inside there are two naves of different lengths. The shorter has stalls against a windowless wall 'for the miners'. There is a notable painting of *The Last Supper* here by Matthäus Günter. Rattenberg is also famous for the finely modelled and engraved glassware.

Just a very short distance upstream is Brixlegg, and just beyond is the Ziller valley. It is worth taking time to go along this road, but turn off south to **Bruck-am-Ziller**. This tiny hamlet sits on the sunny side of the broad valley mouth. It is not particularly notable in this country of so many notable places, but it gives us a turnround point and it is pretty enough. It sits on broad meadows with a mountain at its back and the river Ziller in front. Most of the traffic passes it by on the other side of the valley, rushing up to Mayrhofen. Almost at the turning are the ruins of Schloss Kropfsberg, built to guard the en-trance to the Zillertal. It is at the village of **St Gertraudi**. In the 2-3km (1-2 miles) between here and Brixlegg there are three more castles: Schloss Lichtenwerth and Schloss Lipperhead, sitting one on each side of the road, and nearest to Brixlegg is Schloss Matzen which is situated in Matzen Park where there are tennis courts and a fitness centre.

Brixlegg is a spa town and has a hot mineral bath, Mineralbad Mehrn. Diverse complaints, it is claimed, can be cured by the calcium sulphate waters. The area has an open-air swimming pool, fishing can be arranged, and evening entertainment follows the usual pattern.

Just up the Alpbachtal is **Reith** up on a sun terrace. It is quite small, but welcoming, and was recently voted by an international jury in Brussels 'the best flower decorated village in Europe'. There is a lot to do — walking at both low- and high-level, swimming, fishing and tennis. There is a chairlift going up to the Reither Kogel, 1,337m (4,385ft) which gives fantastic views up the Zillertal and along the Inntal. Also in the town there is a Bauern Theatre (Farmers Theatre) or folk group where everything is done in traditional manner. Often speech is in old dialect which does place most visitors at a slight disadvantage, but hardly detracts from a very unusual entertainment.

Going on up the valley, about 5km (3 miles) from Reith is the Gast Haus Achenwirt and nearby is the valley station for a two stage chairlift, going up to 1,804m (5,917ft), making light work of most of the Wiedersberger Horn which is 2,127m (6,977ft). There are wide ranging views of the Zillertal and the Stubai glaciers, and a choice of paths down for the energetic, with refreshments halfway at the Almhof. Beyond the lift, at Lagerhaus, there is a sharp left turn and the road climbs the last few metres to **Alpbach**. The village is very pretty and there are some wooden houses which are fine examples of the art of building in wood. There is also a swimming pool and sauna, tennis, a programme of walks and evening entertainment.

At **Inneralpbach** there is a rural life museum. This second smaller village is at a point where the valley divides into two, the Greiter Graben and the Lueger Graben. In the latter, less than 1km (just over half a mile) from the village is the Buben chapel.

Back in the main valley go through Brixlegg to cross the Inn and take the minor road through the hamlets of Habach and Asten, through the straggling village of Münster and on to Wiesing. There change onto road 181 to Achensee. From the riverside near Wiesing up to Achensee is a climb of 400m (1,312ft). The journey can be made by bus or car or by a delightful steam driven rack and pinion railway which has its own station, alongside the main railway station in Jenbach, the other end being alongside the lake.

When the Inn valley was carved by the glaciers the Achensee area was left as a hanging valley by a barrier of glacial moraine. The water from Achensee drains north into Germany, not south into the Inn.

The Achensee

The area is delightful and the lake is the largest, and some claim the most beautiful, in the Tyrol. It can be busy at peak times but at others it can be a haven of peace. The lake is nearly 150m (492ft) deep and massive mountains rise almost from the lakeshore in places, while in others there are wide meadows and lovely side valleys.

From **Pertisau** the walk up the Falzturntal is almost parklike, with well spaced mature trees and wide areas of grass, with lots of seats for a nice lazy day. There are plenty of *alms* higher up for the energetic to try to reach. It is only 100m (328ft) climb up to the Pletzachalm, 3km (2 miles) from Pertisau, but the Lamsenjoch hut is 1,000m (3,280ft) and at least 5 hours from Pertisau. However, it is a rewarding walk.

At the head of the lake is the hamlet of **Eben**, on the saddle really, before the descent is made. Here in the tiny hamlet is a church dedicated to St Notburga, patron saint of servants. Next is Maurach, where the road divides, left to Pertisau, right to Achenkirch. In **Maurach** there is a cablecar going up to 1,834m (6,016ft) and the Rofan hut alongside the Erfurter hut, the start of a network of paths going up to the higher peaks of the Rofan group.

From a jetty by the Achensee railway station lake steamers ply the

Achensee railway

length of the lake with four intermediate stops. The road follows the east bank giving intermittent views of the lake. Don't follow the highway, but take the left fork near the Achenseehof to follow the old road through the next three hamlets. Achensee, Achenkirch and Achental all lie within 6km (3¹/₂ miles), below the foot of the lake. There is a camp site right at the edge of the lake near Achensee, with its own bathing facilities. The villages offer all the usual facilities including rowing boats, but no motorboats are allowed on the lake.

At Achental there is a side road leading to **Steinberg-am-Rofan**. This is a beautiful and peaceful area. The road ends at the village, so there is no through traffic. The track to the east is just about drivable, and goes out to the Brandenberg valley. There are two guest houses, a shop and a church at the village. It is possible to sit on the terrace of the Kirchenwirt, in the village square across from the church and the school, and not see or hear a car at all.

Between Achental and the German border, at the Achenpass, there is one more village, Achenwald. At this point the road and the river part company. The road can climb over the Achenpass, the river must flow down into the Sylvenstein reservoir, which is on the course of the river Isar. To the west, on a minor road past this reservoir, is one of those anomalies found in mountain country. The hamlets of Hinteriss and Eng are in Austria but can only be reached, by road, from Germany. The lower section of the main valley is the

Risstal. **Hinteriss** has a few houses grouped round a nineteenth-century hunting lodge where, occasionally, the Belgian royal family holiday. There is a modern guest house and a filling station. The area is a nature reserve and there are plenty of footpaths, both low- and high-level.

Higher up in the Engtal is the hamlet of **Eng**. A collection of holiday chalets line the road and there is a large modern guest house. At weekends there are plenty of visitors down from Germany roaming the footpaths. One favourite from here is up to the Binsalm, which is not far, or even on up to the Lamsenjoch hut. Between the border and head of the Risstal there are many delightful and secluded side valleys such as the Tortal near Hinteriss.

Go back to the main Inn valley, the only line of communication through this part of Austria. It carries the oldest method of transport and the newest, both in close proximity: the river, which now carries no transport, and the motorway. However, retrace the road from Jenbach, through Stans, towards Schwaz but do not cross the river. Instead turn right, on a minor road to **Vomp**. One of those delightful, out of the way places lies north of Vomp. The Vomperberg area, a straggle of hamlets and guest houses set on a terrace 200m (656ft) above the main Inn valley. A wide sweep of meadow gives some very attractive scenes in spring and early summer. There is a nice walk, the Almsteig, of about 4km ($2^1/_2$ miles) to the significant pilgrimage church of St Georgenberg. A little way beyond Vomp lie the twin hamlets of Vomperbach, Ober and Unter, both alongside the stream of the same name.

The next hamlet is Terfens, and take care here to turn north on a minor road into an area renowned locally for its beauty. It is a popular area with the locals from Innsbruck, which is only a short distance away. The road meanders through meadows high above the main river valley, passing the small villages of St Michael and St Martin, and through an area known as Gnadenwald. There is a path through the woods known as the Erholungsweg.

The road leads along, and drops down, to **Hall in Tyrol**. Hall rose to fame and prosperity after 1280 when someone noticed a deer licking a rock. From this lucky chance the salt industry began. The salt road goes due north from Hall into the mountains, the Halltal, and the old salt mines. *Hall* is actually one translation of salt. Also in the old days, river travel was more difficult above Hall, so much of the traffic stopped there. Many goods came on log rafts, and at Hall they were transferred to smaller craft, while the rafts were broken up and used as fuel for the furnaces of the salt works. At one time Hall had a larger population than Innsbruck, but royal preference gave Innsbruck the upper hand eventually.

When the mint was established at Hall in 1477 it remained there for 100 years. Previously the mint had been at Meran, now in Italy. Silver finds near Schwaz meant that silver had to be transported over the Brenner Pass and coins returned. There was a danger of a Turkish invasion along the Pustertal into the South Tyrol and this could have cut off the mint from the rest of the country. The move to Hall made sense. Austrian patriots like to point out that the Innthal coin was probably the ancestor of the American dollar. The town of Hall-in-Tyrol is a wonderful place, with many original fifteenth- and six-teenth-century buildings including the old tower, the Münzerturm.

Quite close to Hall is **Thaur** and to the north of the town the remains of Schloss Thaur and the church dedicated to St Romedius. In 1448 Elinor Stuart, daughter of James II of Scotland, was brought to Austria to marry Archduke Sigmund of the Tyrol. She lived in the Tyrol until her death in 1480, spending some of her time at Schloss Thaur and hunting round Pertisau and Achensee. The village is rich in folklore, as much as any in the Tyrol, and St Romedius figures in this. Said to have been born in the nearby castle, later in life he rid himself of his wealth and lived as a hermit in Nonsberg in the South Tyrol. One day, on a journey, his mule was eaten by a bear. He was able to tame the bear and use it as transport to his destination.

Descending through Rum, take the minor road to Arzl, which will slightly delay the return to the bustle of the main road. Do not cross the river as this will only bring you to Innsbruck. Turn right along road 171. It is only a short distance along to **Zirl**. There is a splendid outing from here up the Ehnbach Klamm where a pathway has been cut out of the rock in this wild and romantic gorge.

Going on up road 313 towards Seefeld and Scharnitz it is quite a climb up from the Inn valley, 622m (2,040ft) at Zirl, to a height of over 1,000m (3,280ft) at Seefeld. The road is good, and the gradients gentle now. In the early days of motorcars locals used to gather at weekends to watch the cars crash on the famous hairpin at Zirlerberg. From close by the guest house on the bend there are some good views along the Inn valley. This in fact is the only hairpin bend left, as the road has also been much improved. In the old days its gradient was 1 in 4 but now it is only 1 in 7.

The hamlet of Leithen is a marker to start looking for the turning to Reith, off the main road. This allows a few kilometres into **Reith**, where the church is worth a visit, and along the old road into **Seefeld in Tyrol**. Seefeld is an elegant place with a high reputation as a ski resort; the Winter Olympics were held here twice. The parish church is fifteenth-century Gothic and there are some interesting murals of the same date which have been restored. This is one of the few places to have a full size golf course, and tourists are well catered for in all the usual ways. There are swimming pools, tennis courts, chairlifts and a funicular railway leading up to the Seefelder range where cablecars go even higher. There is also a network of gentle paths at a lower level.

Going northwards towards Germany **Scharnitz** is the border town. It is a pleasant little place, but people only seem to use it as a border post, stopping to eat or use the banks to change money. However, it is a convenient place from which to explore the Karwendel valley. This valley is reached by path 201, from the river bridge in the town centre. Why not walk up to the Larchetalm, a simple hut serving good food? Or even up to the impressive Karwendel Haus, dramatically situated at 1,770m (5,806ft) almost on the Hochalmsaddle. The two places mentioned are 2 hours and 4$^1/_2$ hours respectively from Scharnitz. Once the initial climb past the little Pürzlkapelle has been made the valley is surprisingly level, only a few ups and downs, until the head wall to the pass and the last slog up to the Karwendel Haus. There are some pretty little cascades as the side streams tumble down to join the main stream, some wide grassy parklike areas and a good forest-type road to march along. It is a good area.

Close by Scharnitz is *Porta Claudia* which was obviously a strategic point to guard the Scharnitz Pass. In the Napoleonic Wars it was commanded by an English colonel and the garrison successfully defied a large French force under the command of Marshal Ney. There is a pathway up to the remains from the village.

From Scharnitz pop over the border into Germany, take the turn off the main road towards the centre of Mittenwald but just after crossing the river turn left towards Leutasch (see also chapter 3). This is a wonderfully picturesque and quiet valley with a string of lovely little hamlets set in a broad valley which tempts one to linger. The footpaths are well marked and easy, there is an indoor pool, a climbing school, a riding school and at Moos there is a chairlift going up the eastern slope of the Hohe Munde.

Following the road down from Moos through Buchen and on down to Telfs is very pretty with one or two good views. **Telfs**, like Zirl where the route left the Inn valley, is a typical market town. There is a superb swimming pool with, like many others, a huge window wall giving lovely views. A nice, fairly level walk goes past the swimming pool to the west of the town, over meadows with a line of tiny chapels, to the church of St Moritzen at the edge of the woods. Another exciting walk goes north, following the Griesbach. This is footpath 19. It goes through the Zimmerbergklamm and it is quite a climb if a different return is to be made, by path 32, for example, to the Gast Haus Lehen or the guest house and church at St Veit.

Take road 171 out of Telfs, and is not very far to Stams. The thirteenth-century Cistercian abbey at Stams will be a must for all those with any interest in architecture. It is one of the largest baroque churches in the Tyrol. There are guided tours and a brochure in English. Though the present structure dates only from the early eighteenth century, the abbey dates back long before that. In 1268 Konradin Hohenstaufen was tortured by order of Charles of Anjou and later beheaded. Konradin was the son of King Konrad IV and Elizabeth of Bavaria, though by this time Elizabeth was married to her second husband Meinhard II, Count of Gorz. At that time she was living in the old fortress at Petersberg and she ordered the abbey in memory of her son. She herself did not live to see its consecration in 1273. In 1362 Emperor Karl IV left the imperial insignia at Stams for safekeeping. Until 1600 all the sovereign princes of the Tyrol were buried at Stams.

Follow the 171 west from Stams to the outskirts of **Imst**. The main roads bypass the town leaving it peaceful. In the upper town there are many attractive houses nestling round the imposing Gothic church. Imst has a museum in which some of the masks used in the carnival are on display. Unfortunately the carnival does not take place each year but it is quite a spectacle. The fearsome gigantic masks represent ghosts but some of the figures represent bird sellers. In the seventeenth century canary breeders from Imst were selling as far afield as St Petersburg and London, where they even had their own depot at Moorefield Square. At the beginning of the eighteenth century the popular singing birds from the Harz mountains were taking a lot of the trade but following a disastrous fire in 1822, when many of the breeding houses were burnt, the trade ended. Modern Imst provides in many ways for tourists and is popular. There are many walks, swimming, riding, tennis, minigolf and much more. A chairlift goes up from near the Gast Haus Sonneck, to the west of the town, to the Untermarkter Alm from where a good path goes even higher.

A minor road leaves Imst and makes the only road crossing of the Lechtaler Alps by way of the Hahntennjoch (*joch* means pass). From the parking spaces near the pass summit there is a good easy path

The Blindsee on the Fernpass

northward to the Anhalter hut. The area round the summit is interesting. It is just about at the tree line, just below 2,000m (6,560ft), and
has broad grassy areas among the last trees, which are the dwarf pine
(*latschen*). Descending over the pass in a north-westerly direction
brings the road into the Lechtal near Elmen, passing the pretty little
hamlet of Boden on the way.

From Imst it is only about 3km (2 miles) to **Tarrenz**, which is a
medium sized village beautifully situated with broad meadows on
one hand and mountains and woods behind.

Nassereith is an interesting place. The main square is the stopping place for postbuses on the Innsbruck to Reutte route, and
behind the square the old part of the town has some nice houses and
a tiny lake. Nassereith also has its turn at holding the masked procession, sharing this distinction with Imst and Telfs. There is a heated
indoor swimming pool and a sunbathing lawn. Close by Nassereith
is the tiny hamlet of **Dormitz**, set on the west facing slope as road 189
sweeps down in a great loop from the Holzleithensattel, taking a
shortcut in from Telfs. It is a sleepy little place happily resting just off
the main roads.

From Nassereith the ascent of the Fernpass begins. This is an
enchanting area dotted with lakes like turquoise jewels set in the
dark green of the woods. There are bathing stations at the Fernstein-
see and the Blindsee, and refreshment stops at Fernstein, Fernpass

Biberwier

and, just on the descent side, at the Restaurant Zugspitzeblick above the Blindsee.

There is a lovely walk through the woods, starting from the castle and Hotel Fernstein and following the Römerweg until it joins path 601. Then turn left, cross the road and follow the 601 back down to Fernstein again.

Beyond Fernstein the Hotel Fernpass is almost at the summit of this pass which at 1,218m (3,995ft) is the lowest pass leading from the Inn valley into Bavaria. It is also often claimed to be the most beautiful. In Roman times it was known as the Via Claudia Augusta after Emperor Claudius who had the road rebuilt in AD46. Below the summit, on a broad sweeping curve, is the 'rest house' and Restaurant Zugspitzeblick, and from the terrace there is a wonderful view of the Zugspitze rising massively above the surrounding trees. This huge thrusting mass of limestone will dominate the last remaining miles. This is the Wetterstein group and forms the border with Germany on this stretch. Having left the restaurant the last few sweeping bends are soon taken and the straighter sections in the valley are ahead. There is a fairly new tunnel which bypasses Lermoos on road 314 so take care to take the turn to Ehrwald.

There is much to see in this area and the scenery is superb. **Ehrwald** is a lovely place to spend a weekend, a fortnight or even a month. The area is at a junction of valleys and there is a large flat area

*On the Grubigstein
above Lermoos*

in the middle known as the *moos*. This is criss-crossed with paths leading from village to village. **Biberwier** is the smallest one and is reached first on the way in by car. The new bypass has made quite a difference to the peace and quiet. **Lermoos** lies to the west of the open space and Ehrwald to the east, 'the sunny side of the Zugspitze' according to the brochures. There are low-level walks, and apart from the *moos*, the larchwoods close to Ehrwald offer a superb gentle stroll and a chance to feed the red squirrels, if you have enough patience.

Ehrwald has a lovely little cablecar going just above tree level up to the Ehrwalder Alm. From here it is a good idea to go up the valley. There is a path going all the way to Scharnitz. Just about 1km (just over half a mile) from the cablecar station there is a tiny plague chapel which is almost at the summit of this pass. A little way on there are open spaces in among the trees where it is possible to picnic without seeing a soul. Though there are people about, the mountains and the woods absorb them. From the valley station of the cablecar a path goes up to a waterfall, and though the last section is a scramble the lower section is delightful. There is a splendid swimming pool, and adjacent tennis hall, and a number of shops. There is a cablecar going

Ehrwald and the Zugspitze

up to the summit of the Zugspitze, with two changes on the way. At the top, right on the border, there is a complex of buildings with a restaurant viewing terrace and a catwalk to the German side. Take your passport as the border is manned sometimes. The German summit is actually the highest mountain in Germany and is quite popular. It is accessible from that side by both cablecar and railway and though the railway comes in lower down at the Schneeferner hut, a cablecar goes up to the summit from there as well.

The actual summit is marked by a cross and it can be reached by a scramble across fixed ladders, but only by experienced scramblers. The cablecar ride is quite exciting as the trees give way to bare rocks and snowfields once over 1,829m (6,000ft). It is possible to walk, or scramble up, but the ascent will take 7 hours and is only for very experienced mountain walkers. Long distance path 801 uses the path from Ehrwald to the summit.

Across the valley at Lermoos there are a few shops, a splendid café from where there is a good view of the Zugspitze, and a chairlift. This goes up, in two stages, almost to the summit of the Grubigstein, 2,233m (7,324ft).

There is a lovely walk all round this splendid area called the Panorama Weg. Properly timed one could have coffee in Lermoos, lunch at Biberwier, and be back in Ehrwald for tea. The Austrians have a word for this sort of comfort, which also embraces the calm relaxed atmosphere of the country and the pleasant manner of the people: they call it *Gemutlikeit*.

Further Information
— St Johann, Kitzbühel and the Inn Valley —

Activities

Achensee
Steam cog railway from Jenbach to Achensee; Lake steamer trips; fishing, bathing (in the lake or indoors at Maurach), tennis, bowling, nine-hole golf course at Pertisau, cablecar at Maurach, chairlift at Achenkirch, walking.

Brixen im Thale
Tennis, fishing, chairlift, walk programme.

Brixlegg
Tennis, swimming, fishing.

Ebbs
Riding, swimming, cycle path, tennis.

Ehrwald
Swimming, tennis, riding, guided walks, cablecar.

Erl
Swimming.

Hall in Tyrol
Swimming, riding.

Hopfgarten
Tennis, riding, swimming.

Imst
Swimming, riding, tennis.

Itter
Swimming.

Jenbach
Swimming.

Jochberg
Swimming, tennis, walking programme.

Kelchsau
Swimming, steam trains to Zillertal and Achensee.

Kirchdorf
Swimming, riding, cycle path, fishing, tennis.

Kitzbühel
Fishing, boating, bowling, riding, cablecar, chairlifts, walking programme.

Kössen
Swimming, riding, tennis, cycle hire.

Leutasch
Riding, swimming, fishing.

St Johann
Swimming, fishing, riding, tennis, golf, cablecar, chairlift, level walks.

Scharnitz
Centre for walking in the Isar valley and Karwendel mountains.

Scheffau
Lakeside walks.

Seefeld
Boating, fishing, walking, riding, tennis, golf, swimming.

Thiersee
Bathing lakes, swimming, fishing, boating.

Walchsee
Swimming, tennis, fishing, guided walks.

Wildschönau
Swimming, riding, tennis, chairlift.

Wörgl
Tennis, swimming, cycle hire.

Places to Visit in the Area

Aurach
Wildlife Park
Open: daily 9am-6pm.

Brandenberg
Peaceful, unspoilt village.

Brixlegg
Schloss Matzen (grounds only); Ruined Schloss Kropfsberg.

Eben
Church dedicated to St Notburga.

Erl
Passion Play theatre.

Erpfendorf
Modern church.

Hall in Tyrol
Medieval town. Parish church (fifteenth century), town hall, Stiftsplatz, ecclesiastical buildings, Damenstift (Ladies' Abbey), boulevards, museum, mining museum.

Hasegg Castle
Open: mid-June to mid-September. Guided tours 9.45, 10.45am and 2.30, 3.30, 4.30pm.

Imst
Old upper town, museum.

Jenbach
Useful centre, just off the motorway, for touring in all directions. Main line trains and buses. Steam trains (see chapter 4).

Kitzbühel
Parish church of Our Lady; local museum, closed Sundays.

Kössen
Folk theatre.

Kramsach
Freilichtmuseum Tiroler Bauernhof Open-air farm buildings museum in a natural setting.
Open: most days.

Kufstein
Fortress, housing the town museum.
Open: daily except Mondays 9am-6pm.

Guided town walks.

Leutasch
A lovely, unspoiled valley.

Mariastein
Castle visited by arrangement at local tourist office.

Oberau (near Wildschönau)
Rural Life Museum
Open: July and August daily except Mondays 10am-12noon and 3-5pm; June and September, Saturday and Sunday 3-5pm.

Rattenberg
Glass workshops.

Scheffau
Peaceful mountain village.

Stams
Monastery

Steinberg
Beautifully unspoiled, peaceful
village.

Thiersee
Passion Play theatre.

Tourist Information Offices

Achenkirch
☎ (05246) 6270

Aurach
☎ (05356) 4622

Brandenberg
☎ (05331) 5203

Brixen im Thale
☎ (05334) 8111

Brixlegg
☎ (05337) 2581

Ebbs
☎ (05373) 2326

Ehrwald
☎ (05673) 2395

Erl
☎ (05373) 8117

Erpfendorf
☎ (05352) 8150

Hall in Tyrol
Wallpachgasse
☎ (05223) 6269

Hinter Thiersee
☎ (05376) 5597

Hopfgarten im Brixental
☎ (05335) 2322

Imst
☎ (05412) 2419

Itter
☎ (05335) 2670

Jenbach
☎ (05244) 3901

Jochberg
☎ (05355) 5229

Kelchsau
☎ (05335) 8105

Kirchdorf
☎ (05352) 3136

Kitzbühel
☎ (05356) 2155 or 2272

Kössen
☎ (05375) 6287

Kramsach
☎ (05337) 2710

Kundl
☎ (05338) 326

Landl
☎ (05376) 5880

Leutasch
☎ (05214) 6207

Mariastein
☎ (05332) 726116

Maurach/Eben
☎ (05243) 5340

Pertisau
☎ (05243) 5260

St Johann in Tyrol
☎ (05352) 2218

Scharnitz
☎ (05213) 5270

Scheffau
☎ (05358) 8137

Seefeld
☎ (05212) 2313

Stams
☎ (05263) 6511

Steinberg am Rofan
☎ (05248) 205

Thiersee
☎ (05376) 5230

Walchsee
☎ (05374) 5223 or 5775

Wildschönau
☎ (05339) 8255

Wörgl
☎ (05332) 2122

7 • Southern Carinthia

This area, which occupies the south-eastern corner of Austria, is well served with good communications. Klagenfurt, to the south, has an airport, although international flights may arrive via Vienna. Similarly, rail links are via Klagenfurt or Klagenfurt airport. St Veit has a railway station and local trains can be used to get to some places of local interest, especially if you are proposing to walk on the many footpaths in the area. There are bus services to Villach and Klagenfurt. The motorway from Salzburg links up with the E7 motorway (Villach to Klagenfurt), and the Spittal-Radenthein-Feldkirchen route (routes 98, 88 and 95) offers an alternative. The direct road to St Veit from Villach via Feldkirchen can be slow, with heavy traffic impeding progress. Although longer, the motorway route via Klagenfurt may be preferred. There is no bypass around Klagenfurt, but there appear to be no undue delays and the route is well signposted. Take the E7/Route 83 north of the town, signposted Vienna. This road is of motorway standard from just north of the airport.

Carinthia is one of the federal states of Austria. It is saucer shaped, in so far as it is surrounded by high mountains with lower mountains and hills in the middle. It is a beautiful area of wooded terrain, rounded hills and rougher mountain peaks, with over 200 turquoise lakes dotted with white, moving specks, its water flashing like miriad diamonds in the sun. Carinthia even has the right climate. Its temperature climbs to respectable levels early in the year and given a certain amount of tolerable rain it is ideal for exploring. The midsummer climate may even be too hot and the sun dictates one's movements on occasions. This is a minor problem however; one can compensate either by having a few lazy days or by going high.

The surrounding mountains are indeed high — Austria's highest mountain lies in north-west Carinthia. The Grossglockner soars above the Pasterzen, the biggest glacier in Europe, to a height of 3,797m (12,454ft). Its snow covered features provide a backcloth of

One of southern Carinthia's many lakes

staggering dimension and beauty when viewed from **Heiligenblut**, with its tall church and slender spire dominating the village, and the Mölltal. Mountains of a lower, but still respectable height are much closer to St Veit. The southern edge of the saucer is the Karawanken range of mountains, such as Hochobir, rising to well over 2,000m (6,560ft). Even closer, to the east, rises the Saualpe, again to over 2,000m (6,560ft).

Carinthia is an area of breathtaking beauty. It lacks the vertical scale and therefore some of the 'chocolate box' appeal of the Tyrol valleys; its hills and mountains are more rounded and lower. Its architecture is similar, with its churches, capped with the ubiquitous 'onion dome', only occasionally broken by slender spires reaching towards the sky; its chalets no different to the casual glance. Its climate is as warm as anywhere in Austria — you are not that far from the Adriatic Sea or western Hungary. The lakes are incredibly warm, often over 21°C (70°F) in the summer. The warmest is apparently Wörther See, and it has been suggested that this lake is fed by warm thermal waters.

The most fascinating aspect of the area, and the reason for its inclusion in this book, is the fact that it is largely devoid of tourists. It has been a different story in the past, however. The large number of 'Zimmer Frei' signs, the car parks (now empty) and facilities for tourists indicate that this was once justifiably a tourist trap. Unfortu-

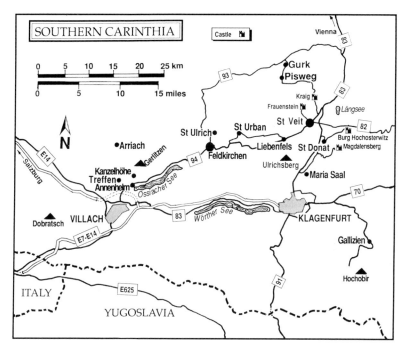

nately for the local economy and fortunately for the discerning visitor, the winds of change currently no longer blow in Carinthia's favour. The mass exodus of Dutch and German holidaymakers with their powerful cars and caravans, still head south for Austria. They now continue on, however. The *guilder* and *mark* buy more *lire* and *drachma* than Austrian *schillings* and the sun seekers are going further south. Consequently, one has all the advantages of an area adapted to accommodate tourism, coupled with the even better advantage of having the area almost to oneself. This is even more so when one moves away from the lakesides which act as a magnet to most of the visitors. It is marvellous to have the choice of lakeside recreation, its lazy social life and sporting activity coupled with the quiet mountains, tranquil alpine meadows prolific with flowers and a network of footpaths adequate for anyone.

This tranquil scene did not escape early visitors, and it comes as no surprise to find that the Roman province of *Noricum* had its capital just outside St Veit. The city of *Virunum* is no more, and there is precious little of it for the visitor to see. It existed in the Zollfeld, a small plain consisting of the river meadows of the river Glan between St Veit and Klagenfurt. Arable fields now cover the site but its stones and carvings can still be seen incorporated into local build-

The village of Velden on the Wörther See

ings. The most famous of these stones is the carving of the two post
horses, their covered wagon and driver. The stone is built into the
south wall of the Gothic church of Maria Saal to the right of the main
church entrance. The delicate pattern on the wagon and the general
attention to detail are a small, poignant remnant of what must have
been an interesting and well executed freize.

To the west, on the ridge that extends to St Veit, is **Karnburg**, with
more Roman stones. Here was the castle of the rulers of *Carantania*,
(the early name for Carinthia). The investiture of the rulers took place
in the open near Karnburg. The stone chair or throne (made from the
base of a column robbed from *Virunum*) on which the investiture
took place was the Fürnstenstein or Prince's stone. It is now preserved in the Landesmuseum in Klagenfurt. A similar throne exists
close to the main road in a clump of trees north of Maria Saal. This
double-seated throne is the Herzogstuhl — the Duke's chair — and
is also made of old Roman slabs of stone from *Virunum*, situated
across the maize fields a little to the north-east. The Landesmuseum
also preserves a mosaic floor found at *Virunum*.

During Roman times the local inhabitants, as well as their Roman
rulers, lived a sophisticated urban lifestyle. Much excavation work
at nearby *Magdalensburg* has revealed a whole town. The site is of
major importance and excavation still proceeds (see page 136).

Much later, in medieval times, the dukes of Carinthia had their

Nesselwängle, Tannheimertal

The Tauern valley and Gross Venediger

Lachesee and the Rote Spitze, Tannheimertal

Roman carving in the side of the church at Maria Saal

capital at St Veit. The castle remains are now somewhat insignificant, owing to fire in the early nineteenth century which destroyed much of the town. In fact, only a tower survives, and this now houses a museum. There are, however, quite a few castles in this area, the majority medieval and some still well preserved. Several are ruinous such as Leibenfels, north-west of the little village of Pulst. Here, the curtain walls survive together with two tall towers. Some restoration work has been going on here, and at the time of writing it was possible to wander around at will. The view over to the Karawanken mountains is particularly memorable.

North of St Veit is the romantic and fully preserved castle at Frauenstein. It has six towers and stands by a small farm and pool. It is also open to the public and was built in the early sixteenth century. Frauenstein is the third castle to be built in this area and its two predecessors are just a little further down the road. The two Kraig castles are not as well preserved as their younger neighbour, but even so the local predeliction for tall watch towers is evident. The earliest castle, Hoch Kraig, was built in the eleventh century and three centuries later work started on Nieder Kraig nearby.

The most famous castle in this area is Burg Hochosterwitz. This medieval castle was rebuilt in the sixteenth century, like Frauenstein. If the latter is romantic, then Burg Hochosterwitz is as dramatic as one can find. It sits on the top of a limestone cliff with sheer walls

Burg Liebenfels near St Veit

some 139m (450ft) high. It has fourteen separate defensive gates which had to be assailed to reach the top. Today it is a pleasant stroll to the top, where one can explore the castle and admire the view from the restaurant in the courtyard. Across the valley is the castle of Taggenbrunn. It sits on the top of a hill surrounded by woodland which makes its location not as easy as one might like to think. Nevertheless, there are the remains of a couple of towers and walls, a large building, reduced to a car park, with the remnant of a once substantial fireplace in an upper floor. It is now a restaurant and one can gaze out over St Veit and the valley of the river Glan from the tables outside the bar. The valley is a pronounced U-shape at this point and the view all the better for it.

St Veit an der Glan

St Veit is a small town situated to the north of the river Glan at the eastern end of the Glantal. It is a wide, shallow valley, lacking the dramatic scale of the valley beyond Feldkirchen where the taller mountains drop steeply to Ossiachersee. Its huge timber yard is a reminder of the importance of forestry in the local economy. Indeed, many of the surrounding hills are clothed in timber. The *fôretstrasse* (forest roads) are sometimes footpaths too and give easy access up the hills, especially when time does not permit a thorough exploration on foot.

Much of the medieval town was destroyed in a fire, which must have taken many of the buildings associated with the period when the town enjoyed the patronage of the dukes of Carinthia. Its importance as a medieval town and stronghold was clearly imposed by the residence and castle of the dukes in the town. Some idea of what might have been is the Rathaus. This beautiful building is the gem of a picturesque Market Place. It was built in 1468 although the most attractive baroque façade to the cobbled square dates from the sixteenth century. The main room, the grand hall, has a fine rococo stucco ceiling of 1754 and the building now houses the town's information centre. The main entrance leads through to the sixteenth-century Arkadenhof where buildings at the rear of the Rathaus form a courtyard, the sides being a three storey arcade. The many arches and the intricately painted mock ballustrades, contrast with the red geraniums in the boxes at each floor level. It is a memorable sight which should not be missed.

Back in the Market Place, do not overlook the other buildings. Although not as old as the Rathaus, the whole scene is a colourful backdrop to the quiet business of everyday life. Here one can feel that the rat race of life elsewhere has left the place behind, with pretty overhanging buildings, plenty of flowers and much use of painted stucco. No one seems to be in a rush; only the tourist seems to be interested in the melody of colour, the fountain and the Rathaus façade. One is spared the tourist trade gift shops to a large extent, but if you require maps and cards, they are available in the Market Place. Before leaving, take a look at the large stone saucer on a pedestal at the Sparkasse bank end. It is Roman in origin and was found at *Virunum*.

If you do stay locally, try the Hotel Stern for dinner one evening. You can sit outside at one of the many tables; the service is unobtrusive and the food quite reasonably priced. It is situated opposite the main school building in Friesacher Strasse.

Burg Hochosterwitz

Due east of St Veit is the fairytale castle of Burg Hochosterwitz. Access to it is easy, as it is signposted from St Veit. Take road 82, and the castle comes into view shortly after crossing the *autobahn* and

St Veit an der Glan

going under the railway bridge a mile or so further on. At Launsdorf, a road to the right leads straight to the castle. Alternatively, if you are heading north from Klagenfurt leave the *autobahn* at the first exit for St Veit, proceed to St Donat and turn left for the castle.

The castle sits on the top of a 139m-high(450ft-) limestone cliff. Its defensive potential was recognised at an early stage and the existing castle is not the first. This one dates from the sixteenth century when the fortifications were vastly improved by Georg Khevenhüller, whose descendents still own the castle. The fortifications were built to defend local people against the Turkish army, who had razed the area in 1473, and several other castles in the area were also fortified.

Georg Khevenhüller took possession of the castle in 1571 and spent several years building the fortress. He was the state governor and also chief equerry and councillor of the emperors Friedrich I, Maximillian II and Rudolf II. He was also privy councillor and chief chamberlain to Archduke Charles, Lord of Styria, Carinthia and Trieste. The latter purchased an estate and founded the famous Lipizzana stud at Lipizza near Trieste in 1580. To Baron Georg Khevenhüller lies the distinction of purchasing in Spain (in 1580 and 1581) the nine stallions originally used at the stud and from which the Spanish Riding School in Vienna used to obtain its horses. It took thirteen years to complete the castle fortifications, which must have been due to Khevenhüller's political and court duties. Today it is a

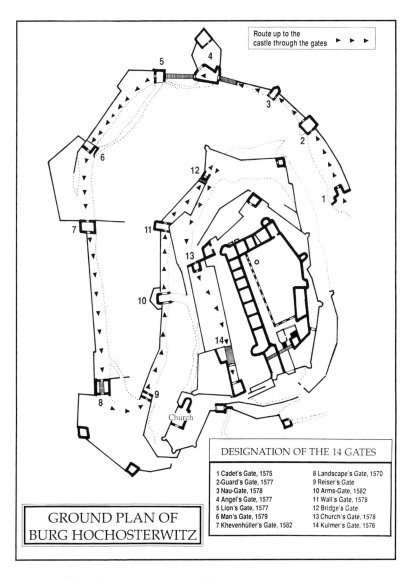

Route up to the castle through the gates ► ► ►

DESIGNATION OF THE 14 GATES

1 Cadet's Gate, 1575	8 Landscape's Gate, 1570
2-Guard's Gate, 1577	9 Reiser's Gate
3 Nau-Gate, 1578	10 Arms-Gate, 1582
4 Angel's Gate, 1577	11 Wall's Gate, 1578
5 Lion's Gate, 1577	12 Bridge's Gate
6 Man's Gate, 1579	13 Church's Gate, 1578
7 Khevenhüller's Gate, 1582	14 Kulmer's Gate, 1576

GROUND PLAN OF
BURG HOCHOSTERWITZ

quiet and fascinating place to explore.

A road leads up to a car park at the rear of the castle and the first gatehouse. From here, access is on foot and the trackway is difficult for wheelchairs. The fourteen gatehouses, cleverly built to take advantage of the precipitous cliffs, made the castle impregnable. The attacking forces had to take each gate at a time and while doing so were subject to attack from elsewhere. Adjacent to the thirteenth gate

Burg Hochosterwitz

is a walled garden and the church, built in 1576. The church has not been open to visitors lately, perhaps to help protect the murals, some of which date from when the building was built.

Today the castle contains a museum, shop and restaurant. The museum contains many items of sixteenth-century armour, cannon etc. The views are memorable as one climbs up to the castle and a visit is definitely recommended.

If you wish to combine a visit to the castle with a good full day's walk, then leave the car or bus at **St Donat**. Proceed up the road towards Burg Hochosterwitz to the last house on the right, before a bend. Just past the house is a signpost to the right marked 'Fussweg Magdalensberg'. Take the unmetalled track up into the wood (do not take the farm track), following green *Wanderweg* signs and then signs waymarked on path 160. The track climbs several hundred feet through the coniferous woodland, with occasional views to St Veit and beyond, and eventually reaches a forest road. Cross this and bear to the left. The way forward is well waymarked with the red, white and red stripes of the Austrian flag. A further climb up the hill brings one to another track (No 106). Join the track and follow path 106, waymarked the remaining short distance to the top. On a hot summer's day the track is a delight. Shafts of sunlight pierce the conifers highlighting the bilberry (blueberry) that can be picked en route. Numerous different species of butterfly dance among the flowers with only the buzzing of bees and the bird song to break the stillness. The path emerges in a field at the rear of the summit, which is crowned by the church at Magdalensberg and an inn at a height of 1,059m (3,474ft), nearly 600m (1,968ft) above St Donat. If heat haze permits, the views from here are magnificent.

From here, descend to St Sebastian and Hochosterwitz, some 6km (3½ miles) away along a waymarked path, 171, which drops through the wood and in and out of farmland. The path emerges in **St Sebastian** to the left of the church. Walk down the road to Hochosterwitz with the castle towering above you. Allow 1½-2 hours to visit the castle and return to the valley road. From here take the road back to St Donat which is about 3 miles away. Clearly, this will need a full day, but it will be a memorable one.

There are important Celtic-Roman archaeological remains below the summit of the Magdalensberg. These are situated chiefly down the metalled road at the bus stop, although excavations have also taken place at the car park adjacent to the church. The remains of a whole village survive, indicating that the local people enjoyed a rich cultural life. Many relics in iron, bronze, clay and glass have been

The archaeological remains at Magdalensberg

found, together with the remains of plaster friezes, mosaic floors, ovens etc. The museum also houses a copy of the full size bronze figure of a nude young man which was found here by a local farmer in 1502. The original is in the Kuntshistorisches Museum in Vienna. Remains of the temple and government buildings can be inspected, in addition to many other interesting features. The site also includes a restaurant and is well recommended. Allow at least 90 minutes to wander around the site, as there is much to see.

To reach Magdalensburg by car turn off the road, two miles south of St Donat, at Willersdorf. Climb up the hill and follow signs for Magdalensburg. The entrance is on the right-hand side of the road near the top of the hill.

Maria Saal and the Zollfield

A further 3 miles down road 83 in the direction of Klagenfurt from Willersdorf lies the little village of **Maria Saal**. It sits on a little knowl on the east side of the Zollfield, crowned by the twin towers of its church, each tower topped by a baroque 'onion'. The large church is just off the village square and the building is one of the best preserved examples of Gothic architecture in the whole of Carinthia, although its dark interior obscures a lot of detail. It was built in the fifteenth century and houses the tomb of St Modestus who brought Christianity to the area seven centuries before this building was erected. The church has some interesting frescoes and carvings together with the Roman carving of the post horses and carriage referred to earlier. If one approaches the church from the square, and through the old building blocking one's view of the church, the carving is approximately halfway down the side of the church as one approaches the porch. There are several old buildings adjacent to the church which are worth looking at.

Just north of the town is the Freilichtmuseum where old buildings from all over Carinthia have been collected together for preservation. Just across the railway line from here, and situated by route 83 is the Herzogstuhl (Duke's Chair) where dukes of Carinthia were enthroned. It is surrounded by a clump of trees which makes identification of the site easy and photography difficult. Although the site of the Roman town of *Virunum* is marked on maps, there is nothing to see there.

Around Villach

Villach is the second largest city in Carinthia, after Klagenfurt, and was originally established as a spa town by the Romans. In fact a spa still survives in the area at Warmbad Villach to the south-west. The town is popular with tourists and has several very old buildings. It makes a useful base if you prefer more social life than that offered by St Veit, but it is hardly 'off the beaten track'. The city stands at a bend in the river Drau at the foot of the Villacher Alpe which rises from the suburbs to the west. The Alpe is almost an oulier of the Gailtaler Alpen; an island of rock bounded to the south and east by the river Gail and to the north by the Bleiberger Tal. It is crowned by Dobratsch at 2,166m (7,104ft), which boasts the highest mountain church in Europe and has an impressive sheer wall to the Unter Gailtal to the south. To the north-east of the town rises the Gerlitzen to a height of 1,909m (6,262ft). Its smooth slopes afford a winter's playground when the snow is firm and deep enough. At its foot is Ossiachersee where water sports and sunbathing occupy summer visitors and locals alike.

Dobratsch

The Villacher Alpenstrasse is a private road which commences in the Möltschach suburb of Villach. There is a toll (it is not cheap) for cars, and the road climbs nearly 1,200m (3,936ft) towards Dobratsch. There are several free car parks on the 13km (8 miles) of road which give ample opportunity of stopping and taking in the superb view. The size of some of the car parks indicates how popular the area has been, and of course, still is in winter. Yet it is possible now in summer to find the whole mountain virtually free of visitors. Car parks five and six are perhaps worth stopping at for the benefit of the view.

Adjacent to car park six is the Alpengarten, established in 1966 and containing many different alpine plants. It is quite extensive and it is easy to spend at least an hour wandering around the garden, set at the very edge of the vertical drop to the Unter Gailtal. The garden is at its best in early summer and there is a charge for admission. Just above the Knappenhütte, the road ends at Rosstratten, with plenty of car parking space. There is a choice here; one can either walk or take the chairlift. The path (No 291) goes to the top of Dobratsch — allow $2^1/_2$ hours to get there. The chairlift goes to Höhenrain and reduces the ascent time by an hour. From the top of the lift there is a choice of paths to the summit.

Path 294 via Zwölfemock is the direct route to the Ludwig Walter Haus just below the summit. A slightly more circuitous route leads to the edge of the escarpment and then follows the edge up to the top. You can use the chairlift to gain height quickly and follow either of these paths to the top. Path 291 can be used to return to Rosstratten.

The paths are very distinct and waymarked, in any event. On a clear day the views are magnificent, with a skyline of peaks along the Austrian border with both Italy and Yugoslavia. If you come up the Alpenstrasse, you get a leaflet which indicates the names of twenty-one of the peaks. There is a bus route up the road to Rosstratten and three restaurants at that point.

Accommodation may be booked at both the Knappenhütte and the adjacent Aichingerhütte if you wish to stay overnight. Bear in mind that the last ascent of the chairlift is at 5pm.

The Gerlitzen

The Gerlitzen rises to a height of 1,909m (6,262ft), yet is entirely covered by meadows or coniferous forest. It is situated to the northeast of Villach and rises from the shore of Ossiachersee and from the Arriacher Tal to the north. There are literally dozens of paths crisscrossing all over the Gerlitzen; two roads which climb a respectable distance up the mountain, and a third, from near Arriach which climbs to the very top. The summit must be very popular in winter for two chairlifts and three skilifts radiate away from it. Yet on a hot day in July, at the height of the tourist season, the mountain can be virtually deserted.

There is a cablecar lift from **Annenheim** on the banks of the Ossiachersee, the third largest lake in Carinthia. This lift will take you up to the Kanzelhöhe at a height of 1,466m (4,808ft). You can reach this height easily by car from **Treffen** (there is a small toll) or leave the car a little higher at the Alpenrose Hotel. From here, a path (No 1763) passes under the chairlift and climbs up into the wood. There is a small housing development in the wood and the track is level and wide enough for the occasional car. Breaks in the wood give good views down to Ossiachersee, to Villach, and beyond to the mountains of the Karawanken.

After a while a path leaves to your left, for the Pöllinger Hütte and the top of the chairlift, if you have had enough. The track from here is fairly level, leaving the wood at a small stream where the path climbs up to the Hotel Berger. Just before the hotel is a small residential development. It is a pity that the mountain has been spoilt in such a way.

From the Hotel Berger, the summit of Gerlitzen rises above you, crowned by the Stifters Gipfel Hotel, radio masts, an observatory and the various lifts. The path rises the last 150m (492ft) amid alpine meadows with tremendous views if the weather is right. If you fancy a break, or if time is short, there is a chairlift from here to the top. There are refreshments at the hotel on the summit. The path back down to the Alpenrose and the Kanzelhohe hotels begins by the skilift near the Gasthof Pacheiner and runs down the hill between the skilift and the chairlift. It descends through alpine meadows and a small stand of conifers to the Pöllinger Hütte, situated at 1,630m (5,346ft) and continues on to the Alpenrose Hotel as a grassy path close to the chairlift.

If you intend to use the chairlifts (to Pöllinger Hütte and the second lift to the Alpenrose Hotel) and the cablecar back down to Annenheim, check the times of the last descent. The summit lift stops around 4.30pm. The route described is quite easy walking but allow about 3 hours to the summit from Alpenrose Hotel and an hour back again; plus any time spent in the summit hotel or resting en route!

St Urban

The road between Feldkirchen and St Veit is a busy one, with heavy vehicles, often pulling trailers, grinding along and often preventing cars from passing them. To the north of this lies a quiet valley which offers an alternative, if slower route. It is not a deep valley, but there are some sleepy villages to explore and the larger village of St Urban and Urbaner See at the Feldkirchen end. Assuming one is starting from St Veit, take road 94 towards Feldkirchen. The village of Lieben-fels is soon reached, where one turns right to Glantschach. However, before doing this, turn right a little earlier along a road marked for Pulst to Burg Liebenfels. Climb out of Pulst village, which is only 2km (just over a mile) from the main road from St Veit, around a sharp bend and look for the two huge towers of the castle ruin high above and to your right.

Park where it is convenient. At present there is no kiosk charging an entrance fee, no postcards or the usual bric-a-brac of commercial-ism. Only a few birds break the eerie quietness. The ruin is used for evening entertainment from time to time, and some buildings at the rear of the castle are being renovated, with floors being replaced etc. Time will tell whether the commercial world has at last caught up with the old castle. In due course the huge watch tower may be refloored again, with a staircase to the top. If it does happen, the view will be magnificent. There are already tantalising views to the distant mountains within the curtain wall.

Returning to Liebenfels and proceeding towards Glantschach, one is soon climbing up the wooded valley with the Liembergbach (stream) close to the road. The valley soon becomes flatter and wider, with the Gösseberg rising to 1,160m (3,805ft) to the north.

Upon reaching a T-junction, the village of **St Urban** can be seen to your right, tucked into the side of the hill, its church spire dominating the village. Turn right here and right again to reach the village. However, if you wish to explore a little more than this, a walk around Urbaner See is not taxing, but offers quiet lanes, a forest trail and a chance to enjoy some lovely countryside. From the T-junction, do not turn right for St Urban, but turn left instead. After a short distance, turn right and there is a large car park on your left. This is chiefly used by visitors to the lakeside with its café etc.

The lakeside is fenced off — you pay to sunbathe by the lake. Continue down the lane with the fence on your left, past a way-marked path (No 1) on your left which crosses the meadows to the end of the lake. Upon reaching the road junction, turn left, and with your back to St Urban walk up the road towards the red-roofed Schloss Bach, now a farmhouse. Below lies the lake and as the road rises, there are good views of it and St Urbaner Berg's tree covered slopes beyond. The road is waymarked, the red and white symbol being painted on trees, telegraph poles etc. There are even the occa-sional seats and tables if you wish to rest.

The Urbaner See

The road climbs up the valleyside and away from the lake, passing a small church at **Kleingradenegg**. Beyond this, bear left at a roadside shrine. At a bend in the road, take the lane to the left signposted to Agsdorf. From here, there is a splendid view down to St Ulrich and across to the Gerlitzen (with the hotel crowning its summit) just beyond the tree covered hill immediately in front of you — the Tschwarzenberg. Beyond the latter and to the left a little lie the Karawanken mountains, heat haze and clouds permitting.

The lane you have just taken is unmade and descends down towards St Urbaner Berg and the path to Agsdorf. After passing an old quarry, take the track to the left. It is marked with the letter A. Bear left when the track forks and walk down the small valley on a forest trail. The track eventually leads to two large ponds. Between the second one and Urbaner See itself is a choice of routes. By bearing left between the two stretches of water, one can return along path 1 through the meadows referred to earlier. The other path continues on through the wood at the side of the lake. It eventually emerges into a lane which brings you back to the car park and your car.

Allow a minimum of 90 minutes for this short but thoroughly enjoyable walk. It is also possible to push a baby's pushchair all round this route, despite the fact that the forest trail is just a rough track. A wheelchair would fare similarly if you are happy with one off the tarmac.

To return to the St Veit-Feldkirchen road, rejoin the road at the car park, turning right to leave the valley and climb over the flank of St Urbaner Berg before descending to Agsdorf and the Glantal just outside Feldkirchen.

The Karawanken

This huge range offers endless opportunities for some energetic — or not so energetic — walking away from the main holiday centres. A perusal of the various maps indicates that there are many footpaths threading their way through the mountains of this extensive range. The mountain tops are often snow covered in mid-summer and should be avoided unless you are experienced in high-level walking or are with an experienced guide. The area described below gives you the opportunity of keeping to the lower slopes or going much higher, and includes a visit to the tremendous waterfall south-east of Klagenfurt known as the Wildensteiner Wasserfall.

The Wildensteiner Wasserfall

From Klagenfurt, the road eastwards to Völkermarkt runs through flattish land crossed by the rivers Glan and Gurk which unite south of Niederdorf before flowing eastwards to join the river Drau where it widens into Völkermarkter Stausee, the large lake to the south and south-west of Völkermarkt. Just after the road has crossed the twin rivers of the Gurk at Niederdorf, take the road to the right which heads for the village of Grafenstein before crossing the river again and heading for the eastern end of the Saltnitz range which is bounded by the river Drau. This huge river is crossed at the St Anna Brücke. Proceed on through Gallizien to Wildenstein. Ahead lies the massif of Hochobir, its lower slopes heavily wooded. As one nears the village of Wildenstein there are glimpses of the waterfall, its water shooting over the precipice and disappearing into the trees below. **Wildenstein** straggles the road in a linear manner and one reaches it at the western end. A lane off to the south leads up through the trees and meadows to Hazar, the end of the lane, where there is a collection of buildings plus a small car park and information on the waterfall.

A well marked path leads up into the wood. It is alternatively numbered 608 or 08 and starts by the car park. Climb steadily and not excessively for about 20 minutes through the wood, suddenly emerging into a clearing with spray rising around you. The Wildensteiner Wasserfall plunges 54m (177ft) over a limestone cliff and into

The Wildensteiner Wasserfall

a small pool below, disappearing down the steep valley amid boulders and trees. You can descend down to the pool where a footbridge enables you to cross the stream in front of the falling sheet of water. You can return via the back of the waterfall — which is quite an experience — but beware of the slippery, wet ground on either side.

From here one has a choice, depending upon time and inclination. There is, of course, the straightforward return to the car by the same route. Alternatively, if you want a longer, but not a taxing walk, climb up the steep path by the waterfall and leave path 08, taking path 07 to Lessiak. It contours through the wood, on the lower slope of Hochobir. Leave Lessiak and take the path to Robesch, bearing left upon picking up path 5 (marked on yellow signs). Walk down the small, shallow valley towards Wischonik. The track descends towards meadowland and upon reaching a minor road at a bend in the valley, turn your right. Follow the road to Wildenstein via the hamlet of Kushnig. Although marked as a road, much of the lane is unsurfaced and makes a delightful path, untroubled by many vehicles. The valley itself is quiet, unspoilt and peaceful. If you car is at the car park mentioned above, from Kushnig take path 6 (becoming path 7) back to Hazar.

If you are used to climbing high, path 608 continues up the steep gorge of the Wildensteiner Bruck towards Hochobir and the Eisenkappler Hütte at 1,555m (5,100ft). In fact the path reaches a total height of 1,714m (5,622ft), with Hochobir rising steeply to 2,142m (7,026ft) on your right. In order to make a round trip, leave path 608 and bear right on path 625 across the northern side of Hochobir up a valley with the Hofmanns Alpe and the Jagoutz huts above your right-hand side. This path descends steeply down to **Jagoutz** at the far end of the Freibach Stausee reservoir. Pick up the road here and walk along the lakeside, and then onto **Raspotnik**, where path 7 returns you to the Wasserfall.

The emerald green lake is used for watersports, and you can park at the roadside to sunbathe at the lakeside if you wish. There are however, no facilities for food or toilets.

Further Information
— Southern Carinthia —

Accommodation

For details of accommodation write for a leaflet from the Information Centre, Hauptplatz 1, A-9300 St Veit an der Glan, Kärnten. The leaflet *Urlaubs und Erholungsgebiet* gives details of hotels, guesthouses and *pensions* plus other essential information eg chemists, banks, doctors, sport facilities etc.

The Reitererhof Gasthof-Pension at St Georgen am Langsee not only offers hotel, bed and breakfast and self-catering accommodation with extensive grounds, sauna, tennis courts and childrens' area but also provides a guide if you wish to go walking in the mountains.

Maps

There are two principal suppliers of maps which are available every-where — the blue covered Freytag and Berndt maps and the green covered Kompass Wanderkarte series. Both are to a scale of 1:50,000 and both include bus stops which can be helpful if you are without a car.

Places to Visit in the Area

Burg Hochosterwitz
☎ (04213) 20 20 or 20 10
Fascinating castle built in sixteenth century with fourteen gatehouses. Situated 139m (450ft) above valley on limestone outcrop some 8km (5 miles) east of St Veit.

Freilichtmuseum
Maria Saal
Open-air museum of Carinthian life. Chiefly old buildings re-assembled on the site.
Open: May to September, 10am-6pm.

Herzogburg
Remains of the castle of the dukes of Carinthia.

Herzogstuhl
Situated at roadside north of Maria Saal surrounded by trees. On road running parallel with motorway. Stone seat used for enthronement of the dukes of Carinthia.

Hörzendorfer See
Small lake between Maria Saal and St Veit, south of Hörzendorf village. Quiet spot for sunbathing by small but undoubtedly pretty lake (with Ulrichsberg rising in the background). Café adjacent. Path around lake not recommended.

Maria Saal
Fifteenth-century church with twin towers and Roman carving of two horses pulling a carriage. Interesting range of buildings separating the church from the market square.

St Georgen am Langsee
Popular beachside area (large car park) with café and toilets. Area nearest monastery is quietest. Lake is warm in summer. Take road to Burg Hochosterwitz and turn left up the hill at Reipersdorf. Benedictine monastery, founded in 1003, has a guest house (*pension*).

St Veit
Rathaus
Built 1468 with attractive sixteenth-century baroque façade and arcade.

Schloss Frauenstein
Preserved sixteenth-century castle with six towers, $3^1/_2$km (2 miles) north of the town. Details of walks on notice near entrance to farmyard adjacent to the castle.

Taggenbrunn
Castle ruins with café/bar. Good views to the Glantal from tables on terrace.

Tourist Information Office

St Veit
Rathaus, situated in the Market Place (Hauptplatz)
☎ (042 12) 3192

8 • Western Steiermark

Western Steiermark or 'Styria' as it is more popularly known, is *not* a land of contrasts. Instead every aspect of life here complements the others. The modern architecture complements the old, as does the attitude and way of life of the area's inhabitants. A sense of natural history is perhaps the most overpowering of all the feelings evoked for visitors here. Life really is tied to the seasons and the people are happy that that is the way it is. The publicity logo dubs Styria 'The Green Heart of Austria.'

This sense of peace is reflected in a lack of industry, and the fact that what minimal manufacturing there is in these parts is closely related to the land. Tourism is, of course, encouraged, but still it is not over-developed, the mountains are not covered with ski lifts. People here talk of the Tyrol as a region that went wrong, overdeveloped in the face of tourist demand and which now can never be the same again.

Taken as a whole Steiermark is geographically Austria's second largest province (after Lower Austria). It is not, however, the second most densely populated and has only just over a million inhabitants, the majority of whom live in the region's major centres such as Judenburg, Knittelfeld and the capital Graz — which are all in the valley of the Mur river in the south-east.

The southern border of Steiermark makes up half of Austria's Yugoslav border, and is defined clearly in part by the widening Mur river as it flows eastwards, once past Graz.

North-western Steiermark, the area covered in this section, is the last bastion of the high calcareous Alps before they begin to sink slowly in the east. The major part of this is the Walzer Tauern and it is the settlements that ring these mountains that are to be visited in the course of the following pages.

The scenery is as dramatic as the Tyrol, often more so, and with both Salzburg and Vienna within easy reach to west and east this is a good central location for striking out to most of Austria's provinces.

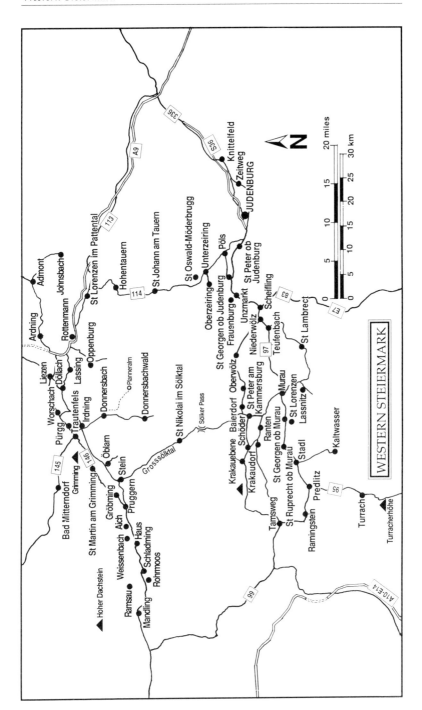

Most of the geology is 'typically alpine', and there is also an increase in the more rugged and erratic rock formations as the land slowly changes. Between the high mountains there are fertile valleys with stretches of surviving forest in places — still the largest in Austria, and possibly the oldest and densest.

The signs of man are again not wholly dissimilar to the Tyrol, in Western Steiermark at least, be it the modern feats of road and rail engineering through the mountains or the chalet-style housing. Away from the tourist centres, with some exceptions, the buildings are perhaps not 'naturally' so colourful as their Tyrolean counterparts.

The Styrians, whose industrial heritage is one of mining for ore, coal and salt, are also brewers of beer and wine — especially down on the southern borders. The inhabitants are as you would expect, a nature loving people. In the western corner especially, the people have for most of their history relied on the land for their survival, not just in terms of farming but also for natural defence against invaders.

Folklore is rife. Carnivals here have mysterious characters such as 'Flinserln', 'Trommelweiber' and 'Pless'. Advent singing in churches is very popular and there are traditional St Nicholas plays or other uniquely re-enacted biblical stories. Summer festivals are equally colourful and full of local interest.

When Austria was briefly divided by the French, British, Soviets and Americans on 4 July 1945, Steiermark went to the British (along with the Eastern Tyrol and Carinthia). During the war there was fighting largely in the east of the region, when major industrial buildings were bombed and much damage done. Like most of the Austrian provinces, some of which are still under 'foreign occupation' of a sort (the South Tyrol, now part of Italy, for example), the people of Steiermark have seen occupation from many foreign powers over the centuries. Among them the Romans, Slavs, Hungarians, Turks, Bavarians, Bohemians and Napoleon. The hardest centuries were probably the fourteenth and fifteenth when much of the invading took place, thanks largely to infighting between rival noble families. Plague, locust infestations and famine were largely by-products of the fighting and whilst other areas were making great cultural advances, the people of Styria battled for their very survival. All these contributing factors have left the population strong and determined, as well as friendly and welcoming!

You may not notice crossing the border from Salzburgerland to Steiermark. You'll have turned off the A10 motorway from Salzburg at Radstadt and headed east on the E651. The tiny village of Mandling stands pretty well on the border before you turn the bend (along with the railway line and the Enns river) into the Dachstein valley, where a host of similar tiny villages lie stretched out in front of you. The first is Puchl Mandling, then there's Rohrmoos-Untertal spread across the hillside above Dachstein's main centre — Schladming. To the north behind a ridge of high hills, lies Ramsau an Dachstein which is dominated by a massive 1,550m (5,000ft) almost sheer wall beneath the Hoher Dachstein mountain (3,100m, 10,000ft). Further to the east along the main floor of the valley lie Haus im Ennstal, Aich Assach, Gossenberg, Pruggern and Michaelerberg before a south-easterly junction breaks away from the main north-easterly valley at Gröbming.

As you would expect from Austrian mountain scenery, the valley is spectacular in both summer and winter. The Dachstein mountains lie to the north and the Schladminger Tauern to the south. Good views are to be found from all angles, but perhaps the best are from the Hauser Kaibling mountain (1,860m, 6,000ft) above Haus im Enstal.

Schladming and **Haus im Ennstal** are internationally famous as ski resorts and are visited by several large British tour operators during the winter months. This need not detract too much from the area's ambience, as compared to most winter sports destinations the Dachstein valley is neither swamped with tourists, nor pretentious; and it's easy enough to break away from the pack if you wish to. Its main claim to fame for skiers was hosting the 1982 World Alpine Ski Championships.

What the skiers tend to miss is the town's history, which is quite interesting. Most of Schladming developed when copper and silver were mined here, originally around the thirteenth to fifteenth centuries. Some old miners' housing still remains, as do several remnants of the old fortifications (seventeenth century). The town's panorama is dominated by the two churches, one Protestant and one Catholic. The latter is late Gothic, largely sixteenth century but with a Romanesque tower. The Protestant church is only 120 years old. It has a winged altar dating from the Reformation and is the largest Protestant church in Steiermark. The old town hall was once a hunting castle.

In common with most Austrians the people of the Dachstein valley are friendly and natural. Perhaps because of the mining history and the harsh winters they're also tough and know how to keep warm — with a nocturnal social life. Night life is very lively, especially with the ski crowd in the winter months who perhaps extend the action later than would be normal otherwise, with many of the festivities tending to occur between 5pm (when the lifts close) and 10pm.

For the skier the valley is best suited to the intermediate, though the World Championship men's downhill course on the main skiing mountain (Planai, 1,953m, 6,300ft) should not be undertaken by anyone other than experts. It is the fastest descent on the international race circuit and the latter half in particular is very steep, and the terrain often tricky. In general the runs are of similar standard and many cut down through the forest, for maximum skiing pleasure. Cross-country skiing is also popular with trails all around the valley.

The Ramsau plateau (see chapter 9) can be reached by roads north from Pichl-Mandling, Schladming, Haus im Ennstal or Aich-Assach. Nicknamed 'Maple Tree Valley' at the turn of the century it runs for about 10 miles at a height of 1,085m (3,500ft). It is a warm sun trap in the summer and normally sheltered in the winter. The settlement is made up largely of scattered picturesque alpine chalet-style buildings, most of which offer tourist accommodation. The 2,000 inhabitants of the valley can provide nearly four times that many tourist beds. It's an extremely pleasant place, in the summer months particularly, with lush flower filled meadows and leafy glades beneath the maples, and the conifer forest then mountain cliff backdrop behind.

At the western end of the plateau a road climbs up a further 620m (2,000ft) to **Turlwand** from where a modern cablecar scales the Dachstein. The lift ascends some 1,550m (5,000ft) of largely sheer cliff face (which very experienced climbers might attempt in 6 to 7 hours). It's an awe-inspiring piece of engineering and though there are many similar feats, this is one of the most amazing. Many may discover that previously unknown vertigo becomes a problem!

Behind the peak is a glacier with lifts for summer skiers. In fact the Ramsau plateau is an excellent place for a summer sports holiday. Besides all-year-round skiing, there are obvious climbing possibilities (Dachstein Climbing School has offices here) and walking. The Sporthotel Matschner (☎ 03687 81721/2/3) has a huge indoor tennis hall and numerous other sports facilities.

Across the Enns valley, **Rohrmoos** is a small village spread out across the hillside above Schladming. It's well placed for skiers and for those who want to look across at the Dachstein.

Back on the E651 the next village to the east is **Haus im Ennstal**. A quieter and smaller village than Schladming, its history is one of farming rather than mining. It has its own skiing on the Hauser Kaibling mountain to the south (2,061m, 6,650ft).

Further on there are a few small villages — Aich-Assach, Weissenbach, Pruggern, Michaelerberg and Gossenberg. All have very limited skiing of their own but easy access to the Hauser Kaibling and Planai ski mountains. Lift passes can be purchased to cover the whole valley. At **Pruggern** the choice of travelling north-west or south-west must be made. This isn't really a major decision unless you want to visit a particular village because otherwise the narrow roads can easily be followed back to meet each other once again within a few miles. The village itself is very pleasant to stop in whilst you ponder your decision.

If you decide to stick on the main valley road you soon come to **Gröbming**. Many of the buildings in the village appear quite modern, though not unattractive. Here there is a church dating from 1500. It has a golden altar from the same period and contains figures of the Apostles. Though Gröbming is an all-year-round tourist resort, it is also famous in Steiermark for its horse breeding.

Tourism, sports and health facilities are well developed in Gröbming. Apart from access to the Dachstein valley's 100 ski lifts and 150km (93 miles) of downhill pistes, plus 200km (124 miles) of cross-country skiing, there are numerous summer sports available, including fishing, riding, hiking, canoeing and cycling. Top class hotels such as the Spanberger and the St Georg offer solarium, sunbeds, indoor pools, whirlpools, massage and sauna. Just above Gröbming to the south and off the main route is the little village of **Mitterberg** which is an alternative, quieter place to stay for ski lovers.

Two or three miles back down on the main road you come to a minor left turning which can link you to Bad Mitterndorf on the main road back to Salzburg, which you will otherwise meet in 10 miles or so just before Stainach. The short cut climbs a corner of the Grimming region and is best avoided in the winter.

A further half mile past this turning is another small village, **St Martin an Grimming**, situated on a gentle hillside which gets steeper as it rises to the left of the road. It is an attractive place with whitewashed buildings topped with grey slate roofs. The church at the top of the village, surrounded by some of the older wood fronted barns, is designed in similar style. Facilities are basic although there are a lot of sporting activities available at the main and only star-rated hotel, the Gasthof Mayer. Summer facilities include a large open-air swimming pool and tennis courts but the emphasis in both summer and winter is on 'back to nature' activities, with cross-country skiing, curling and sleigh rides when the snow falls and horse riding and prepared walking trails in the warmer months.

At Trautenfels, a comparatively small round hill marks a cross-roads in the valley, and you have the option of turning back north-west towards Salzburg through the Salzkammergut. Alternatively you could continue along the road eastwards to Stainach and beyond, or cross the river south to the town of Irdning with the Donnersbach valley opening up behind it.

At this point the valley floor is criss-crossed with roads linking the various villages in a network across the Enns. **Trautenfels** itself is dominated by its impressive thirteenth-century castle which formerly commanded the valley and still contains richly decorated rooms. The original castle was first mentioned in documents in 1260 as 'Neuhaus Fortress'. In 1664-73 it was made into a manorial seat and the rooms were furnished with baroque paintings and stucco ceilings. Since 1959 it has formed part of the Styrian provincial museum, housing landscape museums and presenting exhibitions of folklore and customs of the Enns valley. The emphasis of the collection lies in local labour and implements, household items, traditional costumes and so on. There are also examples of flora, fauna, rock types, fossils, minerals, ores, timber and traditional alpine farming and forestry methods, including bee-keeping.

This crossroads area is historically important. Apart from the castle emphasising the geographical interest there are other monuments to the past. Just to the north-east of Trautenfels lies the medieval village of **Pürgg** up on the wooded mountain hillside. Across to the west, Mount Grimming rises majestically. The village has two important churches. First, to the south, is the tiny chapel of St Johann which is Romanesque and covered with twelfth-century frescoes. The parish church of St George, which dates from 1130, was originally Romanesque but modified during the Gothic period. This contains further fine frescoes from the twelfth century. Of course the village also has modern interests with tennis, walking and climbing (including a 'practise crag') with outdoor swimming in the summer or cross-country skiing and a ski lift in the winter.

To the east of Trautenfels is Stainach on the valley floor. Another interesting village, **Stainach** is most noteworthy for its traditional masked procession (Glocklerlauf) on Twelfth Night. These are not any old masks either, but rather elaborately decorated hats in the shape of many-sided stars up to 1.5m (5ft) high carried on the heads of men dressed in white with bells strapped to their waist (rather like heavyweight morris dancers). If you are not lucky enough to be there on 5 January, Stainach offers similar facilities to Pürgg but is rather modern and less interesting in terms of olde-worlde charm.

That statement is rather ironic however, because Stainach is one of the oldest settlements in the Enns valley, and is historically important as the region's administration and spiritual centre. It only won market-town status in 1985 though, and has a population of 2,000. The administrative importance is not much diminished today with the district control of water, agriculture and forestry inspectorate here, as well as secondary and high schools. There is a modern sports centre in the town as well as more traditional sports available.

Road 308 continues on to Liezen, passing Worschach to the north of the Enns, but first, crossing the Enns by Trautenfels, you come to the large village of **Irdning** which is rather spread out along the road. Sports facilities here are well developed with one of the best eighteen-hole golf courses in the region by the five-star Pichlarn Castle Hotel. There are also indoor and outdoor swimming pools, grass tennis courts and the usual selection of walks (picking the odd mushroom), and an international hiking day is organised for the first weekend of September each year. Other sports include horse riding, skittles and cycling. There is a discothèque in the village and International Chamber Music Days are arranged every other year. The village also shares the large Puttersee natural pleasure lake with neighbouring Aigen. Irdning also has cross-country ski trails in the winter.

From Irdning it is possible to travel back on the south side of the Enns to Gröbming, to continue downstream on the south side of the Enns towards Liezen via Aigen, or to go up into the mountains to the area's best developed alpine skiing area above Donnersbach.

The Donnersbacher valley runs south from Irdning up into the mountains along the side of the Gewasser, a tributary of the Enns. The valley road comes to an official end at the village of Donnersbachwald, although neighbours such as Pusterwald and St Nikolai are only 5 or 10 miles away over the mountain.

The valley itself is particularly popular with holiday-makers, partly due to the fact that it is not on a through-route. There's also the fact that the setting is typically beautiful by Austrian standards and that leisure and hotel facilities are well developed here. For the past few years the region has published its own quarterly newspaper for visitors (in German) which contains extremely useful calendars of events, maps, advertising for local amenities and a services directory.

The main village is **Donnersbach** itself and this might be the best place to stay as there is a wide choice of accommodation. Whether you're here for the winter sports or summer activities the main centres are reached from Donnersbach, although in terms of skiing there is little or none available around the village itself. The flower-decked chalets here seem more Tyrolean than Styrian in style and many are hotels or restaurants.

A toll road runs south from Donnersbach to **Planneralm**, a scattering of about a dozen buildings, mainly hotels, which come to life for the ski season. Indeed the two main ski areas are above Planner-alm and Donnersbachwald, though a ski bus (which runs three or four times a day at peak periods) links Irdning and Donnersbach to the main slopes. There are also good car parking facilities at the ski lifts. Planneralm is the higher of the two (1,600m, 5,248ft) with skiing on four lifts up to 2,200m (7,216ft) and therefore reasonably snow sure. The pistes are largely 'blue' or easy, with a couple of reds and a short black. It's a very peaceful area and therefore very good for families of mixed abilities.

The skiing at Donnersbachwald is similar in standard and facilities but the altitude range begins down at 950m rising to 2,370m (3,116 to 7,774ft) which means the tree cover is more dense and for many rather more attractive and less bleak. The main areas are the Riesneralm (which has a special Styrian award for high quality ski runs) and Premalm. Skiing is suitable for all standards and there is a ski school with ski kindergarten. There are also more extensive cross-country trails around the valley.

Donnersbachwald itself is at the top of the main road which leads up through Donnersbach. Unlike Planneralm this is a proper little village with a very attractive church, whitewashed within and containing a beautiful gold framed picture of the *Virgin and Christ* above the altar.

Though the village promotes itself mainly as a winter sports resort, there is still plenty to do in the summer. Apart from soaking up the atmosphere of an alpine summer, there are many sports facilities available, including tennis courts.

The road from Gröbming to Irdning on the south side of the Enns is the less well developed. If you're not bothered about going anywhere fast it's usually possible to cross backwards and forwards to villages on either side. The villages you'll have missed if you travelled up the north side are Stein and Öblarn.

Stein is more important if you're planning to take the road across the Tauern because this is where it separates from the valley road and heads off south towards Murau. Be careful which turning you take however, as the first takes you up to the tiny village of Kleinsolk. The Grosssölktal road however, takes you ever up, first through Grosssölk itself, then a few more tiny villages before reaching St Nikolai. It's still uphill from there, round a few hair raising bends to the Sölker Pass at more than 1,700m (5,576ft). Then downhill at last into Schöder, above Murau, which is dealt with later in this chapter. The other road from Stein follows the Enns to the south through Oblarn before rejoining the 146 just before Irdning.

Crossing back to the south of the Enns and driving through Irdning, then keeping south of a small thickly wooded hill in the centre of the valley, the Kulmberg (914m, 2,998ft), and following around the Puttersee, you come to **Aigen**. It is the Puttersee that is the village's main attraction for most visitors, fully developed for swimming, wind surfing and boating and with a specially divided childrens paddling area. If you're lucky you'll be there on a summer's day when the temperature of the water can reach 26 °C (79 °F), making it the warmest alpine lake. There are windsurfing and swimming schools based on the lake. The usual complement of summer and winter sports can be found, including superior indoor and outdoor tennis facilities at the Eisenhof sports centre, and the chance to ride Haflinger horses. Fishermen are also well catered for with the fast flowing Gulling brook which rises to a torrent through the centre of the village during the melt water season and is (hopefully) rich with trout. Organised evening entertainments include folklore evenings and barn dances. There is a discothèque and a bowling alley in the village. Aigen is also the place for campers, with a substantial caravan park, the 'Seeruhe im Talgrund' on the banks of the Puttersee.

Leaving Aigen you can stay to the south of the Enns river, passing through tiny villages like Ketten, Aiglern, Fischern and Döllach, then bypass Liezen before joining the road on route 113 south-east via Lassing to emerge near Rottenmann, providing you keep right. This road takes you through the mountain village of **Oppenberg**, yet another treat for flora and fauna lovers. Gentian, anemone, Turk's cap, alpine rose, spikenard and edelweiss are all blooming in this protected high moor. You can observe deer, stags, chamois, marmot and even eagles. The parish church houses the famous altar shrine of Erasmus Grasser, dating from 1480. There are Romanesque frescoes and bells from the period around 1350.

Back in the Enns valley you can also re-cross the river to Golfplatz and **Worschach**, the last major village before the town of Liezen. Rather too regular and modern to be picturesque or romantic (at least

after you've seen all the other villages) and with the view across the
Enns valley marred slightly by massive red and white electricity
pylons, Worschach would probably not be your first choice to stop.
However, there are spectacular waterfalls above it and good sports
facilities available nearby (tennis, riding, golf, swimming, sailing,
skiing).

It is a good base for climbing in the Warscheneck group of mountains to the north, the highest of which — Warscheneck itself — is not
a particularly difficult climb at 2,385m (7,823ft). Above Pürgg and
Worschach, before the mountains, lie the Worschachwald hills and
Spectensee, which is used for recreation. Below Worschach there is
a gliding school which is situated between several of the villages
including Stainach, Irdning and Aigen and can be easily reached
from any of them. The major restaurant and hotel in the village is the
Panoramablick, which has sauna, solarium and fitness room. Elsewhere in the village there are tennis courts and golf facilities. There's
a single drag lift for alpine skiers in the winter and prepared trails for
cross-country skiers.

Liezen lies just before a major crossroad on Austria's old and
modern travel routes. The Enns valley federal highway 308 meets the
Pyhrn Pass federal highway 138. The half complete (at time of writing) A9 motorway from Graz to Linz passes a few miles to the east.
Travellers from Graz heading for Salzburg and north-western Europe are also likely to turn off the A9 by Liezen and take routes 308
and then route 145 into the Salzkammergut towards Bad Ischl.

The result of such a fortunate position is an old town with modern
development, something of a rarity in this part of the world. It also
has some industrial development (another rarity) which benefits
from the good communications. This is the region's administration
and educational centre.

Whether this is an ideal holiday stop for those wanting to stay
away from any threat of modern living is another matter. Looking on
the bright side, there are still literally hundreds of beautiful, picturesque, virtually unspoilt mountain villages, with Liezen being almost unique with its modern shopping centre and ugly modern
rectangular concrete blocks (only a couple).

If you can stand such concessions to the twentieth century you'll
be able to enjoy the positive side of Liezen — much of the older part
of the town remains up on the hillside including the onion domed
late Gothic church containing altar paintings by Kremser Schmit of
Krems. The town also has reasonable sports facilities and it should be
pointed out that whilst many of the other villages in the Enns valley

are tiny settlements surrounded by spectacular scenery, Liezen is merely a rather larger settlement surrounded by spectacular scenery. It ends quite abruptly within half a mile or so and you're back in the same natural environment, with the same choice of walks, fishing, cycling and so on. There is also tennis, cinema, golf and a substantial outdoor pool with diving boards. Slightly more unusual attractions include an aerodrome for model aeroplanes and a dog training ground! Liezen is also frequented by climbers, taking their chances in the Warscheneck mountains to the north of the town. The Hochmobling mountain (2,371m, 7,648ft) is particularly popular.

From Liezen the route takes the E57 south-easterly, but first of all it's well worth a brief detour of 19km (12 miles) along route 112 to the north-east and the Gesause mountains. In fact that road stays with the river Enns which the main route now leaves. River and railway, and a main-enough road, go up towards Admont.

First stop though, is **Ardning**. Here the beauty of neighbouring Purgschachen Moor has been listed by the World Wide Fund for Nature because of the rare flora. Also by Ardning is the twin spired church of **Frauenburg**, a popular destination for pilgrims. Originally of late Gothic design, it was largely altered to baroque in the seventeenth century. The church contains notable frescoes and a fine baroque altar by Stammel. It is also of interest that pilgrims traditionally leave gifts of silver rather than wax here.

A few miles along the road, **Admont** is well worth a visit because it boasts a lot more to see and do than many much larger centres. Equally important the scenery is spectacular in summer or winter, as the Enns valley widens out leaving an expanse of fields and mainly deciduous trees. In the summer the valley is very green so that if you kept your eyes downward you could believe yourself in a rural English town. Look up to the magnificent backdrop of snow-capped mountains and that image is lost.

In the winter the area is, of course, snow covered and draws large numbers of skiers, especially the nordic variety, to follow the many trails around the area which includes the adjoining villages of Hall and Weng. There are also a few ski lifts for alpine skiers. Summer activities are centred on health and fitness, with three heated open-air swimming pools, as well as an indoor pool with sauna, tennis courts, horse riding, cycle track and climbing. Curling is possible all year because there's an artificial rink for use in the summer. For the walker and nature lover there are 200km (124 miles) of well prepared footpaths above the town, and plenty of mountain huts to rest in.

But the highlight of any visit must be the Benedictine convent founded by Archbishop Gebhard of Salzburg in 1074, thanks to a donation from St Hemma of Gurk in 1045 (Hemma was a Carinthian countess, who founded a convent at Gurk and was canonised in 1938). During the twelfth and thirteenth centuries it became one of the most prosperous and influencial religious centres in Austria. Much of the original buildings were destroyed by a fire in 1865, and were then rebuilt in neo-Gothic style. The only building not to be destroyed was the library, designed by architect Joseph Hueber and completed in 1776. The library hall is 70m (230ft) long, 11.5m (38ft) wide and 11.5m (38ft) high. This makes it the biggest monastery library in the world, and for most people it is the most spectacular.

Ornament and decoration are everywhere, with many of the ceiling frescoes by Bartolomeo Altomonte and sculptures by Joseph Stammel. Entering the first section of the hall the relief above the entrance shows King Solomon's judgement on the two women arguing over the child. Even today the books match the pictures and in this section of the library only books on secular science may be found, as the theme is human wisdom. Other pictures are of Moses receiving the ten commandments, St Peter with his keys and St Paul with the sword. The ceiling frescoes include personifications of various sciences (medicine, pharmacy and chemistry); and theology with faith, hope and charity.

The central domed section of the hall runs the theme of 'The Four Last Things', these being death, the Last Judgement, hell and heaven. Look particularly for the Devil carrying an account book, in the *Last Judgement* who, according to tradition, the artist gave the features of a disliked treasurer at the abbey! *The Hell* is Stammel's most expressive work and along with *The Last Judgement* it was recreated for the 1937 Paris World Fair. The work contains images of the seven sins. Finally *The Heaven* shows the human figure in magnificent dress rising to God on a cloud, the three angels represent Christian piety, prayer and charity.

The ceiling frescoes in the centre represent the fight for true faith. In this part of the hall there are only editions of the Bible and early religious works. The final section of the hall shows Jesus and the disciples and the books here are volumes on theological sciences.

For those interested in more unusual details the library also contains sixty-eight busts of well known artists and scholars and illustrations show the world with four continents (prior to the discovery of Australia). There are secret doors in the library which lead up to galleries. Above the main entrance is a bust of the abbot Matthew Offner who was in charge when the library was built. Over

The monastery library at Admont

the rear door there is a beautiful clock which was made in 1801 and only needs winding once a year.

The library contains about 150,000 volumes with special collections of theology and history. It's main treasures are 1,450 original manuscripts and 900 early prints. Apart from surviving the fire, the manuscripts survived the Nazi occupation and confiscation of the abbey beginning in 1939. After the war the abbey's librarian journeyed to Dachau, to where thousands of the books had been removed, and managed to recover them.

Also in Admont is an art history museum and a natural history museum. The latter contains Austria's second biggest collection of insects — 250,000 specimens to enjoy! There is also a good collection of local history from the region.

Since 1977 Admont has been a 'Euro-community'. The practical upshot of this title is that every year the 'Admont Musical Summer' is organised and young people from all over the world arrive for the festivities. They stay in Rothelstein Castle which is claimed to be 'Europe's most beautiful youth hostel' by the locals, and there is a baroque chapel attached.

If you decide to go further up the Enns valley you will find the river becomes an increasingly wild foaming torrent as it cuts its way through the Gesause (wild-water canoeing is available in Admont for the brave or foolish). Stark limestone crags overhang the river and the surrounding mountains of Himberstein (1,240m, 4,000ft), Grosser Buchstein (2,263m, 7,300ft), Tamischbachturm (2,069m, 6,675ft), Planspitze (2,158m, 6,960ft) and Hochtor (2,413m, 7,785ft) make the whole scenario doubly spectacular. The crags are much more reminiscent of the Dolomites to the south than the central Alps to the west.

The road and rail lines themselves, which pass back and forth over the river gorge clinging to the cliff sides, are a great feat of engineering and not for the faint hearted.

The last stop in this direction is **Johnsbach** which really is off even the secondary route with a right turning about 7 miles past Admont. The road goes up quite steeply from the valley into the mountains. You should not be disappointed with the fruit of your labours however. It is a tiny but wonderful village in stunning mountain scenery. It's a haven both for those wanting to get away from virtually everyone and for mountaineers. The small church's cemetery, Bergsteigerfriedhof, contains several of the more intrepid climbers. But don't be put off, there's no need to conquer the Hochtor on day one, there are plenty of gentler walks for those wanting to relax.

The river Isel

Kufstein in the Inn valley; the town centre and fortress

Folklore dancers and concerts happen regularly in the summer and during Advent and the nice thing is that they might well do so without tourists. Skiing is, of course, possible in the winter.

From Johnsbach you must go back to the valley road and to regain the route you must retrace your path back through Admont and Ardning to the E57.

The choice of roads south-east is rather confusing at this point, with bits of motorway, route E57 and route 113 all going in the same direction until Trieben. Which you take depends on whether you want to move quickly or pass through the next few villages rather than seeing them as a blur from the main road out of town.

To the south (right) of route 113 is a high, winding and by far the most picturesque route. The first village is **Lassing** made up of the five parishes of Kirchdorf, Alt Lassing, Burgfried, Moos and Doldach. It is situated in the high valley and celebrated its 950th birthday in 1986 (plans are afoot for 2036). This is the last village before the route begins to drift south of the Enns valley and makes the most of the fact with a large bathing lake, The Badesee, which is particularly popular in the summer for boating and bathing. Otherwise there is the usual complement of sports facilities such as tennis, a crossbow shooting range and a nine-hole par seventy golf course on the outskirts of the village. In winter there is cross-country skiing in the valley and a forest trail, ice sports, sleigh rides and a ski lift.

The village is an old one and is first mentioned in records in 1036 when it was visited by Kaiser Conrad II. The Gothic parish church, Jakobuskirche, was originally built in 1515 and contains frescoes from that period.

The road winds round past Selzthal and passes Burg Strechau to the south, an impressive castle perched on a precipice above the valley. Just past the castle a minor road leads off up into the mountains on the right to the village of Oppenberg, another natural retreat.

Back on route 113 (the high mountain road rejoins it quite quickly) you pass **Rottenmann**, which is actually just off rather than 'on' the highway. The town lies in the Palten valley at the end of the Niedere Tauern and is one of the oldest villages in Styria. So old in fact that the local mountains are named after it (or vice versa) — the Rotten-manner Tauern. It is a good base for walkers and climbers and has an interesting old centre, although there is the odd ugly concrete block. Facilities include indoor and outdoor tennis, a swimming pool and a training area for climbers.

Further along route 113 you pass the quiet village of **St Lorenzen** on the right shortly before arriving in Trieben. This large settlement boasts an ultra-modern swimming pool complex, complete with sauna, solariums and so on — there's even a crazy-golf course outside in case visitors become bored with lying around sweating. The village is another good climbing base, and from here your car will have to do some climbing too, either continuing along route 113 to Graz over the Schober Pass, or following this route and turning south onto route 114 and up the long climb to Hohentauern.

Hohentauern is a village of white houses with grey roofs stretching along the roadside. Some of the buildings are rather too regular and uniform to be called attractive, at least in comparison with what's on offer elsewhere. There is quite a steep hill before you reach the village, which is the first along a pass that has little other than mountains for fifty miles east and west. The scenery is spectacular of course, with thickly pine-forested lower slopes and the regular mountain peaks behind, purple and green in the summer and white in the winter.

The villagers are trying hard to provide tourist facilities and succeeding — with the usual swimming, tennis, fishing, climbing, walking, pony trekking and even cross-bow shooting. Package holidays are available through the tourist board and include children's farm holidays, young persons, old peoples and family holidays.

Hohentauern does have above average winter sports facilities for a very small and relatively unexploited village. There are six ski lifts and pistes are well maintained. Alternatively there are 8 miles of cross-country ski trails and other winter facilities include a toboggan run (popular at night) and a separate ski school for children.

Continuing for about 5 miles along route 114, which follows the valley floor side by side with the river Polsbach, the road reaches the village of **St Johann am Tauern** which stands alone at 1,047m (3,434ft) as the valley descends towards Judenburg to the south. Alternatively, if there's snow on the ground and a *loipenplan* (cross-country trail map) in your pocket you could always ski on the specially prepared route to St Johann. This is probably the least known of Austria's three or four 'St Johann's' (probably many more) and should not be confused with the more famous winter sports resort of St Johann in Tyrol. This tiny village, however, has instant appeal both in summer, when the main hotel, the Zur Post, is bedecked with flowers, and in winter when the area is snow clad. It does have winter sports too, traditional curling, cross-country skiing of course, and limited downhill ski possibilities.

Summer activities are again based on getting back to nature — you can watch it, ride through it, fish for it or shoot it! But mostly you just relax in it. The village is dominated by its sand coloured church, which contains some beautiful carvery around the elaborately decorated altar. Other summer pastimes organised locally include flower arranging courses, as well as crossbow shooting, minigolf and golf-driving.

The countryside here is particularly 'untainted' by mankind with the 'new road' cutting through the Tauern range. The Triebener Tauern reaches a height of 2,448m (8,029ft), with Mount Bosenstein to the east of the road.

Next stops along the road are **St Oswald** and **Möderbrugg**, small adjoining settlements just off route 114. These are pleasant enough villages with basic winter and summer facilities, together with the beautiful scenery and abundance of fresh clear air that one would expect. St Oswald is particularly scenic and compact. It can offer farm holidays, with mushrooming and blackberry picking.

Oberzeiring is an old silver mining town and it is possible to visit the former mine with a small museum attached. The mine is one of the oldest and biggest in the eastern Alps and its beginnings are lost back in time, though records exist for the past thousand years. The mine was at a peak in 1361 when water broke through and flooded much of it, killing 1,400 miners in the process. It is 3km (2 miles) long and 2km (just over a mile) wide. It is difficult to judge its depth due to flooding but estimates make it 100m (328ft) below the town, with the water coming up to 35m (115ft) below ground.

Local archaeological digs have revealed the presence of the Illyrians around 900BC. Even in those days the dead were buried in urns and one such urn is on display in the museum. The Illyrians were followed by the Celts and the Romans.

The silver from the mine contributed greatly to the power of the Habsburg dynasty. Rudolf, the first Habsburg emperor, visited in 1279, 6 years after his coronation, to see the deposits of silver for himself. Oberzeiring was granted privileges during his visit. It became a market town that year and 5 years later was granted the right to mint its own coins. The miners also had their own law courts! Because the town was not walled, a free zone of about 10sq km (4sq miles) was established around the town and everyone who lived in the area and worked in the mine was a freeman and not in bondage. It was hard work, in virtual darkness, with hammers and chisels. Dogs were used to transport silver in sacks on their backs, spending all of their lives underground. After the accident most of the town's privileges were removed, making the disaster doubly harsh.

Because of the town's popularity there are several buildings which housed nobility, particularly through the centuries following the disaster when various fruitless attempts were made to pump the water out. At the beginning of the sixteenth century Emperor Maximillian took charge of drainage attempts at the mine. Empress Maria Theresa also spent a great deal of money on her unsuccessful attempt. Many of the old buildings are in neighbouring **Unterzeiring**, and here there is also a fifteenth-century castle, Hanfelden which was used by Maximillian. It is now very obviously a formerly rich village which today is in something of a decline.

Iron ore was still mined up to 1889, and the mine was re-opened as a museum in the 1950s. Between 1958 and 1960 barite was briefly mined, more than fifty different ores and minerals have been found in the mountain. It was then discovered that the conditions in the tunnel were good for healing bronchial asthma and the mine has since won a new lease of life as a health treatment centre.

The village itself has an excellent medieval central street with the twelfth-century miners' church at the top. This is the Elizabethkirche and dates from AD1111; it contains some interesting frescoes. Also in the main street is the tobacco museum, a very interesting and comprehensive exhibition of everything to do with the tobacco trade, put together by a man who has worked in the business all his life.

Entering Oberzeiring from the Judenburg road shortly after passing St Oswald and Unterzeiring on the left, you pass the small attractive lake of Gellsee (for fishing, not bathing) and then a couple of stone pillars in a field which were formerly a gallows. One of the first houses you come to on the right on entering the village is that of Jakob Diethart. It's worth giving him a call in advance and popping by to see him because the man is the wood carver (Giuseppe) in Pinnochio personified. Outside you will see various pieces of trees that at second glance appear as creatures or faces. Beneath the house in his workshop there is a fantastic selection of wooden toys, some powered by electric motors, and other wooden objects. Mr Diethart is happy to show people around on an informal basis, but unfortunately none of his work is for sale.

The road through Oberzeiring runs a few miles north of the main route 96 from Judenburg through Murau alongside the river Mur. It is possible to rejoin this road on several occasions, which are detailed later. A mile or so along it after leaving Oberzeiring you reach a right turning which takes you up a steep winding trail to the Klosteuneuburger at 1,879m (6,163ft).

The right turning in Möderbrugg (before St Oswald) takes you on a dead end road which forks after a few miles, giving the choice of turning left to tiny **Pusterwald** or going right to miniscule **Bretstein**. Conditions permitting, both routes become tracks up into the mountains reaching over 1,300m (4,264ft).

The valley in which Pusterwald is situated has thickly forested slopes towering steeply up on either side. The valley is surrounded by twelve mountains, all above 2,000m (6,560ft). Its floor is up to half a mile across and largely given up to arable land. Facilities are limited mostly to hiking, with well marked footpaths; there's also canoeing and dancing to the local band who perform on occasion. Cross-country and some alpine skiing is available in the winter.

South of Oberzeiring the road runs downhill towards Judenburg. A turning right a few miles along at Katzing takes you to Pöls and then straight down to Judenburg. **Katzing** contains a factory for kit homes, and there's a ruined chapel nearby. **Pöls'** main claim to fame is an unpopular modern paper mill, which uses local wood, that many of the locals fear may be polluting the streams. Also at Pöls route 114a turns right along the Mur valley and joins route 96, avoiding the need to go on to Judenburg if you don't wish to visit there. For those with the time though, this town is well worth the visit.

With a population of 11,000, **Judenburg**, on the banks of the Mur river, is by far the largest settlement featured in this region of Styria. It also marks the south-eastern corner of the Tauern mountains. From here the mountains become gradually lower and the settlements larger, with Styria's capital Graz less than 50 miles away and several other comparatively large towns (Kolflach, Leoben, Knittelfeld) nearby.

Judenburg has a Jewish name and a Jewish history. The stone head of a Jew is the town's badge, positioned on the old Post Hotel. However it is now believed incorrect to think that the name 'Jude' relates to the past Jewish settlements, as the original castle of 1073 was built by a man named 'Jutho' and the town's name derives from him.

Today the town is an interesting mix of old and new, with past divisions overcome. Approaching from the west you will pass through unattractive urban and industrialised areas, but the town centre is pleasant with good shopping and plenty of interesting buildings. The major church, St Nicholas, originally dates from 1148 but was altered in the seventeenth and nineteenth centuries. It contains a rococo pulpit and some interesting sculptures of the Virgin made from stone and wood. In the chapel to the west of the church is the *Beautiful Madonna* by Hans Von Judenburg. At the south end of the church there is a beautiful rose window. The yellow building behind the church is the restored rectory which was once used by Napoleon.

Another church, the Gothic Magdalene, contains wall paintings and stained glass dating from the building's fourteenth-century origins. The story goes that after the war the window was going to be removed as war booty, but an American general, who had been stationed in Judenburg, bought it for one million *schillings* and gave it back to the town. The former monastery was another victim of Josef II's roof tax in the eighteenth century. It now houses a cinema, and the blue building next door is due to open as the town's museum (in 1990).

Another interesting monument is the Romerturm (Roman Tower), which visitors can climb. It was constructed between 1449 and 1509 and is 74m (240ft) high. From the top there is an excellent panorama — popular with pigeons — of the whole of Judenburg. It was built largely as a sign of the towns' prosperity at that time, though it was also used as a fire-watch tower. Traders came from Venice and the town had exclusive trading rights as well as the right to mint its own coins. The two main streets meet at the tower.

Judenburg's history is not a particularly happy one, with the eternal division between the Jews and the rest of the town's population. Originally the Jews — hated as money lenders and of course said to be poisoners or baby killers — were not allowed into the town, but after paying the Prince Regent large quantities of cash in the fifteenth century, they were allowed to move into the street to the west of the tower. Dividing markers still exist from where the Jewish communities started and ended, one still has a large hook in the ceiling from which scales were hung for carrying out trade between the two groups. One legend has it that about this time the Jews plotted to kill all the Christians on Christmas Day by poisoning them, but a Jewish girl who loved a Christian boy told him and instead most of the Jews were wiped out. Tragically the last forty or so were marched away during World War II, never to be seen again, although it is not known if all ended up in concentration camps. At this time certain members of the town also tried to change its name from 'Town of the Jews' to 'Town of the Forest' or similar, but the new name failed to stick.

After the war the town was again divided, this time between Russian and British occupying forces. The Russians had the area north of the river, the British were in the south, and the two forces had their border on the iron bridge over the Mur river. Judenburg has clearly flourished since the war and is a major area for shopping and

Judenburg

education in Western Steiermark. There is also a major steel working industry.

Around about Judenburg, which makes a good base for excursions in the area, are several places of interest. The church of Maria Buch on route 77 to the south-east is a pilgrimage church first documented in 1074 and recently restored; the design is late Gothic. The legend here is that Kaiserin Eleonores lost a book containing a letter from or to an admirer. In her prayers she promised that if she got the book and letter back she would build a church. So we assume she got her book back.

North-east of Judenburg is the village of **Frauenburg**, formerly famous for its coal mining. Now there is a museum on this topic which shows the development of the coal mining industry, including the traditional work, tools and lives of local miners. There is also a 'show mine' tunnel for visitors.

To the east is **Zeltweg**, a small industrial town with a history of steel working. Nearby is the Osterreichring motor racing circuit, a full 4 miles long, which has been the scene of grand prix and the Austrian National Championships. 'Racing car taxis' are also available in which you pay a professional driver to take you for a spin round the circuit at high speed in a racing car. Other races of vintage vehicles, trucks, motorbikes and so on may be organised and there are safe-driving schools as well as the possibility of taking your own car around the circuit. The airfield at Zeltweg is a military one so be careful with your camera.

East of Zeltweg is the town of Knittelfeld and then Leoben, both worth visits but off this beaten track, as it heads back west.

The main road due west back out of Judenburg passes first the tiny village of St Peter on the left and then St Georgen on the right. The church at **St Peter** dates from 1779 and is baroque, it is quite remarkable in that the architect, Johann Nischelugtier, has incorporated the design of a ship. The church at **St Georgen** was first documented in 1277. As recently as 1988 frescoes were uncovered that show the story of St George and his martyrdom under Kaiser Diokletian. Near St Georgen is the Schloss Thalheim, built in 1552 by Franz Freiherr Von Teufenbach. The design is pentagonal, so that all areas around can be seen clearly. It was one of the first castles to be built with running water on tap and the cellar also contained twelve mineral springs.

The road and narrow gauge railway continue into the Mur valley with its increasingly steep hillsides, thickly forested on the upper slopes. At some points the mountains overshadow the valley for a good proportion of the daylight hours. **Unzmarkt** is an attractive, well spaced out village, though with a compact centre. It stands across the Mur from beautiful Schloss Frauenburg. The castle is one of several built by minstrel Ulrich von Liechtenstein and the one where he died in 1275. There are various versions of a love story involving him, and the love songs he wrote to one (or some say several) women. He is also said to have fought more than 300 knights. There are apartments to rent in the village. From here the valley floor is quite wide and flat and the road is raised above the fields due to the rare possibility of flooding.

At Scheifling, route 96 turns off from route 83 which continues on towards Carinthia. If you stay on this road you enter the nature park Grebenzen which includes seven villages (Teufenbach, Mariahof, Neumarkt, St Marein, St Blasen, St Lambrecht — see later — and

Zeutschach). The park covers 20sq km (8sq miles) and contains more than 250 types of bird, as well as deer and other wildlife. In the summer there are hiking trails, in the winter, cross-country skiing.

The first village on route 96 is Niederwölz and from here another road branches off to the right again, road 75, which heads up to Oberwölz Stadt. Oberwölz can also be reached along a high minor road from Oberzeiring taking a right turn off route 114 before reaching Judenburg. There is, however, a turn left a few miles out of Niederwölz at the tiny settlement of Teufenbach.

Teufenbach, which has a few industrial units in the village, marks the end of the flat agricultural land and the valley walls suddenly come together with the forests sweeping down and a craggy cliff face above the village getting the best of the morning sun. This road climbs into the hills, bends right to arrive at St Lambrecht and then continues back round and up to Murau, should you require another alternative route.

The Oberzeiring-Oberwölz road passes a north turn to Lachtal 1,570m (5,150ft) which has been turned into a mini alpine ski resort, with some large purpose-built hotels. This phrase conjours up images of huge French 'ski stations' for many experienced skiers but in fact Lachtal 300 is quite a small apartment block, very attractively designed with stepped sun balconies and dark wooden cladding. However, such a building would look rather out of place in most of the traditional villages in the area. Its size alone would dominate them and of course the architecture would be out of place.

There are six main lifts, mostly on the south-facing slopes of the Zinken (2,212m, 7,255ft) and the Klosterneuburger (1,879m 6,163ft) which has a small café on top. It is also feasible to ski down to Oberwölz or Oberzeiring if conditions are right. The main ski area is at an altitude sufficient to ensure good snow conditions throughout the winter.

Oberwölz is an attractive 800-year-old walled village, with good modern leisure facilities (tennis, large outdoor swimming pool). Some of the medieval walls remain, including the three original gates, and formerly there was a moat. It is the smallest town in Styria with a population of 985 and so the two large neighbouring churches are particularly remarkable. The older Stadspfarrkirche (1280) is still the town's church, and the neighbouring Spittalskirche (1430), which was restored in 1986, is used mainly for concerts as it has particularly good acoustics.

The only reason for the existence of the two churches that local people know of is a former period of wealth in the fourteenth and fifteenth centuries when the town was a centre for the salt trade. There is still a 'street of salt' containing older buildings from around 1335. The statue in the centre of the town stands against the plague.

There is a particularly good inn/restaurant in the town, the Gasthof Graggober, which is especially popular in the winter for skiers in Murau and the Lechtal. There is also a castle called Rothenfels on a clifftop above the village, affording spectacular views and where rooms are available for rent at ridiculously low rates. Finally, there is the highest naturist camp site in Europe here!

There are no major settlements between Niederwölz and Murau so it may be worth staying up on the high road from Oberwölz and following on to the village of **St Peter am Kammersburg**—where the former castle is now a girls school—then turning south to the Murau valley and to Ranten and Schöder, which are north of Murau. The Schöder and neighbouring Baierdorf are the arrival points if you cut across the Tauern through St Nikolai from Gröbming and the Dachstein. **Baierdorf** contains a wood mill and an old defence tower. It's easy enough to reach Murau from here, by rejoining route 96 a few miles south of Schöder and heading back in the opposite direction into Murau. **Schöder** is worth a stop though because of the dramatic scenery, including the Gunsten waterfall, and its late Gothic church which contains some delightful frescoes.

The high valley in which Schöder and the other little villages are set is a pleasant sun trap in the summer, largely given over to rural use on the low rolling hills before the forested valley sides begin to climb. This is a gently sculptured green valley with few shows of strength visible from the mountains beyond. Traditions remain strong and it seems that virtually every member of each community has their own traditional clothing, colourful tall hat or festival costume tucked away ready for the occasional event.

If you wish to stay north of Murau then your route to the border with the province of Salzburg lies along road 96, turning right rather than left upon rejoining it. This will eventually take you to Tamsweg via Ranten, Seebach and other small villages with Krakaudorf and Krakauebene off on minor roads to the north. **Ranten** is the birthplace of fifteenth-century author Martin Zeiller and there is an occasional exhibition based on his life and work arranged here. The church is unusual with a double onion-dome, and there are winter and summer sports facilities, but these are not as extensive as you might expect.

Around Seebach the road becomes very narrow and twisting, with lots of logs lying around bearing witness to the traditional and

The Gunsten waterfall, Schöder

continuing lumber trade in the region. This is a good place to examine the traditional local architecture too, with house roofs designed to survive heavy snowfalls. On many, the little bell towers with which wives used to call their husbands and sons back from the fields or forests to eat still remain.

Krakaudorf contains a fifteenth-century parish church with a beautifully painted ceiling. It also contains a recent addition to the Guinness Book of Records — Mr Ernst Spreitzer of the Gasthof Guniwirt who in October 1988 cooked the longest apple strudel in the world at more than 70m (230ft)! A proud sign outside announces the fact. The village offers the usual selection of summer and winter sports, including crazy-golf.

The woods and hills are very beautiful around here and popular with nature lovers all through the year for hiking and cross-country skiing. Two small lakes, the Prebersee and the Schattensee (the former 6km (3³/₄ miles) from Krakaubene, which has a very good sledging run, amongst other things), are the home of a unique sport, *Wasserscheiben Schiessen*. This involves shooting at a reflection of a target in the mirror-like waters. If your shot is on target the bullet will skim off the surface and hit the metal target across the lake. It is amazing but true, and needless to say swimming in this part of the lake is not advisable.

Murau is the major centre of the western Mur valley. As the district town it has thirty-two villages in the region. It is a medium-sized and highly attractive town built into the hillside above a bend in the river. The town has grown up on a crossroads, with the only road running through the Solker-Tauern Pass, which runs north across the Tauern to Gatschberg by Gröbming. Fifteen kilometres (9 miles) south-east stands the Benedictine abbey of St Lambrecht.

The area is of course beautiful, with heavily forested rolling hills to the south and north, and mountains behind. Situated at the southern border of the Alps, it is climatically protected by them. Since the turn of the century the excellent quality of the air has brought visitors from far and near for climatic health benefits.

The town, founded in the thirteenth century, is made up of narrow streets centred around a pleasant square and contains several beautiful churches. Originally two castles were built on either side of the river Mur and the town grew up between them. The people hold a love of their environment in common with much of the Styrian population. There is no industry. Though tourism is far from frowned upon it is clear that the people know just how far they want this area of their economy to develop — that is, not to an unlimited degree. Most of the tourists currently visiting in summer and winter are from Germany and other parts of Austria.

The church of St Matthew, the most important in the town, was founded by Otto von Liechtenstein. It was built in 1296 below the castle. The church has a short dark tower and is built in a simple Gothic style, making a major contribution to the village panorama. Inside there is a Gothic carvery on the altar. The central cross and three figures date from 1500 and originate in southern Germany. In 1656 the other parts of the altar were added. This is a comparatively simple baroque altar as it was constructed during a period of comparative poverty. The frescoes to the left of the altar show important dignitaries from Liechtenstein standing with Anna Neumann (see later). They were painted in 1570 by a Carinthian artist. The woman depicts the qualities of God. There are also white statues of the twelve Apostles. The original church organ was constructed in 1446, the present one dates from 1770.

The frescoes on the southern wall were uncovered in 1947 and have been dated between 1370 and 1377. In the centre there is a tower built like a wall. The bell in the tower is from Turrach, the only one in middle Europe. First renovations of the church were made in 1605

Murau

and there is a plaque to commemorate this. At the front of the church there is a 'lantern of the dead' dating from the Gothic period.

The major building is Obermurau castle, which belongs to the Schwarzenberg family and overlooks the town. Prince Shwarzenberg is a member of the fifth biggest landowning family in Austria, owning some 57,000 acres of the country. The current prince is an important human rights campaigner and sat next to Soviet premier Gorbachov in major East-West conferences.

The castle was built in 1258 by Ulrich von Richtenstein during a period of major prosperity in the region, with wealthy traders from southern Germany passing through. Such was Murau's early significance that it became a town in 1298. At that time it was walled, and taxes were payable by those passing through. A small iron industry grew up by the river and items were exported to northern Germany and the South Tyrol. The iron ore was mined in Turracher Hohe (see later), and there is a Bessimer Convertor in the castle courtyard today, a witness to the past importance of the industry here. Many of the older houses still standing today were originally built into the wall and sections of it have been preserved within them. The wall was broken up in 1860 however, because the gates were too small for vehicles at the time.

The castle's history is quite a colourful one. Between 1250 and 1300 it was linked to the castle across the valley by a tunnel. Then in

1556 Anna Neumann, who is very popular in Murau (the main street is named after her) and quite important to Austrian history, made her second of six marriages, to Christoff Von Liechtenstein, and soon inherited the castle. She became very rich and started a private banking system, thereby gaining influence over the people to whom she lent money. She spent much of her wealth on charitable projects and helped to protect Protestants in the Catholic community. For her pains she was accused of being a witch, but survived. At the age of 82 she married 52-year-old Prince Schwarzenberg and the castle has been in his family ever since. After the last war a regiment of Scottish soldiers were stationed in the castle; they were apparently popular with the local people as they gave sweets to the children.

From the castle walls you can see a monastery founded in 1648 where the Shwarzenbeck family are buried, and at the top of the hill to the north-east, a hospital, built there in 1929 because it had a good climate and more sun than the valley.

Murau has a total of seven churches, six Catholic and one Protestant. Besides those mentioned, other churches include St Agidus, which is one of the oldest (fourteenth century); there is also St Leonards church and St Anne chapel — only a little younger than St Agidus. Other interesting buildings include the first hospital, on Anna Neumann Street, which closed in 1684 and now contains flats, and the now Protestant church where Anna Neumann lay in state after her death. She was laid half in the wall and half out to symbolise her support of both faiths. Her body was later taken to a Protestant monastery. The street also contains the town's brewery and the building that was the Rathaus until the eighteenth century. The pink building is a house belonging to a bishop, consecrated in 1266. Between 1278 and 1300 the walls of the building were burnt down three times. Across the river Mur is the animal market, the youth hostel dating from 1311, the surviving Friesacher Tor (ninth town gate), and some of the 101 houses that still have the medieval rights to get wood from the forest for building and heating.

In the winter most of the town's skiing is on the Frauenalpe mountain (2,038m, 6,575ft) to the south-west. Facilities are well above average for a small town that doesn't specialise in the sport. Lift queues are uncommon. Ice skating on frozen ponds and ski jumping is also available. Murau is one of the major centres of Nordic skiing in Styria, with wonderful tracks through the snow-clad forests. In the summer there's climbing, cycling, hiking, boating, fishing, hunting and plenty of prepared walks. There are numerous ponds and lakes in which it is possible to swim. The 'Schroder' waterfall is well worth a visit. The river Mur runs crystal-clear beneath the town and you can take a canoe on this if you wish. The latest idea is the mountain biking holiday, with bikes to rent. There are, rather surprisingly, a few small cosy discothèques, mainly active in the winter months. The best hotel in Murau is the four-star Gasthof Lercher in a quiet street beneath the castle. This mixes excellent cuisine with friendly service and beautiful rooms in a lovely old building.

Hobby holidays in Murau include engine driving and hand crafts. Yes, at last your childhood dream to become a train driver on a steam train can come true, detailed information is available from the tourist office. Indeed, one of the summer highlights is the narrow gauge steam line, opened in 1894, that runs from here to Tamsweg. Brightly coloured carriages include a bar and a brass band. On Corpus Christie (15 August) each year there is a major festival when the town guard parade in traditional uniform of red, green and white. The traditional 5m-high (16ft) wooden figure of Samson is carried by a strong man as a traditional part of the festivities. There are also street parties organised most Friday afternoons during July and August each year.

From Murau you can take a road up northwards towards the high valley, housing villages such as Oberwölz and Krakaudorf previously mentioned. If the road is open (in summer) you can even continue over the Solker Tauern Pass to the Dachstein valley and on to the Salzkammergut. This route goes westwards, however, but first take a short detour south and east which goes through a very small corner of Carinthia at Lassnitz, and then back into Styria and to **St Lambrecht**.

The St Lambrecht abbey is the cultural centre of the region. Dating from the eleventh century there have been numerous architectural additions through the centuries. It was established in 1006 by the dukes of Carinthia and shortly afterwards other monasteries were founded from it, including the famous pilgrimage destination of Maria Zell. The abbey is situated about 13km (8 miles) south-east of Murau. The main church has twin onion dome spires; it was begun in 1421 and took 100 years to complete. Much of the building was restored in the late 1970s, with the towers restored in 1988. Several fourteenth- and sixteenth-century frescoes were discovered during the restoration. Now Gothic, it was originally Romanesque; its present design dates back to 1645 when it was re-designed by Domenica Sciassia and lavishly decorated.

Attractions for enthusiasts of church architecture, art and history

St Lambrecht

are numerous. They include a fourteenth-century wooden crucifix and a seventeenth-century statue of the Virgin Mary. The pulpit was added in 1730. The interesting collection of gilded figures above are supposed to represent different parts of the world. Clearly however, the artist did not have too good an idea of what went where and what some of the newly discovered exotic creatures actually looked like. Hence you have Indians standing by lions, and elephants with pig like noses. The church windows are small and high up, making the interior rather dim with just the daylight. The 22m-high (70ft-) altar is baroque, it was added in 1632, constructed from marble on wood, with the painting depicting Mary ascending to heaven. To the right of the altar the figures of local tradesmen represent patron saints. Other notable features are the 1640 St Benedict altar, and the 1902 Hopenweiser organ above the door. Elsewhere there are more excellent frescoes.

Behind the church is an older Romanesque chapel, and to the left of it is the former corn house and stables. Parts of the old castle and walls still remain, but these were ruined in 1786 with Josef II's roof tax. This problem was a common one for monasteries 200 years ago. A common problem today is a shortage of monks, only seventeen remain in this massive building, with income coming in from lands owned by the monastery.

There is also a school and a small museum collection of art from the thirteenth to nineteenth centuries. However the museum is not just limited to paintings and sculptures, there is everything from love letters to confessionals to be seen here. A second museum contains about 500 indiginous birds, all killed and stuffed by a monk named Blasius Hanf in the last century.

Though St Lambrecht is totally dominated by the abbey, the tiny village also has its own parish church, St Peters (1424), which contains a high altar from 1515 and a Gothic winged altar (1435). The chapel contains some interesting pictures by an Italian artist, who did some work for the abbey in 1906 and returned as a prisoner of war in 1916. He chose to keep painting whilst a prisoner and the large picture of *Jesus with the Fishermen* is his work. Rather cheekily the man has painted himself into the picture; he's the one sitting behind the tree. Anyone interested will not be surprised to hear that there are a couple of small drag lifts by the abbey.

Back to Murau and continuing westwards on road 97 you arrive at the small villages of St Georgen, St Lorenzen (just to the south of route 97 on a minor road), St Ruprecht and Stadl. The fourteenth-century church at **St Ruprecht** is Gothic and has a lovely organ loft. **St Georgen** has a fifteenth-century church containing a sixteenth-century winged altar and a painting from 1450 by Konrad von Friesach.

A minor road ascends from Stadl to the peaceful little village of **Kaltwasser**. This is also an alternative route over into Carinthia, though in winter the road may be blocked by snow (it reaches an altitude of 1,240m, 4,000ft).

There are quite good alpine skiing facilities above **St Lorenzen**, to the south on the Kreischberg mountain (1,860m, 6,000ft), with most of the skiing around the Rosenkranzhohe area. A chairlift departs from the west of the village, and in the summer this can be used by those who want to sightsee in the mountains without the tiresome uphill climbing! This is also a destination for the popular Austrian 'holiday on a farm' concept. Children will especially enjoy holidays here; in the summer they play on a fire engine and sleep in a log cabin, in winter they build igloos!

The road makes a north to south crossing of the Mur at **Stadl**. Here the Renaissance Schloss Goppelsbach dates to 1595 and there is also a fifteenth-century church.

At Predlitz road 97 meets road 95. At this point you can head over the border due west in to Salzburgerland following the faithful river Mur towards its source. The first village you will reach is **Raming-stein**, which has good skiing in the winter and good white-water canoeing or fishing in the summer, and nearby is the twelfth-century Burg Finstergrun now used as a youth hostel. **Predlitz** itself is a comparatively large village and contains a church with an interesting panelled wooden ceiling and a painting by Gregor Lederwasch. There are a couple of short drag lifts operational when snow is in the valley, which can be used by beginners or cross-country skiers.

The 95 road bends due south and keeps within the south-western peninsular of Steiermark before climbing the extremely steep (up to 1 in 4) Turracher-Höhe of the Gurktal Alps, the local area known as the Nock mountains, past Turrach (1,311m, 4,230ft) to enter Carinthia.

The Turracher-Höhe is a high valley, usually warm in the summer and increasingly popular with skiers and climbers. It also provides more leisurely pastimes and a range of summer sports including giant slide, crazy golf, bowling, cycling, boating and fishing. There are also indoor sports and fitness facilities including several hotel pools and saunas. The area promotes itself as both Carinthian and Styrian; it does in fact straddle the border. There is a small lake — the Turracher See — and the area is also well know for its wild flowers.

In the winter alpine skiing is possible from the lake 1,446m (4,665ft) to 2,314m (7,465ft) (Kornock mountain). Most of these runs are enjoyable intermediate standard or easy blues, though there are steep runs from the Paullift. Snow conditions are usually good. There are eight drag lifts and two chairs. Cross-country skiing is also popular, with a short loop around the frozen lake or full 16 mile circuit, again starting and ending at the lake, with a vertical difference of only 115m (370ft). The steepest climb is 62m (200ft) over just under 32km (20 miles), so the route can be attempted by anyone with a little experience and a lot of energy. Turrach is the closest village to the area.

Further Information
— Western Steiermark —

Places of Interest in the Area

Admont
Benedictine Abbey and Library
Open: mid-May to mid-October
daily 10am-4pm. Rest of year daily
(except Monday) 10.30am-12noon
and by appointment.

Local museum
Open: summer from May, 10am-
1pm and 2-4.30pm
(except Mondays).

Mautern
Alpine nature park.
Open: beginning May to end
October, Monday to Friday 9am-
5pm; weekends, 8am-6pm.

Murau
Steam train runs afternoons to
Tamsweg mid-July to early September on Tuesdays. Also possible
to rent the train and drive it yourself with up to 50 passengers.

Oberzeiring
Silver mine.
Guided tours: November to April
11am and 2pm; May to October
9.45 and 11am, 2, 3 and 4pm. Other
times by arrangement. Admission
fee.

Tobacco Museum
For opening times ☎ 03571 308

Jakob Diethart
Wood Carver
☎ 03571 308

St Lambrecht Abbey
Open: daily May to October, tours

10.45am-2.30pm. Also Bird
Museum.

Trautenfels Castle
Open: April to October 9am-5pm.

Turracher Höhe
Mineral Museum
Open: daily (except Wednesday)
9am-12noon and 2-5.30pm.

Zeltweg
Racing car taxi rides from Walter
Penker
☎ 03577 22928

Tourist Information Offices

Admont
Fremdenverkehrsverband
Alpenregion Gesause
A-8911 Admont

Aich — Assach
A-8966

Aigen im Ennstal
A-8943

Ardning
A-8904

Barnköpf
Herbert Lackner Esquire
Langlaufschule
Barnköpf 134
A-8765

Filzmoos
A-5532

Forstau
A-5550

Gnadenwald
A-6060

Gröbming
Ms Andrea Fucik
Verkehrsverein Gröbming und
Umgebung
Gröbming
A-8962

Haus im Ennstal
A-8967

Irdning
A-8952

Judenburg
Ingeborg Hirsch
Freindenverkehrsverband des
Bezirkes Judenburg
Bezirkshauptmannschaft
A-8750 Judenburg

Kleinsolk
A-8961

Krakaudorf
A-8854

Krakauebene
Ms Andrea Siebeuhofer
Fremdenverkehrsverein
Krakauebene
A-8854 Krakauebene

Liezen
A-8940

Murau
Ms Martha Wuitz
Verkehrsverein Murau und
Umgebung
Am Bahnhof
Murau
A-8850

Oblarn
A-8960

Oberwölz
Heinz Graggober Esquire
Graggober Gasthof-Pension
A-8832 Oberwölz 56

Pichl-Mandling
A-8973

Predlitz-Turracherhohe
A-8863

Pürgg-Trautenfels
Fremdenverkehrsverein Pürgg-
Trautenfels
Post Leitzahl A-8981

Pusterwald
A-8764

Ramingstein
A-5591

Ramsau
A-8972

Rohrmoos-Unteral
A-8970

Rottenmann
Anton Stadler
Fremdenverkehrsverein der stadt
Rottenmann
Postfach 39
A-8786 Rottenmann

Schladming
Dir Georg Bliem
Gebietsverband Dachstein-Tauern
Coburgstrabe 52
A-8970 Schladming

St Andrä
A-5580

St Johann am Tauern
Siegmund Klakl Esquire
Fremdenverkehrsverein St Johann
am Tauern
A-8765 St Johann am Tauern

St Lorenzen on Murau
A-8861

St Marein bei Neumarkt
A-8820

St Nikolai im Sölktal
A-8961

St Oswald-Möderbrugg
Verkehrsverein St Oswald-Möder-
brugg
A-8763 Möderbrugg 140

Scheifling
A-8811

Schönberg-Lachtal
A-8831

Tauplitz
A-8982

Tauplitzalm
A-8982

Trautenfels
Petra Pitzer Esquire
Fremdenverkehrs-Gebietsverband
Mittleres Steirisches Ennstal
A-8951 Schloss Trautenfels

Zeutschach
A-8820

9 • Ramsau and the Surrounding Area

Access to Ramsau and the surrounding area is simple. By road the route is east along the European motorway system via Munich and Salzburg, then south along the A10 *autobahn* (Villach and Klagenfurt) as far as the Radstadt interchange. Follow road 308 to Pichl-Prennegg and turn left up the steep access road into the Ramsau basin.

By rail the route is similar, via Salzburg to Radstadt or Schladming, use the postbus service into the valley. The nearest international airport is at Salzburg, again with rail and postbus connections.

Driving south from Salzburg along the A10 *autobahn* and on nearing the Radstadt-Schladming interchange, motorists will have been aware of steep wooded slopes on the left leading to snow topped heights. These high mountains are the Dachstein range, dolomitic ramparts guarding a series of north-flowing glaciers and an area of all-year skiing. At the foot of their almost 914m (3,000ft) limestone walls lies a high sunny valley hidden from the view of travellers speeding along the *autobahn*; this is the Ramsau valley.

To reach Ramsau, climb a steep zigzagging road from Schladming, or take one of two easier but longer routes from either Haus about 8km (5 miles) to the east of Schladming, or from Eben 23km (14 miles) in the opposite direction. Once in the upper valley it is difficult to imagine that one of the busiest north-south European thoroughfares is so close. A gentle stream, the Ramsau Bach, flows east through flowery meadows dotted with traditional Austrian timber barns and colourful farmhouses with venerable *Gasthöfe* lining the roadsides. Although flower boxes filled with bright red geraniums and massive trumpetted petunias are a major feature throughout the Austrian countryside, those around Ramsau manage to surpass the rest of the country. Balconies seem to groan under the

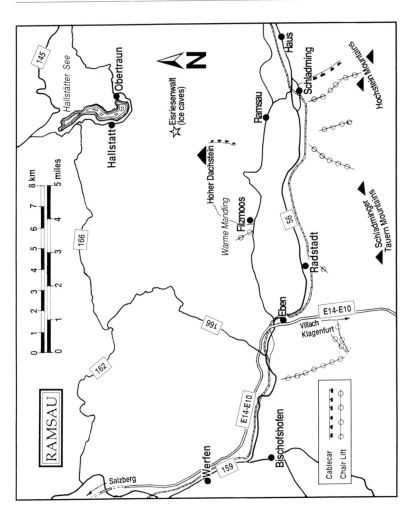

weight of colour and the locals appear to vie with each other in order to fill more ledges and window sills than their neighbours.

There is no real village of Ramsau, and the valley has two churches both sporting traditional onion domes. The area around the more easterly church is where the post office and tourist information bureau can be found; the western church is surrounded by the shops, hotels and the valley school. Ramsau has something to offer everyone seeking a quiet relaxed holiday in the mountains.

To the south a low range of forested hills criss-crossed by easy-to-follow tracks act as an elevated viewpoint to admire the majestic grandeur of Dachstein's southern walls. The view has as its foreground a wide smiling basin backed by forested slopes, slopes which lead directly to the foot of these seemingly impossible walls. To the left and at the head of the Mandling valley is Filzmoos, the only village of any size on this elevated sunny terrace. As well as the forest tracks, paths along the valley bottom follow river banks, leading to conveniently placed little *Gasthöfe* and restaurants which will make an ideal introduction to this delectable area. As with most mountain resorts in Austria, a convenient bus service can be used to return to base. In this way fairly long linear walks can be planned throughout the area.

This is an old area, and its sunny potential was quickly exploited by the earliest settlers who cut the forest to create the now fertile meadows. Generations of 'muck spreaders' created a natural garden where masses of wild flowers bloom until haymaking. Several old watermills line the river banks and the Warme Mandling, above Filzmoos, has four in the space of less than a couple of kilometres. Why the Warme Mandling should be considered warm is a mystery. There is a Kalte (cold) version to the east of Filzmoos and having tried both streams, the author can categorically say that there is little difference between them — they are equally cold!

If the massive south wall of the Dachstein mountain — 3,004m (9,856ft) is out of bounds to mere hill walkers, its summit glacier is not. The Schladminger Gletscher is an extensive uncrevassed glacier, unlike its neighbour the Hallstätter, and perfectly safe to cross. There are organised tours led by local guides and to enrol you simply book through the local tourist office. However, a word of warning. Austrians and Germans seem to enjoy long coffee breaks and periods of involved lectures when walking in groups, so unless you prefer this and your German is perfect, then perhaps it is better to enjoy the walk in the company of your own kind.

To climb the mountain, first take the bus to the bottom station of the Dachsteinsudwandbahn by the Dachstein Hotel and then the cablecar to the top. The cableway is breathtakingly steep and one is in close proximity to the vertical south wall almost all the time. Not a ride for anyone who suffers from vertigo! From the top, or Bergstation, bear half right, away from the rocky ridge and aim for a group of ski tows. If they are operating, keep an eye open for downhill skiers, as they are a hazard not normally encountered on summer mountain walks. There is also a cross country ski track where the Austrian national squad frequently train.

Heading north-east, go steeply down off the snowfield into a wild rocky corrie. Far from a barren wilderness, this corrie is filled with

The Dachstein mountains

pockets of alpine flowers, many rare, and their brilliant colours contrast sharply with the pale yellow limestone. The waymarked path gradually turns south-east and loses height until it reaches a broad col, the junction of four paths. Turn half right here and go steeply down a grassy slope to the welcome shade and hospitality of the Guttenburg Haus, one of the chain of huts in the Austrian Alps. From the hut an even steeper path zigzags into the main valley, joining the shade of increasingly taller pines the closer one gets to the valley bottom. A restaurant, the Feisterer, will make an essential stopping place at the end of a very hot and tiring though exciting day amongst the high mountains and glaciers.

North of the mountain range and only reached by a long drive, is the well known Hallstättersee, one of Austria's prettiest lakes. About halfway along its west bank is what is considered to be the oldest habitation in the country. This is **Hallstatt**, a village where salt mines have been worked for thousands of years, in fact the earliest settlers have their own classification — the Hallstatt epoch. Today the little village is built on a series of steep sided terraces. Land is so scarce that when anyone dies in Hallstatt their bodies are only left in the grave-yard for 10 years and the skeleton is then dug up with the bones preserved in a charnel house behind the church. Each skull is deco-rated with the owner's name and usually an intricate floral design, a unique if macabre custom still necessary in the twentieth century. The salt mines which gave rise to this community are high above the village and reached by funicular railway. A trip through a small part of the 32km (20 mile) complex of tunnels is a must. Fascinating formations and reflecting pools can be found at every turn and in one place it is necessary to slide down a polished wood shoot. Fortunately overalls are issued to protect everyday clothing!

To the east of the lake is **Obertraun** (see also chapter 10), the start of a cable ride to the famous Dachstein ice caves which cut deeply into the Hallstätter glacier. Strange natural and manmade ice carvings are their major features.

There is another ice cave, this time to the west of the Dachstein massif, the Eisriesenwelt, or the 'world of the ice giants', a huge system of rock and ice reached again by cablecar from **Werfen** high above the Salzach valley. Werfen has its own interchange on the A10 *autobahn* to the north of Bischofshofen.

Back towards Ramsau, the main valley to the south is the Enns, a valley dotted by ancient towns. The two major centres of population closest to Ramsau are Radstadt and Schladming. The first, picturesque **Radstadt,** dates from the thirteenth century and still retains much of its original defensive wall. Corner towers built in the sixteenth century, even today manage to impose their massive threat on potential attackers. The parish church is Gothic and two others baroque. Once an important commercial and administrative centre, Radstadt still has an old law court and two castles built in the romantic Renaissance style. One of the reasons for Radstadt's important past is that it marks the northern end of a route through the mountains used at least since Roman times. This is the Radstädter-Tauern Pass — 1,739m (5,705ft) — a motor road now mostly superseded by the Salzburg-Villach-Klagenfurt *autobahn* further west.

Schladming, equally picturesque, is further east and again was once fortified; the town gate (the Salzburg Gate) is its major feature. The town hall was once a hunting lodge and the church is Gothic. Both towns are well supplied with shops for essentials, but also have many attractive boutiques and high quality souvenir shops.

To the south of the Enns river and reached by conveniently placed cablecars and chairlifts, (Planei, above Schladming, is the best served) is a series of roughly north-south ridges which can be explored from Ramsau. The hills and ridges above Radstadt are gentler and mostly covered by forest, but those to the south-east of Schladming culminate in higher rockier peaks, the Schladminger-Tauern. With the exception of their lower northern ridges, most are beyond the scope of a single day's expedition, but the Hochstein, 2,543m (8,343ft) should, by using the Planei lift on the ascent from Schladming and the Krummholz to descend, be within the capabilities of strong hill walkers.

Further Information
— Ramsau and the Surrounding Area —

Accommodation

Either three or four star hotels, *Gasthöfe* and rented apartments. Camp site at Schladming close to the western turning for the bypass. Further details from local tourist offices.

Places of Interest in the Area

Eisriesenwelt
Ice and rock caves above Werfen. Access by cablecar.

Hallstatt
Colourful village built on a series of terraces above its lake. Ancient church with macabre charnel house full of painted skulls. Famous salt mines with guided tours, access via funicular railway from lakeside. Cruises and rowing boat hire on the Hallstättersee.

Hellbrunn Palace
On the outskirts of Salzburg. Oldest baroque park in Europe, the one-time home of a delightfully eccentric archbishop. Seventeenth-century water displays, grottos, sculptures.
Monatsschlössen folklore museum.

Obertraun
Ice caves — access by cablecar from eastern end of Hallstättersee.

Radstadt
Ancient fortified town at the northern foot of the Radstädter-Tauern Pass. Shops, interesting architecture.

Salzburg
Easy drive (or bus) along the A10 *autobahn*. Baroque city with beautiful old buildings. Mozart's birthplace. Shops, restaurants. Guided tours of the town. Music festivals, concerts.

Schladming
Attractive old buildings. Ancient hunting lodge now used as town hall. Good base for exploring the Schladminger-Tauern mountains.

Recommended Maps

Kompass Wanderkarte 1:50,000 series Sheet 31 Radstadt-Schladming or 1:50,000 Ramsau Dachstein

Tourist Information Offices

Ramsau
Verkehrsverein Ramsau
A-8972 Ramsau am Dachstein
☎ 03687/81925, 81833

Schladming
Verkehrsverein Schladming
A-8970 Schladming
☎ 03687/ 22268

Hallstatt
Fremdenverkehrsverband Hallstatt
Seestrasse 56
A-4830 Hallstatt
☎ 06134/ 208

10 • The Salzkammergut

An appropriate phrase to describe the Salzkammergut might well be, 'salt mines, scenery and stories'. Austria's Lake District, a region 2,500sq km (961sq miles) in size, has some of the most spectacularly beautiful landscape in the whole of Austria; deep lakes that reflect craggy mountain summits in their still waters, flower-filled meadows, shadowy woodlands, and a heritage of archaeology and historical remains as rich as anywhere in central Europe.

Surprisingly enough, compared with the Tyrol, Salzburg or Carinthia, this is a region which is comparatively little known to visitors from outside Austria, yet for variety of scenery and cultural richness, it is perhaps without equal in the whole of Austria, and held by Austrians in exactly the kind of affectionate regard which Britons reserve for their own not dissimilar Lake District in north-west England. British visitors, it is true, flock in very large numbers to St Wolfgang and Fuschl on the outskirts of Salzburg, and the lakeside resort of Gmunden is becoming increasingly popular. But these centres are on the edge of the region, and just a few miles beyond St Wolfgang's crowded streets you'll find yourself in a landscape of breathtaking grandeur. This is 'authentic' Austria, a place where you'll hear relatively little English spoken and where it is easy, if you choose, to get well off the beaten track or at very least enjoy a holiday area which is both typically Austrian and full of delights for anyone with a feeling for European culture and history.

The Salzkammergut is often confused with the adjacent Land Salzburg to the immediate west. Salzburg and the Salzkammergut are in fact very different regions, though they do have some features in common, including salt or *Salz* — the common factor in their names and indeed in former times the main source of wealth of both regions. Just as the prince-archbishops in Salzburg monopolised the salt rights in Salzburg at Hallein, so the emperors of Austria received their revenue directly from the salt rights earned from the Emperor's

Salt Estates — the Salzkammergut. The Salzkammergut was a region
which was formerly totally under imperial control and just how tight
these controls were has an important bearing on the history of the
region.

But where exactly is this area which in fact owes its identity more
to history than any modern administrative boundaries? The
Salzkammergut sits astride three Austrian states, by far the greater
proportion belonging to Upper Austria, and the other two sections
belonging to Styria and Land Salzburg respectively. Its approximate
boundaries are the Salzburg-Vienna motorway to the north, the
Tennengebirge (Tennen mountains) to the south-west, the Totes
Gebirge to the east and the Dachstein Massif to the south. The heart
of the Salzkammergut lies in the upper reaches of the river Traun
valley, surrounded by numerous lakes. Some are of considerable size
and include the Attersee, Traunsee, Hallstättersee, Wolfgangsee and
Mondsee among the better known. Most authorities speak of at least
forty major lakes, though the full total including many of the smaller
mountain tarns is reputed to be seventy-six.

The splendid limestone Dachstein range of the eastern Alps, with
its high karst plateau, dominates the region. The mountain itself is
famed for its sudden swirling mists, honeycombs of caves and pockets of snow which remain even in high summer and of course its
glaciers. The name Dachstein means 'roof stone' and is referred to by
the locals in deliberate wry mockery of its impressive brooding
presence as 'the stone'.

It was the glaciers that created the lakes in the narrow valleys.
They date from at least 70,000-10,000BC when a thick ice crust 1,000m
(3,280ft) in depth lay over the Salzkammergut valleys. As the glaciers
retreated, moraines of glacial debris created natural barriers behind
which the lakes were formed. There is an alpine character to the
whole area, with its mixture of peaks, foothills, dairy meadows and
woodland.

The inhabitants of the Salzkammergut came originally largely
from Bavarian stock and there are a number of similarities of dialect
and customs, though there is, at the same time, a very strong Austrian and Salzkammergut identity. The traditional costume, the
Dirndl, is worn with pride, as is the smartly cut Styrian-inspired suit
or costume. Look out for examples of the elaborate Linzer gold
bonnets in local folk museums. These were made of gold thread,
some with gold plates, and showed how wealthy some of the salt
manufacturers became so that they could afford to deck out their
wives in this way. Old traditions and ways of celebrating are kept up

Hay drying in the Salzkammergut

not just to impress the tourist, but as meaningful additions to the calendar of the seasons, with Fasching (the carnival before Lent), Corpus Christi or Fronleichnam (on the Thursday after Trinity Sunday) where the Hallstatt and Traunsee lakes are used for religious processions and ceremonies, and the Festival of the Three Kings in early January. In times past when the Salzkammergut was an enclosed, strictly controlled area under imperial rule where passes were issued to anyone who went in and out, salt smuggling formed its own sub-culture.

Millions of years ago, the Salzkammergut was covered by a great salt sea and as its subterranean basins dried out, their salt concentration increased over a period of time. Rock movements raised the salt levels which were deposited especially in the mountains around Hallstatt, Bad Ischl and Bad Aussee areas. Salt had been discovered in prehistoric times as a flavour and preservative and the prehistoric miner was actually able to tunnel through the rock with primitive tools in order to reach it. Later the Celts discovered that it was easier to loosen or dissolve the salt in water and then evaporate the water in giant vats. Mountains, lakes and swift-flowing rivers with treacherous currents are difficult terrain through which to transport goods and people, and a walk on at least part of the famous old saltway between Hallstatt, Bad Ischl and Ebensee, which follows the line of the world's oldest pipeline carrying brine from the saltmines to the

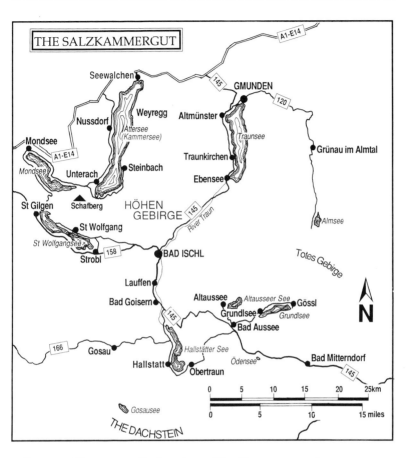

refinery at Ebensee on the borders of the Traunsee, make one appreciate some of the difficulties endured by those early salt producers, miners, refiners and traders.

A visit to one of the historic salt mines of the Salzkammergut is an experience not to be missed.

Just as a decline in the demand for salt seemed to be heralding a decline in the region's fortunes, towards the end of the eighteenth century the Romantic poets and writers began to discover a new world of mountains, lakes and woodlands so that it became fashionable to explore Switzerland and its dazzling mountain ranges. The Salzkammergut, awakened like a latter day Sleeping Beauty from the encircling Kammergut briars which had helped to isolate it for about 250 years, was soon discovered to be the Austrian Switzerland. Between Lambach and Gmunden in 1752, a postchaise connection linked Gmunden to the European travel network, bringing the first

real travellers including artists, explorers and writers of travel books
to this formerly enclosed terrain. Topographic writers such as J.A.
Schultes (1794-1808) exclaimed 'I would gladly give a year of my life
for one moonlight night on Gmunden's lake.'

But the Salzkammergut's reputation was secured when it became
the favourite summer resort of Habsburg Emperor Franz Joseph I
who delighted in the peace and beauty of the area away from the
summer heat of Vienna, centring his court annually on Bad Ischl and
delighting in the many opportunities available to hunt in the region's
forests. Pictures or statues of the emperor clothed in his hunting
uniform of *Lederhosen* (short trousers of soft leather) and feathered
hat, (actually a Gamsbart or chamois tuft) are as much a part of the
Salzkammergut experience as its salt mines and mountains. And
with the emperor came the great and famous, the fashionable and the
artistic, to enjoy the mountains and the lakes and to take the waters
and the 'cure' in one of several elegant and well appointed spa towns
of which Bad Ischl is only the most famous. It is a reputation among
Austrians at least which has never declined, as the more active sports
of walking, skiing and mountaineering have taken over (though not
entirely) the habit of enjoying a 'cure' in pure air and incomparable
mountain scenery.

Early summer is perhaps the best time to see the alpine flora in all
its glory, but the beauty of the area lies in the fact that it is very much
an all-the-year-round region. Each season has something to offer —
December through to March for winter sports, including cross-country skiing (*Langlaufen*) which is very popular, spring to early summer
for walking, climbing and enjoying the flowers, summer itself to take
full advantage of the lakeside bathing facilities and many other
water sports, and gentler walking, and autumn for its glorious colours and encouragement to ramble through miles of waymarked
paths by the lakesides and through the woodlands. Deer, marmots,
chamois, eagles and wild boar are all to be seen in their appropriate
habitats as well as a wide variety of animal and bird life.

As is usual in an alpine area, weather can sometimes change
unexpectedly from idyllic clear blue skies to a sudden thunder
storm, but the many sheltered valleys are often sun-traps in spring
and autumn, and these in turn can experience high temperatures in
the summer making lake bathing a welcome way of cooling down.
The intensity of the sun's rays should also not be underestimated if
you are walking on the mountains. A variety of protective clothing
is sensible and necessary to take account of all possible weather
conditions and remember that warmer clothing is also generally

The Coburger hut near Ehrwald, North Tyrol

Looking towards the Kaisergebirge from St Johann

Eng in the Karwendel group

The terminus of the Achensee narrow gauge steam railway at Jenbach

The Dachstein glacier

advisable when visiting caves or salt mines. Winters in the area are cold with a high snowfall which provides ideal skiing conditions but mountain passes and tracks can be closed for months at a time.

Northern Salzkammergut — Gmunden, Ebensee and the Traunsee

The first town in the Salzkammergut to be reached either by train on the Salzkammergut branch or by turning south either at the Regau or Steyermühl intersections off the Vienna-Salzburg motorway, is the lakeside resort of Gmunden.

First mentioned in 1270 as an important Celtic settlement, **Gmunden** owes its importance to its salt trade connections when it became the administrative centre of the salt trade and organised weekly markets. Two ancient Roman salt roads led from the banks of the Traun to the north. But the salt trade flourished long before, between 1000 and 400BC under the Illyrians. Salt originally from Hallstatt and later brine from Ischl and Ebensee which was transported via the river Traun to other parts of the region or on to the Danube and beyond, had to use Gmunden as a trans-shipment area where a toll was charged and salt dealers had their administrative centre. Salt was stored and kept dry in the cellars and attics of the medieval houses not far from the Rathaus (town hall). Gmunden's former wealth is demonstrated in the number of superb late Gothic houses still to be seen, with their narrow side facing to the street and the marble facings on windows and doorways. The Kammerhof build- ing with its Gothic frescoes, ceilings and pillars is a particularly fine example of this kind of craftmanship. The building is now a museum and art gallery, its collections include drawings and pottery and an excellent Brahms and Hebbel collection, since its famous visitors included the writer and philosopher Friedrich Hebbel and the composer Johannes Brahms. Richard Wagner, Franz Schubert and the regional writer Adelbert Stifter were other celebrities associated with Gmunden. The Brahms collection is noted not only for its memorabilia, but also for its musical insights as regards letters and manuscripts. Although it was actually Bad Ischl that was Brahms' summer home for many years, he also had close connections with Gmunden, regularly staying with his friends the von Millers who after his death established a Brahms Museum at Gmunden contain- ing many mementoes from his rooms at Bad Ischl. Much of this material, together with collections linked to the town's history and artistic life and about the salt industry in particular, can be seen in the Gmunden Town Museum in Kammerhofgasse.

The Rathaus, another splendid building, has elegant stucco deco- ration and on the third story an unusual carillon of ceramic bells, made of the famous Gmunden pottery, which chime musically five times a day in the style of one of the composers associated with the area such as Brahms, Schubert or Bruckner. There is also a plaque depicting Johannes von Gmunden who is remembered as an as- tronomer and professor of Vienna university who produced the first printed calendar.

The Traunsee, through which the river Traun flows, is first re- corded as *Trunseo* in AD909 and later as *lacus felix* (the lucky lake). It is over 12km ($7\frac{1}{2}$ miles) in length, and is one of the largest and most beautiful of the Salzkammergut lakes, its southern end dominated by high peaks including the Traunstein itself, which is 1,691m (just under 5,000ft high).

Gmunden's career as a spa began at a slow pace largely because imperial patronage favoured nearby Bad Ischl. Nevertheless, by the early nineteenth century a private brine-bath was opened at the Traun bridge and proved so successful that the premises soon had to be extended. Initially the people of Gmunden were somewhat reluc- tant to let their homes or rooms to summer visitors. The development of a horse-drawn tram to Lambach for passengers and goods in 1836, one of the earliest in Austria (which still exists as the railway from

Gmunden

Seebahnhof station), undoubtedly aided the town's prosperity while the *Sophie*, a Vienna-Gmunden steamer which operated along the Danube and the river Traun calling three times a day from May to October, sailed to Ebensee and back taking the mail coaches on board. From 1839 there were through steam trains to Linz and Vienna.

Among various artistic and aristocratic people who came to Gmunden were the exiled Hanoverians, relatives of the British royal family who had been driven out by Prussia to Austria, and who built Schloss Cumberland, their handsome country home, by the Traunsee. The town grew rapidly in the nineteenth and twentieth centuries with hotels and fine villas in the popular Biedermeier style spreading along the lakeside and up the hillside.

Gmunden is now a popular boating and sailing centre with a long, lakeside promenade and an excellent choice of hotels, cafés and guest houses, but the character of the medieval town with its narrow streets and courtyards, marketplace, old inns and merchant's houses, remains unspoiled.

Not to be missed is Gmunden's parish church, founded in 1301 with a magnificent high altar by Thomas Schwanthaler as its centrepiece, dated 1678. It is of the Three Kings, and it is said that these figures form the prototype for the famous Salzkammergut Christmas cribs. Additional statues of St Elizabeth and Zacherias by the baroque master Michael Türn are also noteworthy. A charming ceramic Madonna over the south gate is from the Gmunden ceramic works and is of fairly recent date. Epitaphs to old salt merchants and dealers also make interesting reading.

You'll see examples of Gmunden Pottery in many local shops. This is made in a traditional but distinctive style with green whorls and bands on a white ground — teapots, plates, cups, jugs. It is possible to visit the works in Keramikstrasse during the summer months to see pots being thrown.

As you walk along the promenade, you will see a bronze sculpture of a salt miner with a large rock crystal poised on his shoulder to represent rock salt. There is something rather moving in that squat figure and the 'white gold' which represented so much of the town's former prosperity. You will also find a memorial to the composer Franz Schubert who stayed here during the summer of 1825. Fascinating to speculate if any of the famous Schubert songs or symphonies were at all influenced by this setting.

Gmunden also has one of the Salzkammergut's most famous cake and coffee shops — Grellinger's *Konditorei* in Franz Joseph Platz, noted for its ice cream specialities, its walls plastered with photographs and souvenirs of the great and famous who have called to sample the delicacies on offer.

Gmunden is also distinguished by having the smallest tram network in Europe. Opened in 1894, it is the oldest electric tramway in Austria, beating Vienna by 3 years. A little vintage car winds its way steeply up to the main railway station from the town centre, some 60m (197ft) above the Traunsee, to link with trains on the Salzkammergutbahn. Its oldest vehicle still in regular use dates back to 1911 and it is estimated that some 30 million people have used the tramway since it opened.

The best way of all to explore the lake and lakeside attractions is to take one of the regular little motor launches which serve both sides of the lake. During the summer months you can catch the *Gisela*, the oldest coal-fired paddle-steamer of its kind in the world still working. It took 6 years to refit her at enormous cost, but she is a wonderful sight as she chugs gently across the quiet waters of the Traunsee.

The Landschloss Ort by the lake, formerly a palace, was built by Count Herberstaff in 1626, and is reached by walking along the promenade or catching the steamer to Toscana. It is now an agricultural college. Features of special interest are the banqueting hall with a superb wooden ceiling and a beautiful wrought iron fountain in the courtyard dating from 1777. This seventeenth-century building has

Seeschloss Ort, Gmunden

four wings and is really an extended version of the *Vierkanthof*, a characteristic farm building of the Traun valley, with a square court-yard. Members of the Habsburg family lived in the *Schloss* for a time, but none of the original furnishings remain.

The companion piece to Landschloss Ort is the highly photogenic Seeschloss Ort, linked to the mainland by a wooden causeway which is open to the public. It was originally the site of a Roman fort, also first mentioned in 909. Its huge tower, windows and doors date from the time of Emperor Friedrich II, 1400-1493. The picturesque three sided courtyard with its passageways suffered a fire, but was then rebuilt. In the small chapel, again of the late Gothic period, there is some splendid stucco work on the ceiling and a charming picture of the *Madonna and Child*. Remains of Renaissance frescoes are also visible. The building was the responsibility of the chief salt admin-istrator of Gmunden as part of the emperor's *Kammergut*.

Archduke Johann Salvator, son of the Archduke of Tuscany and
a near relative of the Emperor Francis Joseph I of Austria, inherited
the castle in 1878. His army career had caused some controversy in
imperial circles and his increasingly liberal views alienated him
further from the court. He was also a close friend of the ill-fated
Rudolph of Mayerling, (Johann was actually his uncle though only
6 years older) who shared many of his views. After his marriage to
dancer Milli Stubel, he renounced his claim to the throne, took the
name of Johann Orth after the *Schloss* and later set sail for South
America, having obtained his captain's certificate. Fierce storms
wrecked the vessel and he was presumed drowned, though there are
still tales of the former archduke landing on some remote island and
living out his days there.

Johann Salvator Orth's family resided at the Villa Toscana, a
golden yellow building in neo-Renaissance style set on a peninsula
by the lake. The building is now used as a conference centre and there
is a path through the park to the lakeside which gives a splendid view
of the Traunstein mountain.

Take the Traunsee boat across the lake to **Weyer** to catch the
Grünberg cablecar (*Seilbahn*) whose valley station is a short walk
from the landing stage to the summit of the Grünberg, a magnificent
viewpoint.

It's only a short walk of some 4km (2$^1/_2$ miles) along a well marked
and broad path from the Grünberg cablecar to Laudachsee, a beautiful mountain lake which reflects the summit of the Katzenstein in
its limpid waters, an alpine meadow in the foreground. The
Ramsauseralm café-restaurant overlooks the lake — an excellent
place for *Sachertorte* and coffee.

To reach the Laudachsee you follow both the Waldlehrpfad — a
forest nature trail — and rather more unusually, the Märchenpfad.

The Märchenpfad or Folk Tale Path has a series of enchanting
wooden sculptures in the forest which culminate in a little stream-
powered xylophone whose chimes can be heard some distance
away. You come across the sculptures of *Giant Erla and the Nymph
Bloudchen*, a famous local legend and then the *Seven Springs of the
Seven Brothers*. A feature of these folk tales are that they are bound up
with natural features in the area itself and are an attempt to explain
them.

Giant Erla fell in love with a water nymph Blondchen and built
her a beautiful castle on the lake. He married her and they were very
happy till the nymph became fatally ill and died. The grieving giant
carved her likeness in the Traunstein mountain and you can still see

The Traunstein

the profile of the classical features of a beautiful young woman asleep — *Die schlafende Griechin* (the Sleeping Grecian Girl) if you look at the mountain at the right angle. The *Seven Springs of the Seven Brothers* on the other hand is the story of an evil king punished for his ruthless behaviour by finding his sons changed into natural springs that suddenly gushed out of the ground.

Another place best explored by taking the Traunsee boat (though it can be reached by both road and rail from Gmunden) is **Traunkirchen**, an exquisitely beautiful rocky peninsula that juts out into the lake.

The village gets its name from its fine church, Maria Krönung, the church of Mary's Coronation. Originally a convent church founded in 1020 stood on the same site. It was dissolved after the Reformation, but then became a Jesuit church after the Counter Reformation in the sixteenth century and further building took place in the seventeenth century. It is a baroque masterpiece with five altars, but is particularly celebrated for the Fischerkanzel, a richly carved pulpit by an unknown master which represents a boat with a magnificent catch of fish being hauled in by fishermen St James and St John in a net amid a sea of silver. The whole is crowned by the figure of St Francis Xavier, the famous Jesuit missionary who, as the story goes, on one of his epic voyages to South America put his crucifix in the waters to calm a raging storm. As he landed safely, a gigantic crab appeared holding his crucifix in its pincers.

The sculpture is particularly appropriate for the Traunsee which is still justifiably famous for the richness and variety of its fish, including trout, and the local specialities of Reinanke and Saibling (a form of lake salmon) which are not to be missed. A number of restaurants around the Traunsee will give you opportunity to try out these Salzkammergut specialities at first hand.

Not far from the boat landing stage is a winding path that climbs through the trees up a headland crag to the tiny chapel of St John, roofed in pine shingles, which dates from Roman times, with a beautiful painted altar and a magnificent view of the Traunsee and the Traunstein mountain.

There is a rather sad legend connected with the Traunsee concerning a Fraulein von Orth, daughter of a duke who fell in love with a knight and refused to obey her father by giving him up. She was sent away as a punishment to a convent at Obhut, but the knight swam across the lake each evening to see his sweetheart, steering by a light she placed in her window for him. Sadly one night a great storm arose which extinguished the light and the knight drowned on his way across the lake. When the lady saw the body of her beloved washed up on the shore, she threw herself down from her window to join her dead lover, and was battered to death on the stones below.

Also on the shores of the lake, some 4km (2¹/₂ miles) from Gmunden and considerably larger than Traunkirchen, is **Altmünster**, an old market town with a Roman foundation. The town's name gives a clue to its early Benedictine monastery dating from late Carolingian times and called the monastery of Trunseo, the old name for the Traunsee. Graf Herbersdorff's epitaph of red marble can still be seen in the chapel. This former *Statthalter* (governor) of the 'Land above the River Enns' (another name for this part of the Salzkammergut), was hated for the savagery with which he put down the peasants' rising of 1626, and his body lay in the ground outside for a considerable time, before he was given a formal monument. A Roman gravestone has also now been placed in the church to escape further ravages of the weather. Every year the beautiful Thomas Schwanthaler crib is put on the Josefalter with its *Adoration of the Shepherds*, *Flight into Egypt* and *Circumcision* scenes. There is a similar crib in the Gmunden town museum.

The southern terminus of the Traunsee boat, and also easily reached by road or rail, is **Ebensee**. Though there is a small lakeside resort area, this is basically a salt refining town whose products are used in the chemical industry as well as for household purposes and are exported throughout Austria. A large crucifix on a rock by the Ischl road beyond the town is a graphic reminder of the dangerous and sometimes fatal journeys that the heavily-laden salt boats had to make along the fast-flowing river Traun between Ischl and Ebensee. Nowadays the brine is refined in modern factories and is used, among other things, for glass and crystal cutting. It is possible to visit two such works in the town and watch their manufacture.

Modern industry apart, there is a fascinating old part of the town to explore, with narrow streets and old shops, an eighteenth-century church and Heimat (folk) museum. About 1km (just over half a mile) along the Langbath road east of Ebensee is the cablecar up the Feuerkogel mountain, an outlier of the Höllengebirge range, 1,594m (5,228ft) high and offering a splendid panorama of the Dachstein, as well as a series of safe and easy to follow footpaths around the summit plateau and a choice of café-restaurants.

Langbathsee itself consists of two beautiful and less well known lakes — the Vorderer Langbath See and Hinterer Langbath See set deep in the forest, both with pleasant, waymarked forest paths between and around them.

The Gassl Tropfsteinhöhle is a show cave complex also reached off the Langbathsee road, well worth seeing with the Riesenorgel or Great Organ as a special feature. This is a series of pipe-like formations, closely set together, of stalactites up to 6m (20ft) in length, rather like organ pipes, and your guide may well run a stick across to demonstrate the extraordinary sound they make.

Ebensee also has some interesting traditional customs like a Fasching procession called *der Fetzen*, literally meaning 'rags', but really an uncomplimentary reference to the participants, the Ugly Women, as it is traditional for the muffled figures to make themselves into totally repellent ugly-looking women.

Eastern Salzkammergut — Almtal and the Almsee

The eastern side of the Salzkammergut is dominated by a single valley — the Almtal — culminating in the Almsee and the Totes Gebirge range of mountains. This is an area of dense forest through which that narrow valley runs, a basin of richly pastoral countryside, punctuated with small towns such as Scharnstein and Grüntal, scattered hamlets and farms, and churches with tall, red spires. Lacking the large and popular lakes of the other parts of the Salzkammergut, this is a truly hidden region of quiet and very rural countryside with mountains and forest always close by. It is probably the least known part of the Salzkammergut, verging into the adjacent region of Pyhrn-Eisenwurzen. Yet there is plenty of accommodation, mostly in quiet farmhouses or small villages, making it an ideal area for touring or a quiet walking holiday away from any busy tourist centre.

The easiest route into Almtal is from Gmunden along a switch-backing road which climbs past scattered farms and small villages away from the Traunsee valley over the low pass via St Konrad to Scharnstein in the central part of the Almtal valley. You can also get there from Wels via Pettenbach, from where there is a single track railway as far as Grünau, and there is a direct postbus service from Gmunden to Grünau and Almsee.

Grünau in Almtal is the principal resort as such. Surrounded by green woodlands it has a reputation for rest and relaxation since it is not plagued by through traffic, with a scatter of farms and small guest houses, and a little baroque church, but it is a popular place for winter sports, albeit well away from international circuits.

The Cumberland Wild Life Park, some 7km (4 miles) south of Grünau along the valley floor, is a former hunting area belonging to the exiled Hanoverians of Schloss Cumberland at Gmunden. This is not only an open-air zoo, but a research institute which was till recently under the directorship of the late Konrad Lorenz, the world famous animal psychologist. Here brown bears, wolves, foxes, a lynx, birds of prey and other alpine fauna enjoy the semi-natural setting beneath wooded hillsides and among sections of river and ponds well stocked with fish. It is possible to confine yourself to a tour of the animal life or if you prefer, there is ample opportunity for more extended wanderings — or even drives — in this lovely wilderness area surrounded by mountain peaks.

Opposite the Cumberland Wild Life Park there is a 10km-long (6 mile-) tarmac toll road which zigzags up to the Kaiserbergalm where again there is a splendid mountain panorama to enjoy, and a choice of mountain walks. On clear days you might be rewarded by the sight of the Salzburg and Tyrolean mountains, the Watzmann in Bavaria in nearby Germany, the Bohemian Woods of Czechoslovakia, the Ötscher of Lower Austria, the Dachstein and many more.

At Kinderland at **Schindlbach**, which lies in a side valley about 6km ($3^1/_2$ miles) east of Grünau, there is the Austrian equivalent of a theme park for children, filled with attractions including a miniature railway and the nearby Märchenwald where favourite fairy stories are brought to life.

If you follow the road to the head of the valley you come to the

Almsee, one of the finest of the smaller lakes of Salzkammergut, whose pale green waters mirror the snowcapped peaks and limestone pinnacles of the Totes Gebirge mountains. This is an area famous for its birdlife, and you can leave your car (or catch the postbus) near the crossroads on the Ödenseen road and take a forest path around the head of the lake where you might see the celebrated 'floating islands' which move around the lake, largely consisting of vegetable matter.

This is a cul-de-sac valley with tracks and paths leading deep into the Totes Gebirge mountains — routes strictly for experienced mountaineers, or, in the winter months, well equipped skiers. Less adventurous spirits may enjoy the delights of two excellent restaurants with a postbus service to return you to your waiting car, Grünau or direct to Gmunden. There is also a rail service from Lambach and Gmunden to Grünau.

Central Salzkammergut — Ischl, Hallstatt and the Dachstein

Bad Ischl, because of its central location, is undoubtedly the best centre for touring the Salzkammergut, whether by car, with excellent road links from Salzburg or Gmunden, or by public transport with so many rail and bus and even boat services to the other lakes. Certainly, anyone coming to the Salzkammergut without a car can be strongly recommended to base themselves at Ischl and take advantage of rail and postbus networks. There is also no shortage of accommodation. But there are far more positive reasons than this to discover this charming and sophisticated spa town.

Ironically, an event in this idyllic mountain setting had an extraordinarily far-reaching effect on the lives of countless millions of people throughout the world — the declaration of World War I. With the assassination of the Archduke Franz Ferdinand, Emperor Franz Joseph's nephew and heir to the throne, by a Serbian nationalist at Sarajevo in 1914, the notorious ultimantum to Serbia for this provocation was signed at Bad Ischl where the emperor was staying for his annual holiday. The inevitable outcome was World War I with its massive carnage and political upheaval whose effects are still with us today.

The emperor's mother, Princess Sophie, had been recommended the Ischl brine baths as a cure for childlessness. (It had already been discovered that the warm brine baths were beneficial to the salt miners for various muscular complaints). Within two years Sophie had given birth to a son — Franz Joseph — and to his two brothers a few years later, who were collectively known as the Salt Princes. Bad Ischl's fame was assured and within a relatively short time, it became the centre of aristocratic and artistic activity. Composers, painters, stars of the opera and stage all flocked to Ischl with its glamorous new clientèle. Franz Joseph returned annually to Ischl for his birthday celebrations each summer after his accession in 1848 until that fateful day in 1914, for rest and relaxation from the cares of court life but above all else to indulge his inextinguishable passion for hunting stags, deer, chamois and a number of other wild creatures.

At Ischl the young emperor fell deeply in love with his sixteen-year-old Bavarian cousin Elizabeth (Sissi), instead of her elder sister as expected, and their engagement was announced with due ceremony at the Hotel Austria in 1853 where their families were staying. This elegant building with a rococo façade and triple gables, on the Traun Esplanade, was originally known as the Seeauer House and belonged to a wealthy salt refiner. It has had a further change of use from hotel to town art gallery and museum where interesting modern and period paintings connected with the Ischl area can be viewed.

The Kaiservilla and parkland in Ischl were a wedding present from Princess Sophie to the young couple and a year later the emperor built the Marmorschlössl in the grounds for his young wife where she could read and write poetry. The Kaiservilla is now a fascinating museum of Franz Joseph's life, with 50,000 hunting trophies, wall mounted and carefully labelled, which are an extraordinary tribute to the emperor's passion — some would say obsession — for the sport. The furnishings are relatively austere as befits what was basically a hunting villa, and on the emperor's desk you can see the document which started the war. Among other relics is the cushion used to support the dying Empress Elizabeth, murdered by an anarchist in Geneva. Their son, Crown Prince Rudolph, had apparently committed suicide in 1869 with his young mistress, in circumstances which have never been fully explained. They were undoubtedly violent times.

The museum does give a vivid insight into the character of this lonely and punctilious man, who regularly rose at 4 or 5am to deal with his official documents and who came to be seen as a father figure to the Austro-Hungarian empire. The Marmorschlössl is now a well laid out museum of photography and contains additional imperial memorabilia.

Britain's King Edward VII came three times to Ischl in 1905, 1906 and 1908, hoping to persuade the emperor of the significance of Germany's growing power and to persuade him to help isolate Germany. The occasion of the banquet at the Kaiservilla prepared for the king in 1908 is re-enacted from time to time with suitable pomp and circumstance and replica menu plus the additional thrill of an aperitif with Markus of Habsburg-Lothringen, the old emperor's great nephew (in suitable modern Austrian democratic tradition the present-day curator of the Kaiservilla) who gives a personal conducted tour of the Kaiservilla on such occasions.

Bad Ischl has, of course, other claims to fame. It speedily became a centre for the arts, especially music, attracting composers of the highest calibre to the nearby lakes and mountains which proved to be a potent source of inspiration. Anton Bruckner, the great symphonic composer and organist, played the organ at Ischl parish church while staying with friends, whilst Johannes Brahms stayed innumerable times both at Bad Ischl and Gmunden, composing a number of his chamber works and his *German Dances* in the Salzkammergut. It was said that he drew much of his inspiration for some of the folk themes in his work from the music overheard at a neighbour's house.

But it was the world of Viennese operetta that came to have a particular association with Ischl. Johann Strauss, the waltz king, dined frequently at the Café Ramsauer in the Pfarrgasse (still a pleasant venue for food or drink), and Friedrich Kalman and Oscar Strauss also spent a good deal of their summers in Ischl. The Leharvilla, built in the Biedermeier style, is now a museum to the memory of the celebrated Franz Lehar. This is where Lehar composed two dozen works for the musical stage including the immortal operetta *The Merry Widow*. The villa is filled with the many splendid gifts he received from all over the world as a tribute to his genius and it is interesting to note the decorative iron gate in the house which was closed when he was at work and not available to visitors.

Biedermeier is the name of the nineteenth-century style used to suggest solid middle class comfort of both architecture and furnishings. It is far less massive than baroque and has a distinct charm of its own. It was the Biedermeier painters who began to discover the beauty of the Salzkammergut countryside and encourage the fashionable Viennese in their annual exodus to the lakes and mountains.

Nowadays you can still drink the waters in the colonnaded Biedermeier-style Trinkhalle (Pump Room) and listen to concerts of light classical music on the little stage. Nearby is a splendid *fin-de-*

siècle post office building, a tribute to Ischl's importance as a centre of communications when not only the imperial court, but many other crowned heads, heads of government, diplomats and innumerable prominent visitors flocked to the spa. Between July and August each year there is a summer repertoire of operetta at the Kurhaus where the audience, elegantly dressed, some of the ladies in sumptuous evening style dirndls, promenade in the interval, perhaps drinking a sparkling glass of Sekt (the German and Austrian version of Champagne and much recommended) and walk out to look at the lights glimmering on the fountains of the Kurpark.

Zauner's *Konditorei* in the Pfarrgasse formerly provided the imperial court with wonderful delicate confections of cakes and pastries. (The Zauner Stollen is one of many specialities.) Today you can still have a similar experience by drinking coffee, always served with a glass of fresh clear water to refresh and cleanse the palate, and enjoy a masterpiece of the confectioner's art, probably unrivalled for quality even in Austria, or just an ice or a drink. It was upstairs in the red and gold apartment that the emperor too might sometimes indulge in similar pleasures. Nowadays Zauner's has also opened a charming restaurant by the river Traun esplanade where you can refresh yourself either indoors or out till late evening with a drink, light snack or meal, watching the lights reflected in the river from both buildings and bridges.

Ischl is still a spa. The Kurmittelhaus is one of the best equipped in Austria and has treatments available for respiratory diseases, heart conditions, digestive disorders, skin conditions and many more and the luxurious Kurhotel is directly linked to the various treatment areas by an underground passage. But taking the waters or the 'Cure' is not just simply a matter of medical treatment; it includes facilities for complete relaxation whether this be listening to the Kurpark orchestra or a Trinkhalle concert, attending a stimulating lecture or strolling round the elegant small shops on the Traun promenade and making excursions by train, postbus, coach, chairlift, cablecar, car or boat into a stunningly beautiful landscape.

Among attractive walks in and around the town is a route through the woods by footpath or chairlift to the Siriuskogel, a little peak which overlooks the town, for coffee, cakes and a glorious view or, for the more ambitious, the Katrinseilbahn, (Katrin cablecar) to the summit of the Katrin mountain from where paths radiate through forests noted for the number of wild chamois. It's less than an hour's walk to the little Nussensee to the west of the town, a little lake deep in the forest, whilst a walk of a similar distance by lane or footpath above Perneck brings you to the Ischl Salt Mines where a little train takes you into a remarkable series of well lit tunnels and salt workings where you are shown much of the geology and early history of this fascinating industry.

Lauffen lies some 5km (3 miles) south of Ischl, but is easily missed from the main road which passes above the picturesque village. It has a number of mills powered by the waters of the river Traun. Originally an eighth-century settlement, it boasts a particularly lovely eighteenth-century pilgrimage church known as Maria Schatten (Mary in the Shadows). There is a stone Madonna dating from about 1400 and fine altars, but its particular interest lies in the fact that in late summer a traditional pilgrimage is made by local people to the church at Lauffen to give thanks for the safe return of their cattle from the high pastures after a summer on the heights.

Bad Goisern, further south on the road from Ischl, is a sizeable but scattered resort, with typical alpine-style chalets and farmhouses, often with richly decorated windowboxes crowding along the valley floor and the small hillocks formed by old glacial moraines. There were once-popular sulphur baths to the north of the town, whilst the area remains famous for the making both of violins and hand-made walking boots. An excellent opportunity to test the aforementioned boots lies with mountain paths to the nearby Predigstuhl (1,278m, 4,192ft) along a high traverse known (perhaps ominously) as the Ewige Wand or Wall of Eternity.

Hallstättersee is perhaps the most dramatic of all the larger Salzkammergut lakes, set in a deep ravine enclosed by towering mountain crags and peaks, with all the almost-claustrophobic quality of a romantic painting, a Caspar Friedrich or even Turner in one of his more introspective moods.

Undoubtedly the finest way of all to approach the little town of **Hallstatt**, which gives its name to the lake, is by the ferry which you can catch at the landing stage at nearby Hallstatt railway station, meeting trains in both directions. As you speed across the waters of the lake, you see clusters of houses in almost Mediterranean pink, white and cream stucco and the gleaming spire and tower of the two churches. Everything seems dangerously perched below towering rocks and crowded round the water's edge. When you disembark from the boat you are soon in a pretty town square tightly packed with shops, café, inns, every window spilling with flowers. Behind the square you make your way along the little narrow streets which cling to the rock faces and think yourself in Italy or France. But this is one of the oldest towns in Austria.

It was salt that brought ancient Celtic and Illyrian peoples to this beautiful spot, set between the thickly forested mountainside and the lake. *Hal* is the old Celtic word for salt — Hallstatt means Salt Town — sharing its derivation with Hallein near Salzburg, Bad Hall near Linz and Schwäbisch Hall in south Germany.

Salt was mined in the area from about 1,000BC and by 900-500BC came the great period of the Hallstatt Culture, a time of highly flourishing salt trade with other parts of Europe. Glass beads and bowls and amber were traded from the Baltic while a beautiful sword with sheath (now in Vienna) with ivory inset, indicates the wealth of their operations. Miles of galleries, textiles, leather shoes, wooden bowls, broken axes and even burnt out torches have been discovered in these remarkable ancient salt mines. A visit to the Hallstatt Salt Mine above the town (reached by funicular from Hallstatt Lahn) is something not to be missed.

In addition about 20,000 objects discovered in the burial grounds in the area have enhanced archaeological knowledge of Iron Age civilisation even further. 'The Man preserved in Salt' discovered in 1734 and still clothed, proved to be one of these early people and other objects and bodies indicate that there was a catastrophic landslide which destroyed part of the terrain and blocked many of the mine entrance passages. Food remains indicate that their diet seems to have consisted of a porridge of millet, barley and broad beans and there is also evidence of prehistoric *Almwirtschaft* or alpine dairy farming. Heart shaped moulds have been discovered in the rocks in the mines, which were obviously used as a pattern, enabling an oval shaped fragment on each side to be knocked out and then the central salt layer, with the help of wedges, could be chipped free. Attempts to reconstruct this exactly have failed so far, as obviously a special way of cutting the rock was employed, proving that modern technology has often something to learn even from ancient sources. Even early ladders, in the form of holes hacked regularly into the supporting walls of the tunnels with logs laid across, have been found. In the Hallstatt Heimat museum is a model of an Iron Age miner with his ancient conical carrying sack for rock salt made from goatskin with fur side outermost, stretched on wooden laths. It could easily be emptied in one movement. Many of these archaeological remains, of European if not world importance, including a miner's leather cap, are displayed at the Museum of Pre-History in Hallstatt.

Light seems to have been obtained either by small bunches of wooden spills fastened together or by metre-long spills of fir and pine also fastened together. Although many of the most famous finds

Hallstatt

are in the Natural History Museum in Vienna and elsewhere, there is workmanship of superb quality from the neolithic, Iron Age and Roman periods in pottery, armour, jewellery and various domestic articles to be seen.

It seems that the Romans, who followed the Celts, were able to co-exist peacefully with the miners as their overseers and consolidate the wealth of their skilful subjects. Salt production continued throughout the Middle Ages and during the fourteenth century when the emperors and the prince-archbishops argued over their respective salt rights in the region.

The plaque in the centre of Hallstatt, not far from the market place, commemorates Queen Elizabeth, Albrecht's widow, who helped to increase salt production dramatically by handing over salt rights to certain prosperous burgers able to develop them. Salt was originally carried by boat and horseback from Hallstatt to Gmunden via Goisern and Lauffen. Gmunden was the seat of the *Salzamtmann*, the Salt Controller, who supervised all matters dealing with the mining, refining and sale of salt. Up till the late nineteenth century, the road from Gmunden only went as far as Traunkirchen so that salt had to go by boat down the river Traun and across the Traunsee. It took till 1872 for a road to be built as far as Bad Ischl, and Hallstatt itself could only be reached from the north on foot or on horseback. Sometimes an open carrying chair was used for those who demanded greater comfort. Model figures in the Heimat museum demonstrate the load of rock salt strapped to a person's back on a wooden carrier which was taken over the steep tracks between mine and landing stage before the development of the technique of dissolving the salt in water to make brine and piping it along wooden pipes along the Soleleitungsweg (Brine Pipeline Track) and incidentally this pipeline was the world's first, built in the late sixteenth century. The Soleleitungsweg is still a dramatically beautiful footpath between Hallstatt and Ischl and on to Ebensee.

The Salzkammergut was strongly Protestant at one time, and there are still a number of Protestant churches, as in Hallstatt whose comparative austerity contrasts with the more richly decorated parish churches. The Hallstatt parish church is set on a high point overlooking the lake and reached by an extraordinary ancient covered way up steep steps past houses. The church itself is well worth a visit — pause at its beautiful small cemetery with its wrought-iron crosses and flower-filled graves. Here Catholics and Protestants share the same resting place, religious differences vanishing where space is so limited, and this gave rise to the custom of digging up the bodies after about 10 years and storing them in an Ossuary or Bone House nearby where the further custom arose of painting the name and date on the skulls and occasionally details of their profession or in the case of the skull with the snake drawing, the manner of the person's death. It is an extraordinarily moving experience to look at these faded looking greyish objects with their painted flower garlands for females and oak or ivy leaves for males.

The church itself was enlarged and consecrated in 1320 as Maria-Hilf and was completed in 1505 in the late Gothic style. The strikingly decorated tower was painted after a fire in 1750 and this was complemented by an imposing fresco of St Christopher facing the direction of the lake. The entrance on the south side is framed in red Salzburg marble. Over the entrance are two frescoes depicting the *Crucifixion* and *Christ Carrying the Cross* by an unknown master of the Danube school, while the plaques on the wall and the ironwork all merit attention. The church itself has a neo-Gothic crucifixion altar on the left and on the right a splendid late Gothic winged altar (1510-1520). To the right and left of the choir stalls was the place of honour for the chief salt producers. The late Gothic altar was in fact the work of Michael Pacher's pupil (see St Wolfgang). Above the altar is a wonderfully delicate tracery of carved wood and ten figures of lace-like delicacy with Christ at their pinnacle. The inner wings of the altar are richly gilded relief work, while the outer sides have Gothic paintings. The lower part of the altar contains holy relics such as St Veronica's handkerchief. The winged altar gave the opportunity for varying the scenes according to church festivals and were a dramatic way of informing the less educated members of the congregation. The great centrepiece depicts the Virgin as queen of heaven, the church of course is consecrated to her, while on the left is St Catherine, patron saint of the woodworkers and on the right, St Barbara, patron of the salt miners; both highly appropriate for the area.

A delightful way of discovering the Hallstättersee is by the Hallstättersee Ostuferweg (the east bank footpath) which runs from Steeg Gosau station to the lakeside resort of Obertraun. This way-marked route uses a specially constructed section of path along the edge of the lake and is quite spectacular in places with beautiful views.

Above the head of the lake beyond Obertraun, the valley narrows to marshland and high crags, only a narrow pass (the Koppental Pass) taking road, river and railway through to Bad Aussee.

But this is an area which has a lot to see in its own right, including the Koppenbrüllerhöhle or cave. From the signed entrance to the cave on the main road, (close to the railway station at Obertraun Koppenbrüller) you walk along a narrow gorge above the river. Remember to wear warm clothing if you wish to visit the cave which is normally 6 °C (43 °F) all year round. What makes the visit particularly interesting and atmospheric, apart from the cave features themselves, are the shadows thrown out by the flickering oil lamps given to visitors (no electric lighting here) as you go through the cave complex. The guide will ask everyone to hold the lamps on the same side to guard against accidents. The name 'brüller' derives from *brüllen*, to roar, as the underground waters of the Dachstein flow through this cave and the pounding water is awe-inspiring to see and hear. There is a highly efficient early warning system in case of flooding from melting ice at certain times of year and excessive rain will also cause the caves to be closed. It takes about 4 hours after a thunderstorm for the water stored in the mountain to pour out of the cave.

This spot was obviously a perfect hiding place for anyone on the run. There is a moving story set in the Koppenbrüllerhöhle of an army deserter, one Franz Engl and his intended bride, Hofer Sef. During the Empress Maria Theresia's reign in the eighteenth century, Franz hid in the cave and his sweetheart looked after him in secret and brought him food for many months. One day, however, she fell seriously ill, but in spite of her condition, she knew that she could not abandon her lover. So she dragged herself in her feverish condition through the Koppenwald and waded barefoot through the river Traun and then somehow forced herself on through the Koppen gorge to the cave. Franz, her lover, was overcome with horror as his dying sweetheart reached him. He made a rough bed for her in his damp cave hideout and as soon as it was dark, he went across to Hallstatt to beg the clergyman to help him.

The clergyman was not very pleased to be called out to such a place at night, especially as it was winter. Eventually he was persuaded, and as day broke, they both reached the cave. Sadly Franz's sweetheart was already dead. Franz, who had deserted the army for Sef's sake, found his world had fallen apart. He had lost the only person who gave a meaning to his life. With nothing more to lose, he gave himself up, was arrested and awaited the death sentence.

The Hallstatt priest, who had meanwhile been deeply affected by these events, wrote to the Empress Maria Theresia begging for a pardon for the young soldier. He described what had happened in such a way that the empress was strongly moved and finally agreed to be merciful to this young man.

Not far away but higher up the mountainside are the Dachstein Caves — the Eishöhlen and Mammuthöhlen. They can both be reached via the Dachsteinseilbahn (cablecar) from Obertraun. The whole area is honeycombed with caves; about 400 have been explored but there are countless more. Visitors to the Ice Caves are carefully monitored and numbers are restricted so book your tour as you arrive at the cave entrance. This is necessary so that the finely balanced climate of the Ice Caves remains undisturbed. Although the caves are thousands of years old, recent tests have discovered via a pollen count that the amazing ice structures are only about 500 years old. Since more ice forms each year especially on the cave floors, it is only the circulation of air that ensures that the caves do not ice up completely from top to bottom. A heavy metal door is used to keep the cave complex at a suitable temperature, but in fact there is no ice in the first part, only stalagmites and stalactites hanging in thick clusters as well as ring shapes and spirals of all descriptions. Bones of prehistoric cave bears have been found here and measurements prove them to have been a third larger than today's brown bears.

The caves are brilliantly lit, with various sections named after such legendary tales as Sir Parsifal and the Holy Grail, (part of the Arthurian sagas). King Arthur's Hall is the deepest point of the caves where the temperature reaches about 0° and the ice begins. Ice palaces, ice waterfalls, a gigantic ice canopy, ice droplets hanging from cave roofs all contribute to the magical effect enhanced by lighting as the ice shimmers in shades of blue and green. The Tristandom has ice up to 30m (98ft) in depth on the ground and in the Grosse Eiskapelle visitors are surrounded by ice of great delicacy like gigantic curtains. The whole complex seems like a set for a magical flying ballet, but the scale is gigantic.

Both sets of caves were formed by limestone and dolomite which allowed surface water from the mountain to trickle deep inside the ground through channels, clefts and fissures of all kinds. The caves were formed over many millenia by the chemical action of water on limestone, eating it away, and also by the power of the water itself which further scored deep channels inside the rock, making galleries and tunnels.

The Mammuthöhle is equally impressive in a quite different way, being the deepest cave in Austria. The entrance is 15 minutes walk from the Schönbergalpe cablecar terminus from Obertraun. You climb a number of steps inside the cave up to the Paläotraun, a huge, gigantic, awe-inspiring tunnel. The mammoth of the name in fact refers to the size and scale of the caves and not to the extinct animals themselves. The Mitternachstdom is 30m (98ft) high and as you clamber on through narrowing channels which suddenly widen out to dramatic cathedral-like expanses, you look upwards from time to time at gigantic boulders poised like some latter-day sword of Damocles above your head, and less alarming perhaps, at fanciful shapes coloured by the red and white rocks, suggesting a lady in rococo costume, an Indian, a beggar and many others.

The Dachstein itself is a mountain for experienced mountaineers — an area of high alpine climbs and mountain walking, including glacier traverses which have claimed many lives. Those that reach the 2,995m (over 9,000ft) summit look across the three states within which the Salzkammergut falls: Upper Austria, Styria and Land Salzburg; the Dachstein is an appropriate and potent symbol of the region.

The position of **Gosau**, in its shallow valley between the glittering peaks of the Gosaukamm and the Dachstein with its glaciers, makes it a very popular area for winter sports and a superb walking area. The small town boasts both a Protestant and Catholic church, though the times of the religious wars have long passed when Protestantism was put down with such ruthlessness that the Protestant community retreated up to some of the Dachstein caves to hold their services in secret and a sight of some of these cathedral-like interiors will indicate that this use is not inappropriate.

The Vorderer Gosausee is reached from the top of the narrow, wooded valley and a short walk from the car and coach/bus park takes you to the unforgettable sight of the Gosaukamm and Dachstein reflected in the Gosausee — a vision of water, stone, ice and forest which seems to be the creation of some matchless landscape painter or photographer. There is a cablecar to the Gablonzer hut on the Gosaukamm for further spectacular views of the Dachstein ranges, but little can compare with the walk along the track past the Vorderer Gosausee and the shallow Gosau Lacke before climbing through the forest to the Hinterer Gosausee; a walk of $1^1/_2$ hours to a quiet translucent lake immediately below the great Dachstein Massif, spellbinding in its beauty.

A little *alm* (farmhouse) at the top of the lake offers traditional food for serious mountaineers and casual strollers alike. There is a massive ceramic stove in the corner and postcards from almost every country in the world are pinned around the walls.

This whole area is a geologist's paradise, rich in fossils such as corals and ammonites. The largest complete ammonite known in the eastern Alps, with a radius of a metre, came from the Gosau area and is now in the Vienna Museum of Natural History. Stone cutting and stone polishing are specialities of the region and can be viewed at the Gapp lapidary.

Friedrich Simony, whose name is recalled in such places as the Simonyhütte, was particularly instrumental in getting the Dachstein better known in earlier days and was really an early environmentalist, founding the Austrian Geographical Society in 1856 and the Austrian Alpenverein (Alpine Club) in 1862, and spreading knowledge of the area by means of drawings, pictures, photos, climbs and scientific research into its lakes and glaciers.

A wooden cross on the Dachstein dating from 1954 is to the memory of three German teachers and ten young teenagers on a school trip who were overtaken by bad weather and lost their lives in a blizzard. A sad warning and reminder that the mountains, like the sea, should always be treated with the utmost respect.

Southern Salzkammergut — Ausseerland

The southern section of the Salzkammergut, usually called Ausseerland after the Altaussee lake, lies entirely within the state of Styria.

This was also a favourite hunting area of Emperor Franz Joseph

I and his entourage. But this fairly constant mingling of the aristocracy with simple forestry workers and salt miners dates from well before this time and seemed to engender a rather special kind of social relationship, allowing the salt or forestry worker to say, for example 'Du, Herr Graf' to his social superior. The word *du* is the familiar personal form of 'you' only used to equals and intimates and *Herr Graf* is the respectful 'my lord.' This quasi aristo-republic, beloved of writers and poets like Nikolas Lenau, Adelbert Stifter, Franz Grillparzer and the great writer and librettist Hugo von Hofmannstahl, (who collaborated with Richard Strauss for example in his operatic masterpiece, *Der Rosenkavalier*), has its own dialect and strongly protected traditional customs. In 1945, after World War II, Bad Aussee wanted to become an independent mini-republic of 5,000 people! In some respects Ausseerland has some of the individuality of West Germany's Bavaria on a minute scale.

Its principal town, **Bad Aussee**, a busy market town and mountain resort, is built at the confluence of the upper branches of the river Traun, geographically in the very centre of Austria in a basin between the Dachstein and the Totes Gebirge, surrounded by numerous lakes. It is easily reached from the central part of the Salzkammergut either by the scenic road which climbs from Bad Goisern over High Pötschen, or from Hallstatt via the Koppenbrüllen Pass.

Bad Aussee became part of the Kammergut in 1542 and was administered by the Kammerhof in the town itself, but its market had actually been founded by Duke Albrecht, son of King Rudolf of Habsburg, in 1290.

It is still a noted spa, specialising in complaints affecting the stomach, liver, gall bladder, rheumatism, diabetes and gynaecological disorders. The healing brine comes straight from the salt mines themselves in the Haselgebirge, directly down to the Kur centre. The action of the brine is claimed to strengthen and tone up the whole body system in a gradual process rather than working directly on specific organs. Treatments vary from a variety of baths and inhalations, to being wrapped completely in *Soleschlamm*, the muddy brine residue which still has a salt content of 10 per cent and which is packed round damaged organs and limbs. The mineral springs with their sulphur content are particularly good for digestive disorders, constipation and liver-related diseases.

Bad Aussee is also associated with the famous romantic love story of the Archduke Johann (1782-1859), brother of Emperor Franz and son of Leopold of Toscana, who fell in love with Anna Plochl, the postmaster's daughter about half his age. The Emperor Franz and his

Chancellor Metternich withheld their consent to the marriage for a number of years, but the couple were finally able to marry in 1829 and Anna was created the Countess of Meran. The archduke also became the idol of the liberal middle class, a Biedermeier Prince. He understood the people, delighted in the beauty of the landscape, (his walks and mountain climbs became legendary) and promoted enlightened education, for example the Johanneum at Graz, an academy for further education which he founded. His demand that the peasants should be armed against Habsburg enemies and his support of the Tyroleans under Andreas Hofer in their freedom fight, all ensured that such enlightened opinions were unlikely to be popular in court and establishment circles. After he was asked to resign from court affairs he made Styria his base, and bought 'Brandhof' in 1818, a property which he oversaw and farmed himself as a model farm. He encouraged the iron and steel industry in Upper Styria and he was associated with many projects relating to the welfare of the region. Anna Plochl's descendants still live in the posthouse, which has a number of art treasures and memorabilia on display.

The village of **Altaussee** by the lake is older than Bad Aussee, but its growth was halted round 1147 as work stopped on the salt mines in the area. It is an interesting town with wooden houses decorated with balconies and outside staircases. The wooden balcony, so frequently seen in the Salzkammergut and often beautifully carved, has an interesting history. Originally it was a high walkway which was constructed outside the house so that crops drying in the rafters could be easily reached. The modern transformation of this into suntrap and showcase for potted plants is something of a misuse, albeit a very delightful one. The old parish church is worth a visit and there is a wonderful view from the lake of the Dachstein range. The setting of lake encircled by mountains is particularly enchanting, and the popular circular walk along well marked paths around the lake has benches every hundred metres or so, making it possible to sit and enjoy the superb views. Rowing boats can be taken out on the lake.

A tour of the ancient saltmines at Altaussee, reached along the Steinberg road some 3km (1³/₄ miles) north-west of the village, is highly recommended. You are provided with colourful protective clothing and a lengthy walk inside the mine itself brings you to an interesting exhibition and museum area, a beautifully lit miners' chapel and the Barbarakapelle with its altar framed in translucent rock salt and fir branches which can last up to a year preserved by the saline levels. Exciting slides take visitors the traditional miners' way down to the various levels and a spectacularly lit brine lake make this a memorable trip.

Another spectacular excursion by car or postbus is to the Loser mountain behind Altaussee. An old toll road — the Mautstrasse — ascends to the Lower Hut at 1,577m (5,173ft), from where it is only a short if steep ascent to the summit of the peak, at 1,838m (6,029ft), a magnificent viewpoint.

Worth visiting too, is the Alpine Garden, some 4km ($2^1/_2$ miles) above Bad Aussee on the Bad Goisern road which has both rare and familiar alpine plants and shrubs on display in a natural setting.

The Ausseerland is also famous for its annual Narzissenfest in late May, now well established, but which only started in 1960 and is centred in Altaussee, Bad Aussee and Grundlsee. The narcissii are wonderfully scented wild narcissii, normally native to central Europe, which grow in their thousands on the slopes in the area and are gathered in vast quantities in order to make the gaily decorated floats which are the focal points of the processions. Up to fifty or sixty floats usually participate and there are also parades with decorated boats on the lake. A light wooden or metal frame is covered with wire mesh and small bunches of narcissii are so placed as to give a very closely woven effect. It is estimated that about 30,000 flowers would be used for one of the larger decorations. These can be anything from miners' lamps and enormous elephants to whole scenes such as a horse and cart fully executed in flowers. Traditionally about fifteen people work on one exhibit through the night so that the finished project is absolutely fresh for the procession, usually held over three days. The parades are further enlivened by music, the choosing of a Narcissus Queen, a regatta and quantities of eating and drinking. Between 20,000 to 30,000 visitors generally attend.

A much older custom which obviously has its origins in old fertility rites is the Strohschab. The original meaning of the word was a bushel or bundle of straw, which looked roughly like the shape of a man as it was dried on a support after the harvest in the fields. This in turn became the straw-clad figure with large horns, wielding a long whip which with others similarly dressed, cracks out a distinct rhythm. The traditional time of year is the feast of St Nicholas in early December. A similar custom in the Upper Austrian flatlands is called 'Appa-Schnalzen' which drives out evil winter spirits. At Fasching (early February), the Trommelweiber in Bad Aussee are men dressed as old countrywomen wearing masks, who carry drums warning of their approach.

The 'Flinserl' of Aussee are another local tradition for Fasching. They are figures dressed in costumes glittering with hundreds of

Altaussee

gold and silver sequins, pointed hats trimmed with gold foil and their faces hidden by Venetian style face masks. Their name suggests the constant winking and brightness. As they pass, the onlookers call out 'Nuss, Nuss' and not only nuts, but also oranges and apples are thrown to the children standing by.

The great Austrian composer Gustav Mahler, a frequent summer visitor to the Salzkammergut, found the constant rehearsals of the local salt miners' brass band so distracting to his musical composition when he stayed in the Ausserland, that he solved the problem by incorporating the music into his Fourth Symphony with remarkable results. Artur Schnitzler, the famous Viennese playwright, was also a regular visitor to Altaussee, as was the celebrated founding father of psychology, Sigmund Freud who spent his early summers in a simple farmhouse. The museum in the Kurhaus in Altaussee has a splendid literature section with writings and memorabilia of the many writers and seminal figures of European culture who stayed in the area.

Archduke Johann's statue is in the Kurpark at **Grundlsee** and in the centre of the town is the Plague Column, reconstructed in 1876, a reminder of the terrible scourge of earlier days. The Kammerhof, formerly the palace of the Superintendent of the Salt Mines, was given splendid window-frames of red Salzburg marble in the seventeenth century. The Hofer House, the sixteenth-century home of the

Director of the Mines, has contemporary frescoes of Samson and Deliah and a hunting scene, while outside are frescoes depicting Saints Sebastian, Florian and Anne.

Grundlsee, a mere 4km (2¹/₂ miles) from Bad Aussee by car or postbus, is another delightful lake enjoying a dramatic backcloth of the Totes Gebirge mountains. An excursion which is particularly recommended is to walk along the lakeside path along the wooded south bank or to take the boat trip to Gössl at the head of the lake where after a short walk and ascent you reach the exquisitely beautiful Toplitz See, fabled site of Nazi sunken treasure. A motorised gondola takes you to the head of this lake and then a short ascent of steps through woods brings you to the tiny Kammersee and the waterfall which forms the source of the river Traun as it trickles down a cliff face. This is a magical place full of atmosphere.

South-east of Bad Aussee the main road into Styria follows a tributary of the Traun known as the Kainisch Traun. A minor road from Ausseer Kainish, as the next village is known, climbs up to the Ödensee, one of the lesser known of the smaller lakes but an extremely attractive one, which has a bathing area and a path around its banks.

Bad Mitterndorf lies just across the main watershed on the Styrian edge of the Salzkammergut. Known for its healing mineral springs by the Romans, Mitterndorf has only developed to any considerable degree as a spa from the early 1960s. It was officially allowed to add the word 'Bad' to its name in 1971 and became known for its mineral springs, healing mud and healthy air.

What is particularly interesting about this pretty spa town is the fact that it so nearly fell a prey to the less desirable effects of mass tourism, but stopped just in time. Between 1968-72 a large number of holiday and second homes were built, usually by German developers. Two large pyramid-style buildings which overlook the town, somewhat dwarfing the fourteenth-century church, were then added. At this point a political party unique to Bad Mitterndorf arose in 1975, called 'Gesunder Lebensraum', (The Party for a Healthy Environment). All this helped to bring about the passing of a strict new law which made the sale of land to foreign nationals illegal in Austria, and a development plan carefully restricting any further buildings and use of land for development, was set up by the Styrian regional government.

Western Salzkammergut — Wolfgangsee, Mondsee and Attersee

Most of the western part of the Salzkammergut lies within Land Salzburg and its proximity to the major tourist centre of Salzburg makes it very much better known than other parts of the Salzkammergut.

The Fuschlsee is the first of the Salzkammergut lakes seen by people on the main trunk road to Ischl coming out of Salzburg — a pleasant if unspectacular lake popular for watersports and bathing which probably owes its popularity more to its proximity to Salzburg than to any inherent qualities.

St Gilgen, on the eastern edge of Wolfgangsee also benefits from a Mozart connection, being the birthplace of his mother Anna Pertl and the spot where his sister Nannerl lived for a time. The Mozart House Museum and the parish church, founded in 1376 and renovated in the rococo style, are well worth seeing, though much of the town around the lakeshore has been spoiled by commercialisation. A trip on the cablecar to the Zwölferhorn (1,522m, 4,992ft) is one way to escape the crowds, with the particularly steep ascent up a vertiginous cliff face rewarded by panoramic views.

The lakeside road from St Gilgen passes through **Strobl**, a scattered community and lakeside resort and site of the former station on the much lamented Ischlerbahn, the narrow gauge railway between Salzburg and Ischl, a surviving locomotive of which you'll find by the roadside on the way into Ischl. It is here that buses from Salzburg, St Wolfgang and Bad Ischl interchange with an accuracy of timing and convenience to make British users of rural transport green with envy. There are also superb high-level walks from Strobl itself via the Schwarzensee to the Mondsee and Attersee.

Southwards from Strobl a narrow road, served by regular postbus, ascends a series of spectacular hairpin bends to **Postalm**, a combination of winter ski resort and summer ramblers' paradise high in the mountains with a choice of waymarked paths to nearby peaks.

Strobl is also the junction for the road to **St Wolfgang** whose White Horse Inn (Weisses Rössl) is the hostelry, now much renovated, which gave its name to a highly popular operetta of the same name by Ralph Benatsky and Robert Stolz. Even though this has caused tourists to flock in some numbers, it has to be conceded that the little town itself is very charming and if you can put up with the coach parties for one day at least (and even Hallstatt is overrun in the summer months), there are things which are just too good to be missed if you are in the area.

High on any such list is the fifteenth-century pilgrimage church dedicated to St Wolfgang of Regensburg (see Mondsee section), who gave his name to both town and lake, which has a magnificent altar by Michael Pacher which took 10 years to complete in 1481. This masterpiece of late Gothic art is 6.5m (21ft) wide when its winged sections are fully expanded and 11m (36ft) in height. But it is the quality of the painting and carving which is so breathtaking. When the altar is open, the focal point is the carving in gold and silver of the Virgin Mary's coronation, flanked by angels with St Wolfgang as the patron holding a model of the church and St Benedict as the founder of the order looking on. High above is a crucified Christ on slender carved pillars while at the apex sits God himself. Beneath the main altarpiece is the shrine with the *Adoration of the Three Kings*, while the sixteen painted panels depict various scenes from the life of Christ. Almost as amazing as the masterpiece itself is the story of the journey of the altar from South Tyrol over the Brenner Pass in carts, boats and rafts to the church itself. Not surprisingly, some time had to be spent in minor repairs and retouching after such a journey. A superb altar in the baroque style by Thomas Schwanthaler (see Gmunden) from 1676 is also well worth seeing. When the rage for renovation took over in the baroque era, it was Schwanthaler who defied the church authorities and insisted on placing his altar elsewhere in the church so that Pacher's masterpiece would remain intact.

The quickest way to escape the coach parties, is to walk the ancient Pilgrim's Way via the Falkenstein in the St Gilgen direction. This is a lovely wooded path, clearly marked both by arrows and a series of lovely little painted shrines. At the summit by the Falkenstein rock is a little shelter and shrine which shows scenes from St Wolfgang's life. One of the legends tells how Wolfgang outwitted the devil who attempted to throw him from a high cliff. As his fame spread, he was given the bishopric in 972 by Emperor Otto II. But St Wolfgang found that city life interfered with his desire for peace and meditation and decided to go to the Salzkammergut with a single companion. As he looked round for water one day to quench his thirst, he found a healing spring in the forest and decided to stay there alone. He sent back his companion and became a hermit, later founding the town and church of St Wolfgang (the lake now takes its name from the saint; it was formerly known as the Abersee).

Just before you reach the shrine a steep path with an extended ladder walk takes you to the Scheffelblick, a viewpoint where there is a superb view across the entire Wolfgangsee.

As you descend from the shrine in the St Gilgen direction, you will find a small forest chapel built into the rock by a holy spring with a bell rope inviting you to pull the bell three times and wish — you will probably hear its sounds before you arrive. If you continue downhill to the lakeside to Fürberg you can catch a lake steamer back to St Wolfgang which will sail past the picturesque and characteristic lakeside crosses by the water's edge — the Ochsenkreuz and the Hochzeitkreuz, the latter erected to commemorate the wedding of a seventeenth-century nobleman. Another alternative is to continue by lakeside path and lane into St Gilgen, there to pick up the ferry.

The other pleasure awaiting anyone with a love of mountains and steam railways at St Wolfgang is a trip on the Schafbergbahn which takes you to the summit of the Schafberg mountain (1,782m, 5,845ft) by vintage steam-powered rack railway and gives you wonderful views of the lake and surrounding mountains and a choice of mountain walks. This trip is strongly recommended, but make sure that there are no mists on the tops. There can also be long queues at the stations at busy times.

Mondsee

The crescent shaped Mondsee lake lies at the foot of the aptly named Drachenwand cliffs (literally Dragon's Wall) and the Schafberg mountain, and is one of the warmest lakes in the Salzkammergut, temperatures reaching up to 27°C (81°F) in summer. It is also one of the larger Salzkammergut lakes, 68m (223ft) in depth and 11km (7 miles) in length. From the lakeside, it is a pleasant walk or short drive of about 700m (763yd) to the market town of Mondsee through a beautiful avenue of lime trees.

Regular steamers serve the lake and there is a good choice of walks into the surrounding hills particularly once you have crossed to the north of the motorway.

Geologically, the formation of the lake follows the regular Salzkammergut pattern. During the Ice Age, as the mountains thrust themselves upwards, the valley sank through a section of the Traun glacier. The moraines (the debris left in the wake of those earth movements) caused a dam to form at the foot of the glacier at the end of the Ice Age which then melted and formed a lake similar to a number of others in the region.

Theories abound as to the origin of the name Mondsee which has changed over the centuries from Maense, Meinse, Maninse, Moninse, Moensee, Mannsee, and Mansee to the present spelling. It has been suggested that this was originally Mano's lake, the Mano being a Germanic tribe, or perhaps it was named after one individual. More simply, since the moon goddess was such a potent deity from ancient times, Moon Lake becomes an obvious homage to its shape and the goddess. Finally there is a charming legend related about the Bavarian Duke Odilo who was out hunting in the region as darkness fell. The rising of the full moon opportunely saved him and his entourage from plunging into the lake and almost certain death. In gratitude, he vowed to build a monastery on its shores, known as Mondsee monastery, a foundation which duly arose in 748 and in spite of many changes can still be seen.

Mondsee's history stretches back, however, to far earlier times and is nearly as famous as that of Hallstatt, giving its name to a culture. For it is in the Mondsee area, in the lake itself, that wonderful archaeological finds have been made; remains of neolithic settlements and a rich treasure trove of artefacts of pottery, and bone and stone tools and utensils. Much can be seen in the excellent local museum about the life of these neolithic peoples who lived in the Mondsee area by the lake around 2800-1800BC and gave their name to an epoch which covered the major part of Upper Austria and parts of Salzburg. Most recent research has indicated that the settlements were probably not built out over the lake on stilts as first thought, but were on land near the shore which became submerged as the lake's water level rose.

In contrast there remains little of the cultures which followed, the Bronze and Iron Ages, but rather more evidence has survived of the ancient Romans who colonised the site in their turn and built a road to *Iuvavum*, the Roman name for what is now Salzburg.

But it is with the arrival of Christianity and the founding of Duke Odilo's Mondsee monastery previously mentioned, that Mondsee increasingly becomes a focus of religious and spiritual activity. It is now thought that Mondsee's monks came not from Monte Cassino as originally claimed, but from the old Bavarian monasteries such as St Peter's in Salzburg and that there were highly beneficial exchanges between scholars for a considerable period. Mondsee then came under the imperial control of the Bavarian Duke Tassilo III in 788; the Book of Psalms or Tassilo Pasalter was an early gem of its famous School of Calligraphy and Manuscript Illumination and is the oldest completely preserved book in Austria. Shortly after 800, the 'Mondsee Matthaeus', the oldest German language translation of the Bible, was also produced here, though the original is now in the National Library in Vienna. Mondsee's School of Calligraphy and

Illuminated Manuscripts reached a new high point under Brother Luithold and his twelfth-century version of the Gospel, and the Benedictine monastery continued to grow in influence over the centuries.

From the ninth to the twelfth centuries Mondsee came under the jurisdiction of the Bishops of Regensburg and Wolfgang, as Bishop Wolfgang whose original *see* was Regensburg, had fled from the military disturbances in Regensburg and took up residence for a year at Mondsee; not surprising when one thinks of its religious importance at the time. Wolfgang then went on to found a church on the Abersee which later became known as the Wolfgangsee as his fame spread and the church of St Wolfgang as it later became known, increasingly became a place of pilgrimage. Mondsee monastery was to draw much of its revenue from the Wolfgang area and was to instruct Michael Pacher to design and carry out his masterpiece, the St Wolfgang altar which, of course, is one of the jewels of the Salzkammergut.

The town is characterised by a charming market square, flower bedecked with wrought-iron shop signs and balconies, and houses with rococo and baroque façades. As you perhaps take some refreshment at a pavement café, do consider that this very attractive scene was not always so. At the time of the peasant wars, two peasants were hanged in the market place and many others exiled over the Turkish border. In 1774 a huge fire in the market place swept through the town, destroying many of its medieval buildings and much more.

Today the pale yellow baroque façade of the parish church conceals what was the Benedictine monastery church till 1791 and still has very important elements of Gothic architecture. A large Roman church of 1104 originally stood on the site as part of a larger Roman settlement and other earlier churches undoubtedly occupied the site as well. The great baroque sculptor Meinrad Guggenbichler is responsible for five altars within the church, his *Corpus Christi* in the north nave is reckoned to be one of his masterpieces, while the pillar ringed by *chubby putti* (child angels) entwined with vines prove an irresistible magnet to photographers. Guggenbichler worked for 47 years in the Mondsee area and many examples of his work can be seen in various churches in the region. His final work of *St Sebastian* has a series of strikingly moving figures while the carving of the chancel and even the carving of the prayer stools from his workshop are testaments to his craftmanship. He is also credited as being one of the first of the local baroque artists to suggest the sense of move-

Pisweg, near Gurk, southern Carinthia

Maria Saal's Gothic church, one of the best preserved in Carinthia

ment so dramatically in his figures. Baroque, in sharp contrast to the Gothic style, suggests drama, excitement and a real sense of theatre which the play of light, the use of rich colours such as gold to highlight, and the suffering depicted on the faces of the grieving figures and agonised saints, all contribute to the effect.

The Heimatmuseum is housed in the former Benedictine chapel in Mondsee and has remains of thirteenth-century frescoes of the *Annunciation* as well as painted furniture and utensils and archaeological remains and displays.

In 1959, in order to make way for the extension of the motorway between Vienna and Salzburg above Mondsee, the old Rauchhaus or Smoke House of 1416 was moved to a nearby open-air museum, the Freilichtmuseum. The name of the old farmhouse building comes from the smoke from the open fire which rose to the high vaulted ceiling above, without chimney flue, and dried the grain at attic level, inconveniencing the inhabitants, it is said, relatively little. In addition to the farmhouse utensils and implements on display, are other outbuildings for drying fruit, a grain store, a flax drying room and an old grinding mill. Not far from Mondsee an excursion to the Kolomans mountain enables one also to see the last completely preserved wooden church in Austria.

Near the lake a steam locomotive built in 1893 for the Ischlerbahn local railway has an interesting history. It was used to pull the last train from Bad Ischl to Mondsee in 1957 when the line closed against strong local opposition, and it was also used during World War I in Bosnia and returned in 1920. An early dug-out canoe of the type used by those early neolithic peoples is also displayed nearby.

The Attersee

The Attersee, immediately to the east of Mondsee, is the largest and most northerly of the Salzkammergut lakes with an area of approximately 50sq km and a depth of 170m (558ft) and is the only Salzkammergut lake which doesn't freeze in winter. Its sparkling clear water is of the same standard as drinking water and the lake is particularly notable for its many bathing places and lidos, both public and private, where the water can reach a temperature of up to 22 or 23 °C (72 or 73 °F). Access to the lakeside is possible at many points since most of the lake has little in the way of built up areas round it, and there is an excellent boat service which, because of the size of lake, operates to timetables in both the clockwise and anticlockwise directions, linking with trains at Schörfling and the tram from Vöcklamarkt at Attersee. There is also a good motor road around the shores of the lake and direct, though less frequent, postbus services from both Bad Ischl and Gmunden, both enjoying with the motorist superbly scenic roads from the Traun valley across forest passes.

The Attersee and its surrounding landscape was painted many times by Gustav Klimt (1862-1918), the Vienna Secession (Art Nouveau) painter who was clearly enchanted by the reflection of the mountains in its clear waters. Some of Klimt's Attersee paintings are to be seen in major galleries in Vienna and Salzburg.

The Attersee, like so much of the Salzkammergut, has a long history and was the site of a great lake dwelling culture similar to the Mondsee Culture 4,000 years ago. Numerous archaeological finds are displayed in the Heimathaus at Vöcklabruck and give a very good impression of the lifestyle of those neolithic peoples. There are also remains of Bronze and Iron Age eras which were followed by 500 years of Roman rule which gave way to that of the Bavarians. In 885 the Carolingian palace of Aterhofa was erected on a slope above the town and later expanded to a mighty medieval castle. The three churches of Attersee town are all worth a visit, the parish and pilgrimage church of Maria Attersee was originally Gothic and still has a statue of the period on the high altar, plus additional statues of St Peter and St Stephen and a relief of the Three Kings from those earlier times. In the eighteenth century it was renovated and refurbished in the baroque style. The Protestant parish church, the old Martinuskirche at the foot of the Kirchberg, was rebuilt in the late fifteenth century and it has nineteenth-century additions in the shape of a neo-Gothic altar and chancel. The late Gothic Laurentinuskirche at Abtsdorf has the high altar, side altars and chancel by the famous Mondsee artist Meinrad Guggenbichler.

Seewalchen is the largest settlement on the north shore and apart from its beautiful clear water there is an abundance of fresh fish such as trout and Reinanke. At Kammer there is also a *Seeschloss*, a lake château. To the west of the lake there are farms, woodlands and fields, which at the southern extremity at Unterach overlooks the Höllengebirge and the Alps. If you look down from the heights at the villages below, it looks as if someone had shaken the houses and churches out of their pocket onto the hilly landscape.

Steinbach has a strong connection with the great composer and conductor Gustav Mahler who spent several summers here away from the stresses and intrigues of the Viennese musical world and composed some of his great symphonic work here, notably the Third or Steinbacher Symphony which is so richly evocative of the countryside and of nature itself. It is still possible to visit the little house where he stayed whilst working on the masterpiece. From Steinbach the Wildpark of Hochkreut at 1,000m (3,280ft) has a splendid view of the Salzkammergut between the Traunsee and Attersee. The park had originally been a hunting area, it now incorporates deer, stags, wild horses, eagles and many more alpine fauna. There is little atmosphere of a zoo as the animals appear to roam freely and there is a great choice of routes and walks.

Seewalchen, Nussdorf, Steinbach, Unterach and the other lake resorts are all well provided with good facilities for bathing, rowing and sailing, with electric boats, wind surfing, water skiing, fishing and all the usual sporting facilities. For the less active there are trips on the lake by steamer, *Heimatabende* (folk evenings), lakeside festivals with fireworks, music and dancing. But there is also some excellent walking which can be a gentle amble through all gradations to the fairly strenuous, depending on experience and mood; most notably the waymarked Attersee West Weg, a superb waymarked route through forest and farmland which winds its way along the western side of the lake from Unterach to Seewalchen at the head of the lake.

There is an additional thrill for anyone interested in vintage transport in the form of the Attersee tramway or *Lokalbahn* which is operated by old narrow-gauge electric tramcars of turn-of-the-century vintage which rock their way gently through the fields of deepest rural Austria between Attersee town and the main line station at Vöcklamarkt via St Georgen. Festive occasions with the oldest tramcars in service are arranged, when you can actually drive one of the old tramcars, enjoy a meal on board, even hire a whole train. Or you can simply enjoy a regular trip on any day of the week on this 'old-timer' form of transport.

Weyregg on the east side of the lake is also identified with the New Stone Age dwellings of the Lake Culture, followed by the ancient Celts and then the Romans who built their luxury villas here and obviously enjoyed the facilities of pure air and warm Attersee lake water.

Further Information
— The Salzkammergut —

Places of Interest in the Area

Altaussee
Salt mine
Open: mid-May to mid-September,
Monday-Friday 10am-4pm. Closed
Sundays and public holidays.

Museum of Literature
Open: May to October, Monday-
Saturday 10am-12noon.

Altmünster
Wild Life Reserve Hochkreut
Open: April through October.

Attersee
Parish and pilgrimage church
Maria Attersee
Open: all year round.

Bad Aussee
Tourist information and local
history museum
Open: April to end October every
day 10am-12noon, plus every 2nd
and 4th Sunday in month.

Alpine Garden and educational
trail
Open: April through October
8am-6pm.

Bad Goisern
Local history museum
Open: June to mid-September
9.30-11.30am.

Woodcutters' Museum
Open: June to mid-September
9.30-11.30am.

Bad Ischl
Kaiserpark
Open: all year round.

Kaiservilla
Open: Easter, and May to mid-
October daily 9am-12noon, also
1-5pm till end October.

Lehar Villa
Open: Easter, and May to end
September daily 9am-12noon and
2-5pm.

Museum of Photography
Open: April to end October daily
9.30am-5.30pm.

Hotel Austria
Esplanade
Year round exhibitions.

Salt Mine
Open: mid-May to mid-September
Monday-Saturday 9.30am-4pm.

Cable railway
The Katrin
Open: all year round.

Bad Mitterndorf
Local History Museum 'Strick'
Open: all year round.

Ebensee
Limestone Cave, Gassl
Open: May to end August, Saturday, Sunday and public holidays
9am-4pm.

Local History Museum
Open: July to end August, Monday-Saturday 2-6pm, Sunday
8.30-11.30am.

Lead Crystal Works
Open: all year round, Monday-
Friday 8am-12noon and 3-6pm,
closed Wednesday afternoon.

Traun Crystal Works
Open: all year round, Monday-
Thursday 7am-12noon and
1-4.30pm, Friday 7am-1pm.

Gmunden
Schloss Ort
Open: all year round.

Seeschloss Ort
Open: all year round.

Parish Church
Open: all year round.
Altar by Schwanthaler.

Ceramic Carillon
Town Hall
Open: April through October.
Chimes at 9am, 12noon, 1pm, 4pm
and 7pm.

Kammerhof Museum
Open: March to late October,
Tuesday-Saturday 10am-12noon
and 2-5pm, Sunday 10am-12noon.

Villa Toscana and Toscana Park
Open: all year round.

Ceramics of Gmunden
Open: all year round, Monday-
Friday 8am-6pm, Saturday
8-11.30am.

Pessendorfer Ceramics
Open: all year round, Monday-
Friday 8am-12noon and 2-6pm,
Saturday 8am-1pm.

Gosau
Lapidary G. Gapp
Fossils and semi-precious stones
exhibition.
Open: all year round except Sun-
day, spring through to autumn.

Grünau
Children's pleasureground,

Schindbach/Fairytale Forest.
Open: early June to early September daily 10am-6pm; April, May,
September: Saturday, Sunday and
public holidays.

Grundlsee
Parish church
Open: all year round.

Hallstatt
Prehistoric and local history
museum
Open: April and October daily
10am-4pm; May to September,
9.30am-6pm.

Salt mines
Open: May, mid-September to
mid-October daily 9.30am-3pm;
June to mid September daily
9.30am-4.30pm.

Salt mine cable railway
Open: May, mid-September to
mid-October daily 9am-4.30pm;
June to mid-September daily
9am-6pm, funicular included.

Mondsee
Museum of Lake Dwellings
(neolithic)
Open: May to early September
daily 9am-6pm; August to end
September, Sunday and public
holidays 9am-5pm.

Smoke House, Mondsee
(Rauchhaus)
Open: April and mid to end September, Saturday, Sunday and
public holidays 9am-5pm; May to
end August daily 8am-6pm.

Obertraun
Dachstein Giant Ice Caves
Open: May to mid-September,

daily 9.30am-5pm.

Dachstein Mammoth Caves
Open: May to mid-September daily
9.30am-5pm.

Koppenbrüller Cave
Open: May to end September daily
9.30am-5pm.

St Wolfgang
Parish church with altars by
Pacher, Guggenbichler, Schwanthaler.
Open: May to end October, daily
9am-6pm; November to end April
daily 9am-4pm.

Schafberg railway
Open: early May to early
September.

Steinbach/Attersee
House where Gustav Mahler
composed.
Open: all year round.

Burggrabenklamm (romantic
ravine); Gasthof Fottinger

Traunkirchen
Parish church, fisherman's pulpit.
Open: all year round.

Tourist Information Offices

**Salzkammergut-Verkerhrsver-
band**
A-4820 Bad Ischl, Kreuzplatz 23
☎ (06132) 6909

Altaussee
☎ (06152) 71643

Attersee
☎ (07666) 219

Bad Aussee
☎ (06152) 2323

Gmunden
☎ (97612) 4305

Grünau
☎ (07616) 8268

Hallstatt
☎ (06134) 208

Mondsee
☎ (06232) 2270

St Wolfgang
☎ (06138) 2239

Travelling to the Area

By Air
Flights to Salzburg, then local bus,
train or taxi into the Salzkammergut.

By Rail
The Salzkammergut is served by
the Salzkammergut railway which
runs from Attnang Puchheim on
the Salzburg-Vienna Railway to
Gmunden, Bad Ischl, Bad Aussee
and Bad Mitterndorf, with connecting postbus links to St Wolfgang
and Mondsee. A regional railcard
(*Landnetzkarte*) is available on local
trains including the Schafbergbahn
mountain railway and
Wolfgangsee boats (St Wolfgang).

By Road
The main Vienna-Linz-Salzburg
Motorway the E55 cuts across the
northern edge of the Salzkammer-
gut, linking with major roads to
Gmunden, Bad Ischl and Bad
Aussee. There is a direct road from
Salzburg to Bad Ischl.

11 • Lower Austria: The Danube from the Traisen to the Enns

This 'region' is rather a mixture and is perhaps best observed as a 'taster' for a number of smaller Austrian regions — the Wachau for example, famous for its wines, the Mührlviertel with its woods and rolling hills, or the forests of the Waldviertel. Both extend from the north of the Danube to the Czech border.

The area is approximately that of Ostmark ('Eastern March'). It is the oldest established region of Austria, historically bounded by the rivers Enns and Traisen. It does not exist as a region today, being part of Austria's largest province — Nieder Osterreich or 'Lower Austria'. Back in the tenth century, however, it was the main defence region for Bavaria after the defeat of the Hungarians by Otto The Great in 955. The 'Ostarrichi Document' dating from 996 — the first written reference to Austria — can be seen at Neuhofen, near Ybbs.

Before this, Ostmark had already existed in various forms, with the Romans and the Huns in battle for control up to the fifth century and then the Habsburgs, who used the area for defence against Bohemian and Hungarian invasion. Prior to Otto the Great's retaking of Ostmark however, the region had been largely lost to Hungarian invasion.

Near the end of the tenth century Ostmark became an independent hereditary duchy under the Babenbergs who used it as the central point for their expansion into virtually all of what is now called Austria, with the exception of Salzburg, Carinthia and the Tyrol. However, the area will not be referred to as Ostmark, as Hitler was fond of using that name, and the people here would rather forget it on his account.

The tour begins in Krems, which is really the largest settlement for

nearly 85 miles on the banks of the Danube. The next 'large' settlement is in fact Linz. If you take the train on the north side of the river
the journey takes nearly 6 hours, although it doesn't seem to go too
slowly. The train also follows the banks of the river and stops at most
of the villages and so is quite a good way to travel.

Krems is the district capital and regarded by some as the capital
of Lower Austria, though this title has been officially given to St
Pölten. It stands on the junction of the river that bears its name and
the Danube; it is also the oldest town in Lower Austria, first recorded
in AD995.

Once you pass through the Steiner Tor, or gate (walking eastwards) you are on the main shopping street, the pedestrianised
Landstrasse which is a very attractive area, lined with fine baroque
and Renaissance houses, all well cared for. A few hundred yards
along here will soon take you to the Spitalkirche, a late Gothic
building on the right of the street. You might also be impressed by the
designer telephone boxes nearby!

Opposite is the sixteenth-century Rathaus, which contains an
excellent Renaissance oriel of 1548. Following this side street two
churches come into view. The nearer and larger is the parish church
of St Veit; built between 1616 and 1630 it is one of the earliest baroque
churches in Austria. It is also a very large building but opinion is
divided as to the quality of the vast ceiling paintings by Kremser-
Schmidt. The gilded statues, pulpit and altar were produced by J.M.
Gotz.

The former Dominican church is reached by taking the second
left, about 46m (50yd) after coming through the Steiner gate. This
building dates from the thirteenth century and contains elements of
both Romanesque and Gothic. It was restored in the late 1960s and
now houses the town's museum with antiques, folk art, coins and
sculptures. There is also a wine museum showing the development
of the industry in the region. Not only this, but within the building
there is still space for a small theatre where concerts are sometimes
performed.

There is certainly a lot to see in Krems and there is also a very well
developed leisure area down by the river, with camping and a
motorboat harbour as well. The park area includes a large outdoor
pool complex with diving pools, tennis, minigolf and sports ground.

The Wachau region is Austria's most famous wine producing
area. The region is characterised by quite steep, rocky terraced hillsides to the north of the Danube, reaching up to 496m (1,600ft).
Everywhere there are vines, especially in the heart of the region. The

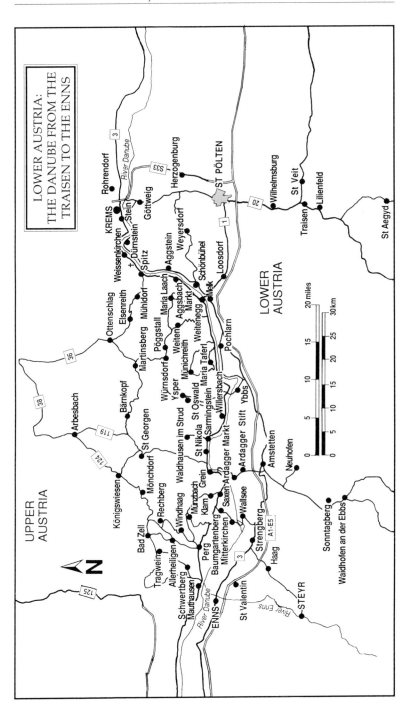

LOWER AUSTRIA:
THE DANUBE FROM THE
TRAISEN TO THE ENNS

Wachau traditionally begins in the east at Krems. In fact it begins at
Rohrendorf just before Krems if you are coming from Vienna, a
famed wine producing village (for at least the past millenium) and
home of vine-growing pioneer Dr Lenz Moser. He pioneered a
method of growing vines to twice their normal height along wires
and in so doing produced a better quality of wine and more of it, with
lower labour costs. His wines are renowned in expert circles and his
methods have been copied all over the world. Rohrendorf is known
locally as the gate of the Wachau and has good sporting facilities for
visitors, including an indoor riding arena.

The main wine is the Gruner Veltliner, also known as 'Schluck',
which is grown with skill and efficiency, largely by the 3,000 grower
members of the region's co-operative based at Durnstein.

Apart from wine, you may well find cyclists omnipresent in the
summer months. There are cycle tracks along stretches of the Danube
and cycling holidays are very popular and well organised along the
length of the river covered in this section.

You do not have to leave Krems to reach Stein, as the two are
joined through an interesting tunnel in the Steiner tower, built in
1480. Stein is very much a riverside town and its three squares
overlook the Danube. There are three interesting churches, one of
which, the Minoriten, houses a museum to local painter Martin
Johann Schmidt, alias Kremser-Schmidt. He lived from 1718 to 1801
and is responsible for numerous altar pieces in Upper and Lower
Austria, being perhaps the most prolific baroque artist. They are not,
however, always highly regarded by critics.

Dürnstein is a treasure worth hunting, though it is not very hard
to find, being the first major stop after Krems. Keeping north of the
river, it appears after a steep northern bend in the Danube. No road
signs are needed to identify it: the town walls are virtually complete,
the streets are narrow and medieval with the cast iron signs of shops
and taverns overhanging them. Such is the tiny town's attraction, it
has drawn tourists through the centuries. Great painters such as
Matthaus, Merian, Rudolf von Alt and Max von Suppantschitsch
painted here.

Rising above the town are wine terraces, sandwiched between
rugged and rocky hillsides and dating back to Roman times. The
famous crisp white wines from here and neighbouring Loiben are
noted for their character and light bouquet. A Dürnstein wine was
served when the state treaty was signed in 1955, re-establishing
Austrian independence. Local inns or *heurigen* serving the current
year's wine may still advertise the fact in the time honoured manner

Dürnstein

— by hanging a bit of fresh greenery above their door. The wines also complement the townspeople's enthusiasm for traditional cuisine. There are few places where you might have such good food and drink, in such beautiful surroundings, with good company.

The terraces are crowned by Kuenringer castle, ruined since 1645, and adding a romantic tale to this already architecturally romantic town. Richard the Lionheart was imprisoned here by Leopold the Fifth of Babenberg, the Duke of Austria, on 22 December 1192. Richard had managed to make himself unpopular with the duke by removing the former's flag from a tower captured in the Seige of Acre in Palestine. En route back from the crusade Richard was ship-wrecked in the Adriatic and headed home through Austria. He travelled disguised as a pauper but obviously wasn't very good at maintaining his disguise and was spotted and caught.

It was several months before Richard was discovered, suppos-edly by his minstrel, Blondell, who was forlornly wandering around Austrian castles singing his majesty's favourite songs, and just happened to walk past Kuenringer (which can't have been too easy given its situation). Given the number of castles he did jolly well to find it so fast. There was no dramatic rescue, just a ransom of 150,000

silver marks eventually paid after thirteen months of captivity. This
turned out to be rather a waste of British taxpayers money as the king
was handed over to Emperor Henry VI who also had it in for poor old
Richard and kept him locked up in Trifels castle in what is now
Germany for a further year before another huge ransom was paid.
Rumour has it that a part of the first ransom was used to build the
walls round the towns of Enns, further up the Danube. But the former
residents of Kuenringer don't seem too popular in Dürnstein today,
where they are referred to as 'The Robber Barons of the Wachau.' The
Pope excommunicated the Babenburg duke for molesting a cru-
sader. Those who make the trek up to the castle will be rewarded by
spectacular views across the valley.

Virtually every building in the town is of architectural interest.
One of these, the Chorherrenstift, is a former Augustinian monastery, founded in the fifteenth century and rebuilt in the eighteenth.
Its church (now the parish church) contains works by baroque
masters such as Prandtauer and Kremser Schmidt. It was designed
by Munggenast and Steindl and its tower is considered one of Austria's most beautiful. The interior too is stunning, with fabulous
stucco reliefs on the ceiling and gilt-laden ornamentation all round.

Apart from historic and romantic interest the town has some good
sports facilities including a large and pleasantly situated outdoor
swimming pool in a nice grassy park, minigolf, bicycle rental, fishing
on the Danube and tennis. A large pleasure boat travels from beneath
the town to Rossatz. It is also possible to take a boat from or to Passau,
Linz or Vienna.

Despite all the attractions of Dürnstein it is worth continuing
round the long westerly bend in the Danube for 8km (5 miles) or so.
The riverside road requires careful driving, but you are again rewarded, this time with the Wachau's largest wine producing munici-
pality of Weissenkirchen, along with its neighbouring villages of
Joching, Wosendorf (baroque church) and St Michael (where the
richly decorated fortified Gothic church is well worth a visit), further
west along the road. The place is of a similar age to Dürnstein with
fifteenth-century buildings. There are many attractive courtyards
and narrow streets. Above the village there are orchards and the
climbing wine terraces which are characteristic along the valley.

Weissenkirchen's most remarkable building is probably the
Renaissance 'Teisenhoferhof' house, dating to the mid-sixteenth
century and now housing the Wachau museum which contains
paintings by local artists.

The church is early sixteenth century but was modernised in the baroque period, though some older artifacts remain. It has interesting architectural features dating back to when it was fully surrounded by battlements.

Today Weissenkirchen offers a good range of holiday facilities including walking paths through the vineyards, bicycle hire and tennis. There is also a delightful promenade by the river.

The river flows north-east from here, and still travelling upstream arrives at **Spitz**, a slightly larger town than the others on this side of the river, but just as old. It first appears in official documents in AD865. Of course it's a wine producing town, with the vineyards almost encroaching onto the central streets. The hill above is aptly nicknamed 'Thousand Buckets Mountain', its official title being the Tausendeimerberg.

The village church, St Maurice, is fifteenth-century Gothic and has a rather unusual design containing three aisles with the choir at an angle to the nave. It also contains some beautiful carvings of Christ and the apostles and is reached by a charming street through the village centre. In common with many of the churches in the area from this period, it contains a painting by Kremser Schmidt. Another interesting building, the Erlahof, is a former monastery farm and houses a shipping museum which has an extremely interesting collection of Danube artifacts, well presented. Five hundred yards to the south-west of the village on a wooded hill there are the Hinterhaus castle ruins.

In more recent times the village has become a traditional health resort and offers paddle boats or bicycles to rent. Additional modern facilities include a discothèque.

From Spitz the Danube basin falls away to the south. An alternative minor road takes you up through the vineyards to the west and you quickly reach the village of **Mühldorf** in the Spitzerbach valley. The area is known as a local sun trap and promotes natural sports again with 24km (15 miles) of prepared hiking trails, a small fishing lake and other basic sports facilities.

Back on the Danube's banks it is another 8km (5 miles) or so to **Aggsbach-Markt**, nestling between the river and the 980m (3,158ft) high Jauerling mountain. The village has a population of just over 700 and first appeared in documents in 830. It has several claims to historical fame. The best known of these was the discovery of the *Venus of Willendorf*—a female fertility idol from the middle stone age now at the Vienna Natural History Museum. The discovery was, to be fair, made in Willendorf, a small village you pass on the way into Aggsbach.

Emmersdorf

Other prehistoric discoveries here include mammoth hunters from the last ice age. Today most of the charming old whitewashed houses with red tiled roofs are typical of architecture in the region. There is a thirteenth-century Romanesque church and the pilgrimage church of Maria Laach can be reached from here.

Across the river Schloss Aggstein stands high on a rocky hill above the valley. Here the Kuenringer (King Richard's 'friends') laid in wait for passing ships to rob. The parts of the castle that survived

Schönbuhel

are now used as a youth hostel. A ferry crosses to neighbouring Aggsbach-Dorf.

The Wachau comes to its end at Melk, across the river from Emmersdorf, where the Danube meets the Melk river. **Emmersdorf** sees the countryside flattening out and is a good spot for a base between regions. It has a late Gothic parish church and a medieval styled central area.

As the Wachau ends the legendary area of Nibelungengau begins. Just past Emmersdorf on the right a road climbs up in to the hills, and doubles back towards Dürnstein. The most notable place you'll come to if you follow this road is the pilgrimage church of Maria Laach. Founded in the fifteenth century the church is Gothic and contains a painting by Maria Sechsfinger which is said to be capable of working miracles. The winged altarpiece is particularly splendid. It was designed in 1480, partly painted and partly carved. The stone pulpit was carved in 1500. The most imposing tomb is that of Georg von Kuefstein dated 1607 and there are also the coats of arms from other members of his family. The village by the church offers hiking, bowling and floodlit alpine skiing on an artificial surface (if the snow is in short supply). It has won awards for its

Würnsdorf

attractiveness. Just over the hill is Aggsbach which can be reached easily from here.

Back by the Danube, further upstream, another road (216) turns north up the hill from the market town of Weitenegg towards Ottenshlag and Zwettl. The Danube is partly hidden here by wooded islands. Take the right turn, then, just past neighbouring Weiten, a further right fork a few kilometres into the hills takes you off towards Mühldorf. From there it is only a short drive east back down to Spitz. First however, you pass through **Raxendorf** a small traditional village in rolling hilly countryside. Horse riding on Halflingers is possible here, perhaps over to the Jauerling mountain, famous for its wildflowers, further on to the right of the road. Alternatively, if you turn left (west) out of Mühldorf you pass Elsenreith, cross the Klein Krems tributary and then come to the town of **Ottenschlag**. Situated in gentle hills with increasingly large areas of woodland, this old market town has long been the district centre. There are five main routes out of it, and one actually goes in a pretty straight line north of Zwettl. The town has good sports facilities, with the usual selection of outdoor pursuits plus clay pigeon shooting. There is an aerodrome to the south of the town from which there is gliding and occasional ballooning. There are several interesting buildings around the main street including the onion domed church with apostles standing out from the exterior of the tower. There is a small lake for boating and swimming in the summer and rather unimpressive alpine skiing facilities from a drag lift on the gentle hills in the winter.

Taking the south-west road out of Ottenschlag you return to the Danube via Pöggstall and Weiten (see later). However, a turning on the left after a few kilometres takes you off towards the forests of the Mühlviertel via Bärnkopf. The first stop however is the small peaceful village of **Martinsberg** with its eleventh-century church and two bathing pools.

If you choose to stay on the original road through Weiten you can do the journey in reverse and come first to **Pöggstall**, which is worth a visit for those interested in churches. The example here has a beautiful late Gothic winged altarpiece, a fifteenth-century Madonna and some excellent stained glass. Nearby the old Schloss Rogendorf dates from the early sixteenth century. It has a charming arcaded courtyard and a strange Rundell, a heavily fortified building which was probably designed by Albrecht Dürer for firing cannons. Just pass Pöggstall the road network, which is difficult enough to follow in any logical sequence as it is (not necessarily a bad thing if you're not in a hurry), becomes even more confusing, with roads going in every direction around Würnsdorf. Once they've sorted themselves out to some extent you have the choice of taking the Zwettl road north, or going west to a further crossroads at Laimbach on the edge of the forest and next to the Peilstein peak at 1,060m (3,477ft).

Back by the Danube the road continues along a straight section of the river with comparatively gentle sloping sides, especially to the south. It's a few more kilometres to **Klein Pöchlarn**, the little brother of Pöchlarn, linked by a ferry over the river. It's not an especially attractive village, with some modern housing blocks and massive industrial development across the river. There are older parts still intact but the whole gives an impression of being rather disjointed.

Just past the village is another right turn, which can again take you towards Pöggstall and from there in virtually any direction you choose. First stop though is **Artstetten** about 3km (nearly 2 miles) into the hills. The castle here is twelfth century and set in parklands, with five onion domed towers and a baroque chapel. This now houses the remains of Archduke Franz Ferdinand and his wife

Sophie who were murdered in Sarajevo in 1914, partially sparking of World War I. There is an exhibition of the archduke's life and the events of 1914. The village itself is very pleasant and offers good leisure facilities. The Danube valley widens further after Klein Pöchlarn with agricultural land spreading out on both sides of the river, though particularly to the south. The twin onion domed spires of the famous pilgrimage church at **Maria Taferl**, come into view high above the Danube. A road leads to it from either side of the hill — something of a strain after the nice flat run for the hoards of summer cyclists. The church was built between 1661 and 1711 by Jakob Praudtauer. The interior contains an eighteenth-century organ loft, heavily decorated in gold and a similarly gilded pulpit, with numerous figures within the design. The nave and the dome contain frescoes illustrating the lives of St Joseph and the Virgin Mary. The high altar was completed by J.M. Otz in 1736. The side altars have altarpieces by J.G. Schmidt and by Kremser Schmidt. Outside there is a Celtic sacrificial stone.

The village here is a popular health resort, thanks to its high location and surrounding woodlands. There are good panoramic views across the valley to the alps on fog-free days and there's also a particularly good hotel the Krone which alone has a wine tavern, modern indoor pool, sauna, solarium, whirlpool, gym, massage room, large outdoor pool and minigolf. It is well equipped for disabled visitors.

The riverside road reaches Marbach shortly after you pass the church (the two villages share a train station). There is increasing industrial development visible to the south of the river. **Marbach** has a population of 1,600 and an attractive old central square. This contains the sixteenth-century Rathaus and opposite the residence of Count Starhemburg and Lowenstein dating from 1575. A road north from Marbach joins up with the one mentioned previously from Klein Pochlarn at the village of Münichreith.

The road cuts off most of a southern U-bend in the Danube before coming to **Persenbeug**, across the Ybbs and reached by a bridge over the dam constructed for the hydro-electric power station. Austria's last emperor, Karl I (1887-1922) was born in the seventeenth-century baroque castle of the same name which looks out above the village and the river basin from a high rock above. The original castle was probably constructed in the ninth century. The most noteworthy building in the actual village is the Schiffmeisterhaus, a highly ornate baroque building.

The road over the dam continues north along route 36 which runs a straighter than average course up towards Zwettl and ultimately on to the Czech border. The road passes **Nöchling** on the left, a typically attractive peaceful village in the Waldviertel, set in the midst of gently undulating countryside, with increasingly dense woodland to the north and west. A wide range of nature-related sports facilities are available. The first village the road passes through is **Altenmarkt** which has a 900-year-old hotel, the Marketwirt, with antique furniture. The parish church of St Amilian contains a fifteenth-century fresco of the Virgin Mary, protecting believers beneath her cloak.

Soon after Altenmarkt a left turning takes you to the village of Ysper on the river of the same name, then to St Oswald and on across the border into Upper Austria and the Mühlviertel, arriving first at the picturesque monastery village of Waldhausen. Meanwhile the Danube road becomes more closely surrounded by hillsides once again and passes through Ispersdorf, where there is an alternative turning to Altenmarkt.

As you follow route 3 along the Danube upstream it bends from south to west flowing and you reach the old shipping villages of St Nikola and Sarmingstein. These are the outposts of Upper Austria, the border of which lies a mile or so before St Nikola. It is the same border for the Mühlviertel region, which swallows up the rest of the country covered by this route to the north of the Danube and a good way beyond, far past Linz to the Czech border.

Mühlviertel is a rich land of green rolling hills and some dense forests. The regional tourist office claims, 'Mühlviertel cannot be defined.' If you'd like a little help with getting into the spirit of the area the tourist office offer organised holidays in the region with subjects from mountain biking, hiking, riding and cultural events through the epicurean specialities, or just gingerbread making, cider pressing and the traditional arts. For those wanting to clear their minds, body, nature, self-awareness and the potentially explosive family-awareness holidays are all available.

From St Nikola a small road runs due north up towards the highlands and Arbesbach, rejoining the main road near to Bärnkopf and passing first through **Waldhausen**, about 6.5km (4 miles) north. This is a beautiful village situated in an area called the Strudengau which borders Wachau. It combines natural beauty with history and is the site of a former Augustinian monastery founded in 1147 and dissolved in 1782. The area is characterised by many wooded hills and valleys, disected by streams and running into a major Danube tributary which sweeps gracefully past the village, much of which is low down by its banks. Waldhausen is very much a summer resort, with sports facilities including a very large swimming lake also used for fishing and boating. Skittles, tennis and cycling are available and there are of course plenty of hiking trails.

There are two churches, the main one connected to an old monastery on a hill above the village. It is early seventeenth century and combines Gothic and Renaissance styles. It contains more than 300 frescoes. The tabernacle is early seventeenth century but the stained glass pre-dates this. The winged altarpiece comes from later in that century. The 'Stiftskirche' is baroque and rococo with impressive stucco and painted ceiling and a massive high altar decorated in white, black and gold, created by Paul Deniff and typical of the period. The organ, dating from 1677, is particularly magnificent and the scene of famous summer concerts.

The monastery building itself had been purchased by outside interests, but has now been bought back by the villagers who are deciding what to do with it. The village church was built between 1608 and 1612 from local granite. It has a Renaissance interior and in 1957 renovations uncovered numerous frescoes. There's a rather incongruous new window and confessional. The south door contains bullet holes from the Napoleonic wars. Look out for local crafts in this village, there's a remarkable candle maker and a woman who makes pictures on cloth using natural dyes.

Back by the Danube **St Nikola** has, like many villages, improved its tourist facilities a lot over recent years. Many of these are situated within the bounds of its first class Hotel Zur Post, a former shipmasters house. They include sauna, solarium, fitness room and minigolf and there is a heated swimming pool and tennis courts in the village. Other activities including walks on well marked hiking trails, fishing and water sports.

Like neighbouring Sarmingstein, it is located in the middle of the legendary Strudengau which characteristically has some of the most picturesque views along the Danube, framed between wooded mountainsides and the famous blue river. It also used to have some of the most dangerous currents and underwater rocks in the Danube. Neighbouring Grein, upstream, had quite a good business going, supplying navigators to passing boats.

The town of **Grein** lies at a junction with the road north to Arbesbach and Zwettl and shortly before a turning to a road south over the Danube to Amstetten. It is situated on a corner of the river which turns from north to west flowing at this point.

The town's most famous attraction is its beautiful theatre, the

St Nikola

oldest and probably the smallest in the German speaking world, designed in rococo style, opened in 1791 and still going strong. Its history and location are particularly interesting. It is found on the second and top floors of the old town hall, which dates from 1563. The theatre building was originally a granary, used to store goods and grain, which was added to the town hall during a period of prosperity. Over the years this commercial trade decreased and the people became more interested in entertainment and pleasure, and so decided to convert the building to a theatre.

The nice part of this story is that the money raised from performances was used to support the poor people living in the almshouse. In its heyday the theatre seated around 200; the wealthy actually bought their seats, all along the front few rows, and kept them locked when not in use so that no one else could sit in them! The keys are still hanging in a glass box on the wall.

A few other delightful historical details include the fact that the

Grein

old jail was situated near to the theatre so that prisoners could catch part of the performance at least through the windows. More delightful still, the toilet on the left hand side of the auditorium has a curtain not a door, so that the devoted theatre goer could watch the performance under any circumstances! There are also remnants of the old winter heating system — hot bricks carried up from downstairs and placed under the seat during the show.

The theatre's history is also linked to various wars. In 1805 there were 13,500 French soldiers stationed in the area and Napoleon is said to have visited the theatre. The box on the right of the auditorium is named 'The Napoleon Box' as a witness to this. After the last war the Russian occupying forces supposedly stole ornamental gold stars from within the theatre, but new ones were made by a local priest.

Everything about the theatre is seemingly in miniature — the lighting, decoration, drop curtain and decorated circle supported by pillars. The artistic history of the theatre begins with amateur performances, but during the last century groups from Vienna and Germany came to entertain. Restored after wartime closure, the theatre is now visited each year by the 'Greiner Sommerspiele' from Vienna who perform comedies most weekends in the summer.

There are several other major attractions to Grein, which was incorporated as a town in 1491 and is one of Austria's smallest with

a population of 2,800. The settlement is much older and was originally an important base for the pilotting of boats through 9 or so
kilometres (15 miles) of the 'Greiner Strudel' or 'Grein Swell'.

The town's parish church was rebuilt in the Middle Ages having
been mentioned first in documents from 1147. It now has elements
from the baroque and late Gothic periods. The high altar picture was
painted by Bartholomew Altomonte.

The picturesque main square contains a lovely old fountain and
houses originally built in the Gothic style. Many more such buildings
were destroyed in various fires during the last century, but as the
houses were not renumbered, you'll notice a rather erratic progres-
sion around the square. One of the buildings — formerly a ship
builder's house — now houses a traditional Viennese coffee house
serving sixteen sorts of coffee; and you get a glass of water with your
cup. It's called the Kaffeesiederei Blumenstraussl and is a century-
old family business.

The Schloss Greinburg is perhaps most famous for its beautiful
triple-tiered arcaded courtyard. There was probably a fortress here
in the eleventh century but the present building, which dominates
the town, was originally constructed between 1489 and 1493. About
500 people worked in the original construction, some paid but some
apparently voluntarily. The five-sided tower gate and the rare cell-
type vault date from this period. Festivals are occasionally held here
in the summer, and the castle's owner, Prince Frederic of Sachsen-
Coburg-Gotha, an uncle of the King of Sweden, is happy to encourage these. His father was a cousin of King George VI and the castle
was owned by Queen Victoria for a brief time.

Among other attractions in Grein is the shipping museum, which
is upstairs in the castle. It houses exhibits of Grein's former importance as a shipping town. Other local attractions include boat trips to
the Wachau, bicycle rental, heated swimming pool, tennis court and
50km (31 miles) of hiking trails.

Crossing the border back into Lower Austria and from the
Mühlviertel to the Waldviertel, the Weinsberg forest becomes denser
still and if you take a turning to the left off the main road a few miles
from St Georgen you reach Bärnkopf. The cross-over point is hard to
miss as Lower Austria has large 'N' signs by the side of the road
announcing that you're entering Niederosterreich. Here the 400
residents are proud of their isolation from main roads and railways,
being at the centre of the largest forest in Austria. It's also the oldest
part of the forest and trees tower above you all around.

The forest is owned by the Habsburg family, an offshoot of the former emperors. It covers the hilly highlands at an altitude of around 930m (3,000ft). Apart from the roads marked on the maps, minor roads in varying states of repair criss-cross the forest back and forth — be careful not to get lost in the woods!

The traditional work here through the centuries has been forestry, a business which kept everyone fully employed until the 1930s. A remnant of this is to be found in artificial channels cut down through the hills for up to 50km (31 miles) to the Danube. Lakes were also created so that enough water was available for floating logs down these channels in the springtime. Many of these lakes are now used for leisure activities such as fishing, boating and bathing. Another typical feature of the area is the *Wackelsteine* or 'shaking rocks', natural towers of rock sometimes 9 to 19m (30 to 60ft) high which have been carved by erosion.

Another interesting geological feature to be found in the region are similar rocks that sometime balance one on top of another, seeming to defy gravity. Many look as though they could be toppled with a quick shove, but in fact they have been there for hundreds or thousands of years. 'Rock hunters' can get rock-spotters books from tourist offices and get them stamped at each rock they visit!

The village of **Bärnkopf** is small and peaceful. Because of its location and history there are few historic buildings. A former signal tower is located on top of the highest mountain, the Weinsberg, though the building has been ruined for almost 500 years. From here on a good day it is possible to see right across to the Alps or into Czechoslovakia. And the population of Bärnkopf are proud of the weather record, often finding themselves in bright sunshine, looking down on the fog in the Danube valley.

The residents of the high ground are proud of the fact that, compared to the valleys, their climate is usually fog free. All the tourist brochures for every village claim that their climate is 'fog free'. In reality the valleys can be very foggy for long periods, particularly in spring and autumn. In these circumstances the 'Highlanders' can look down on a sea of fog. This isn't always the case however, as the fog does occasionally lift and cover the high ground, but it's usually the valleys that suffer.

The main business in Bärnkopf now is tourism, particularly with cross-country skiers who come to one of the largest and best suited areas for this pursuit in central Europe, all situated in splendid isolation. There are some 140km (87 miles) of ski trails.

Even though the village is rather isolated, the residents are not. Herbert Lackner, who organises a local cross-country ski school, once spent a year travelling through all the ski resorts from Alaska to Tierra del Fuego in North and South America — quite a feat. There is a man made lake in the village to laze around in the summer (making lakes is another favourite pastime for those villages hoping to promote tourism!), and log cabins are available to rent.

The strange looking fences by roadsides here, which seem pretty pointless as they have big gaps in them and therefore can't fence anything in, are quite effective at fencing drifting snow out.

About seven miles further on from Bärnkopf is **Arbesbach**. The village was founded in the twelfth century, the late baroque church originally dates from 1246. The ruined castle nearby is known as the 'molar of the Waldviertel', there are also the remains of gallows, stocks and pillory in the old village. Trails from the outskirts pass by the beautiful Hollfall or 'Hellfalls'.

From Arbesbach it is a short journey on north-east to Zwettl (featured in a separate chapter). However, for this route take the second road out of town, route 124, to reach the one in from St Georgen and Bärnkopf (route 119). This takes you back into Upper Austria and the forests around **Königswiesen**.

This old market town has become a progressive holiday resort and has a range of leisure activities organised. There are tennis courts, an outdoor swimming pool, curling alley and a children's play area. For summer walkers there are over 120km (74 miles) of prepared hiking trails and in the winter many of these may be used by cross-country skiers. Riding and fishing are also available.

There are also several places of historical interest which belie the town's local importance in the past. Particularly surprising is the late Gothic parish church of the Madonna. The design is a masterpiece with intricate rib-vaulting (480 sections) and notable buttresses. There is also a very interesting rectory dating to 1658 and an eighteenth-century fountain. If you visit in the summer months look out for the beautiful flower arrangements for which the town has won seven prizes in recent years.

Mönchdorf, three miles south-west, contains two smart discothèques for those wanting a night out in the area. The road south from here leads to Pabneukirchen and on to Grein. Shortly before Bad Zell and Tragwein a minor road turns south and left, which avoids arriving in Linz and keeps the route off the beaten track, returning via Rechberg and Schwertberg to Perg, back above the Danube.

Rechberg was voted most beautiful village in Upper Austria in 1985. As it is difficult to find a village in this part of Upper Austria that isn't beautiful, it would have been tough to be a judge in such a competition. However the winning factor was probably the village's famous floral display. The 50km (31 miles) of signposted footpaths around the village are strewn with massive granite boulders and these and other geological features bring students from far and wide, to study from an observation tower. The village has its own band which entertains at folk dancing evenings, and an artificial swimming lake for the essential refreshing dip. One of the strange 'balancing rocks', known as the 'Schwamerlstein' or 'mushroom rock', is to be found a mile from here; a footpath leads from the village.

Back on route 124 is **Bad Zell**, set in typical Mühlviertel countryside of rolling hills and famous for its thermal baths. The modern version is a Spa Centre complete with radon bubble bath as well as massage, sauna and solarium facilities. Other facilities include horse riding, bowling, cycling and of course cross-country skiing in the winter. One other point of possible interest to wart sufferers: there is a farmer in Bad Zell who apparently has an inherited skill to naturally remove them.

A few kilometres further on you reach **Tragwein**. According to legend the name originated when the residents were building the church. They ran out of water for use in construction and decided to use wine instead, so the name became *Trag* meaning to carry, and *Wein* being pretty self-explanatory. The village was first mentioned in 1287 and contains the castle of Reichenstein. Local antique rocks contain holes which were used in the production of resin by placing pine wood on the stone covering them with earth and heating up the whole lot. A local farmer, Herr Hinterreiler rents horses.

Before Pregarten leave road 124 as it heads on to join the A7 motorway to Linz. The main south turning is route 123 from Pregarten, but prior to that a minor road turns left towards **Schwertberg** and the countryside begins to change as it finally reaches an area of more urbanised land use. It is a fairly large industrial village; half of the population has work in the area, more than a quarter commute to Linz. The church dates back to 1357 and was extended in 1913. There's also a moated castle, ruined fortress and summer festivals arranged, with amateur theatre in the park.

The road joins route 3 near to the Danube. Turn left again, this time following the Danube downstream back towards Grein but coming first to Perg, one of Upper Austria's eighteen regional administration centres and also the main education centre for the area. If you turn left at the junction you come to riverside **Mauthausen** with a history dating back to the thirteenth century. With respect to the inhabitants, as the area was the scene of a notorious concentration camp during World War II, it is a difficult place to go near. There is a beautiful church with some excellent thirteenth-century frescoes there however, for those who are able to put their love of church art before other emotions.

At Perg you reach route 3 above the Danube once more and have the choice of a right/west turn to Linz or turning back left/east towards Grein, this time following the Danube's flow, but not getting near to it until shortly before the bridge that takes you over the river towards Amstetten, just before Grein.

Roads run north and south from Perg. The road south takes you to Perg and then to a road which runs between the main number 3 road and the Danube, although it does not follow the edge of the latter. The road reaches **Mitterkirchen** after a few kilometres, perhaps best known for the Celtic remains uncovered there, including the grave of a king. From here the choice is south over the Danube or back up north towards route 3. This northern road soon takes you past the rarely visited monastery at **Baumgartenberg**. It is an interesting place as many of the original buildings, though still standing, have been covered in elaborate decorations in various colours which include black, gold, white and pink. The monastery is Cistercian and was founded in 1141, although much of the building had decayed by the late eighteenth century. It currently houses a girls school.

The main number 3 road through Perg passes next through **Arbing**, with a fine Gothic church, en route to Grein and on back to Lower Austria and the Waldviertel. Every kilometre or so roads head off north, deep in to the Mühlviertel and reaching typical villages such as Windhaag, Allerheiligen and Münzbach. Apart from a difference in countryside between the Mühlviertel and Waldviertel there is a traditional architectural difference in farmhouse design. In Mühlviertel the buildings are traditionally formed into a square with a quadrangle in the centre; in Waldviertel buildings are normally only built on three sides, in a U shape.

The route has now come back full circle almost to Grein and is about to finally cross the river to the south. But first a short detour up to a rather magnificent *Schloss*.

Schloss Klam is an impressive towering fortress originally built in 1149 by Otto von Machland. It has been owned by the Klam family since 1454 and currently houses some very friendly dalmations as well. It has been lived in and looked after by the same family for more than 500 years and the original deed of purchase is still in the castle archives. As such it is one of the few castles to remain fully intact throughout its history. The last major rebuilding was completed in 1636. The current owner is the chairman of the Austrian Castle Owners Association.

The survival is doubly impressive when you consider the turbulent history it has had right up to the conclusion of World War II. The large courtyard, surrounded by five-storey buildings, has always been a place of safety for the local population. Look out for the coat of arms of the original builder, now also the crest of both the Klam family and of Upper Austria on the tower of the first courtyard. A Renaissance gateway leads to the second courtyard and from there to an arcade-lined inner yard.

The castle contains a Porcelain Room housing an excellent collection of Alt-Wien and Meissen porcelain. The castle museum houses mainly family militaria with many connections with Austrian and European history. For example the uniform of Count Karl Klam-Martinic, which he wore when escorting Napoleon to exile in Elba. There is also a 'Landscape Room' with frescoes from 1803, and earlier frescoes in the Gothic chapel, consecrated in 1491.

Below the castle is the more recent 'Oak Chapel', erected in 1973 from an uprooted 1,000-year-old oak tree. A path runs from there to the Klam gorge, which served as an inspiration to the Swedish poet August Strindberg.

The road back to route 3 goes to Saxen, from where there are three choices for crossing the Danube. Since the route is heading for Enns, perhaps the fastest way is to follow route 3 back through Perg to where it rejoins route 123 and follow that left over the river and into Enns. Alternatively you could take the first left after taking route 3 towards Perg, drive back to Mitterkirchen and across to Wallsee, then join the main road to Enns. The third option is to turn east on route 3 towards Grein, then cross the river a kilometre or so before and follow the main road, or join the A1 motorway by Amstetten and reach Enns that way.

Whichever way you get there, the town of **Enns** is worth the effort you make. This is Austria's oldest town, granted a charter in 1212, and with a history as an important settlement going back much further. The remains of the encircling walls are still here and for those that have visited the Dachstein region or perhaps the monastery at Admont there is a certain satisfaction at reaching the end of the same river, at the point where it joins the Danube.

Enns is built on the site of the Roman town of *Lauriacum*, capital of the Roman province of *Noricum*. St Florian was martyred here in the fourth century and now there's an 11-schilling stamp featuring the town. The Gothic basilica of St Laurentis was built on the site of a Roman temple, which in turn had an early Christian basilica and a Romanesque pilgrimage church built on it. Because of the religious importance of the site the church was designated a papal basilica in 1968 and is now the seat of an archbishop. Inside there are bronze reliefs depicting the life of St Florian. It is a vast church with slender ribbing and long narrow windows. There is a Gothic tabernacle with pinnacles rising towards the roof. In the walled churchyard there is a round chancel house with a pyramid roof; there is also a Gothic column.

The huge sixteenth-century Stadtturm stands 62m (200ft) high in the centre of the town's central square (which actually is very square), surrounded by interesting Renaissance houses. This watchtower was erected by order of the Emperor Maximilian II in 1565 and it now doubles as a clock tower. Just outside the town is the Schloss Ennsegg, built around 1570 with additions in the seventeenth century; it has an attractive arcaded courtyard.

The town's museum is housed on the first floor of the Rathaus, a former mint dating from 1547 (original building 1439), situated opposite the Stadtturm. This is a basically Gothic design, but is fronted by a baroque façade and has an arcaded Renaissance courtyard. The museum itself contains many Roman relics, many of which are in very good condition. They include some beautiful jars, a Roman altar stone from the third century and a decorative Mithraic stone. There are also some prehistoric finds.

The parish church has a double nave and a fourteenth-century chapel and statues from the same period. It was formerly the monastery church of the Minorite brotherhood and was built between 1308 and 1343.

As you would expect from a town with a population of 10,000 there are good shopping and sports facilities. In the latter category there is a large indoor swimming complex near the railway station. There is also a large sports park on the west of the town. The second largest indoor riding school in Austria is to be found here, as well as a shooting range. There are also major conference and exhibition halls. Anyone who suffers from insomnia might be interested in the institute here that attempts to cure sufferers.

If you follow route 337 southwards you come to **Steyr**, one of the most beautiful and interesting towns in Austria. This route however goes back east below the Danube. You can of course follow the A1/ E5 motorway, but you get better views on the main road (number 1 again) towards Amstetten. The road here is very different to that

Steyr

which follows the northern bank of the Danube. Instead this road is often a kilometre or more away from the river banks.

Its worth taking one of the right turns before or after Altenhofen — the border point with Lower Austria (there is also a motorway junction). Here you turn south towards St Valentin, but should usually follow the road through to the main attraction — **Haag.**

Above the town is Schloss Starhemburg which has beautiful gardens and good views across the hills and woods that typify this area. The castle was originally thirteenth century and was extended in the sixteenth. It has a quite important place in Austrian history, formerly being a border post between Bavaria and Austria. The omnipresent Napoleon made it his base on several occasions and there is a room named after him.

The castle has a rectangular courtyard, half of which is arcaded. Its chapel has an elaborate gilt and wooden crucifix in the baroque style but created by a relatively modern Austrian sculptor. There is also a small museum with a collection of local trade signs and glass paintings.

Haag itself is an attractive town with an originally Gothic church modified to baroque in the eighteenth century. 'New' additions include the tower with an onion dome. There is a wildlife park to the south of the village. You can continue from here on minor roads heading south-east towards Waidhofen if you wish. To do so the shortest route takes you past the Benedictine Seitenstetten abbey founded in 1112. It was rebuilt by Josef Munggenast by 1747. The Knights' Chapel is the only original building remaining. The abbey, which also has a good collection of pictures, is situated by a virtual crossroads with the main route 122 towards Steyr. You should continue across towards Waidhofen.

Back in Haag the road out north-east takes you quickly back to the motorway or the A1 at **Strengberg**, a town which offers indoor swimming as well as riding, fishing and so on. There are more sports facilities available at Wallsee however, one of the few major settlements in this area that is close to the Danube. It is reached by taking a left fork a few miles east of Strengberg en route for Amstetten. Damming of the Danube has made this a particularly good area for watersports of which virtually all imaginable are available. There is also a bridge back over the Danube to Mittelkirchen.

Amstetten stands a few kilometres south of the Danube, with the main A1 motorway from Vienna (Wien) to Salzburg passing its northern boundary, and the Ybbs river passing on the south, soon to join the Danube by the town which shares its name. It is frequently ignored in the guide books, perhaps because it does not really fit into any of the regional categories, being just east of the Upper Austrian Border, just south of the Mühlviertel and west of the Wachau region. It is in fact at the northern tip of the Voralpenland or alpine foothills, a far from satisfactory location as it doesn't feel much more alpine than most of the rest of the alpine basin.

It is a good base for excursions to virtually every corner of Austria however, and for sampling each of the local regions. The town itself is a reasonably attractive mix of old and new and the regional administration, education and shopping centre, particularly along the Hautplatz. It also has far above average sports facilities with the modern Johann Polz Sports Hall incorporating large gymnasium, swimming pool and indoor riding school. There are also extensive outdoor swimming pools, a sports stadium, tennis courts and all weather curling amongst other things.

The major church of St Stephen was founded in the eleventh century and Amstetten was first documented in 1111. On 13 September 1276, King Rudolf of Habsburg awarded the town market-trading status. In the latter half of the thirteenth century there was a stone settlement in what is now the south-eastern quarter of the town. This was sited on the former important main street than ran from east to west, and this was where the original market place was situated. Amstetten's rise to modern commercial success began with the construction of the railway and the first station opened in 1858; steam trains are still to be seen there. In 1897 the village was awarded town status by Kaiser Franz Josef. Today there is a small museum, dedicated largely to local farming history.

A few miles to the south of Amstetten along route 121a at an altitude of 1,200m (3,936ft) is **Waidhofen an der Ybbs**, a very picturesque little town standing on a triangle of land formed by the Ybbs river and a tributary of it. It owes its prosperity to the nearby iron works, which went into operation 500 years ago. There are many buildings of note here, particularly the impressive tower, built in 1542 in memory of Waidhofen's successful repulsion of a Turkish invasion. The clock has been stopped at 11.45am, the time of the Turkish defeat.

Even the 'ordinary' buildings in this town are interesting though, with rows of gabled houses from the fifteenth and sixteenth centuries. Many have arcaded courtyards and the whole scenario is very pleasing, particularly on a good day when the town and the green wooded hills beyond are reflected in the river.

Other major sights are the castle tower and the town's churches. The tower is fifteenth century and the castle has an arcaded courtyard with the remnants of frescoes of *The Evangelist* and the *Church Fathers* painted in 1400. The fifteenth-century parish church now contains the Gothic winged altarpiece from the Spital church in which the central panel is *The Crowning of the Virgin* with St Barbara, St Mary and St Katherine. The Gothic Spital church has kept its Gothic stone pulpit, but the *Madonna and Child* from the fifteenth century is part of the seventeenth-century high altar.

The Schafkas Express steam trains run from June to September. Other facilities include minigolf, a heated pool, 100km (62 miles) of hiking paths, tennis and angling. The town's museum has some good examples of ecclesiastical art, including a fifteenth-century *Madonna and Child*, examples of local steel work and recreated former peasants living rooms.

Shortly before reaching Waidhofen you pass **Sonntagberg** to the

The town hall, St Veit

St Peter am Kamersberg, Steiermark

The Vorderer Gosausee in the Salzkammergut
The picturesque little town of Waidhofen an der Ybbs, Lower Austria

left of the road. Here, 620m (2,000ft) above sea level, stands the white basilica on which Josef Munggenast and Josef Praudtauer worked together. The church is visible for miles around. When you reach it you'll find a richly decorated baroque interior with an impressive high altar. There are also side altars containing paintings by Kremser Schmidt, a baroque pulpit, pews and confessionals.

If you travel north from Amstetten you return towards the Danube at the west of the Strudengau and pass the bridge to Grein. The road (119) takes you through Ardagger. Two kilometres (just over a mile) before you reach it however, you'll pass the former monastery, established as a college of secular canons in 1049 and dissolved in 1782. The abbey church is now the parish church of St Margaret. This is late Romanesque but has been modified to baroque, and was built into Gothic style around 1300. There are some excellent mid-thirteenth-century stained glass windows above the altar showing the life of St Margaret. There is also a Romanesque crypt.

There are some pleasant roads through the hilly countryside between Amstetten and Ybbs including one through Willersback which takes you back onto the banks of the Danube. Most of the villages round about are pleasant and can offer good basic tourist facilities; however many of them are also now commuter towns from Amstetten. If you are in a hurry route 1 and the motorway A1/E5 criss-cross each other in their haste to get you off east. Before moving on however, historians might care for a brief stop in the village of Neuhofen, a few kilometres south of Amstetten and not far off the route to Waidhofen. The village is best known for the discovery of a document dated 996 which refers to 'Austria' for the first time. Hence it calls itself the 'cradle of Austria'.

Ybbs is an attractive and now quite large village on the banks of the Danube. However, the Danube panorama is not as picturesque as it should be for those who don't like large hydro-electric power stations to block the view. Tours are organised for anyone interested in a change of pace, and really the dam is not unattractive.

In Ybbs the remains of the village walls and towers are still to be seen and it has a pleasant square containing a Renaissance fountain and surrounded by fifteenth- and sixteenth-century houses. Indeed it is places like this that can leave you wondering what the Austrians have been up to for the past 400 years. Did all the village builders die in a plague? You can find out at the local history museum in Kirchengasse. The parish church of St Lorenz is Gothic and has a notable painting of *The Mount of Olives* from 1500. The church itself is fifteenth century. There are many good restaurants here, and modern sports facilities are well developed.

Ybbs is the start of the legendary region of Nibelungen (heading back east), a race of dwarfs who appeared in the German epic stories. The twelfth-century, *Song of the Nibelungen* relates the overthrow of the kingdom of Burgundy by the Huns in the fifth century. The saga inspired Wagner to write, *The Ring of the Nibelungen* (1869), although he shifted the scene to the Rhine.

The countryside alongside the river Ybbs which joins the Danube at this point is certainly the sort of romantic fairytale stuff that leaves you waiting for one of the Nibelungen to come diving out from behind a tree at any moment.

The A1/E5 motorway runs side by side with the main route and comes close to the edge of the Danube as they run up to Melk. The best road however is the 'B' route that follows the side of the Danube to **Pöchlarn**. This is an attractive village and the birthplace, in 1886, of the painter Oskar Kokoschka. It's also situated at the mouth of one of the Danube's tributaries — the Erlauf. The remains of the fifteenth-century tower and walls still stand and the local museum contains relics from the old Roman port. The late Gothic church was redesigned during the baroque period and contains more paintings by Kremsner Schmidt.

It is impossible to miss **Melk**, 92km (57 miles) from Vienna and 97km (60 miles) from Linz. The vast, famous Benedictine abbey with its towering sandy coloured walls and red tiled roof dominates the skyline. The monastery building sweeps majestically forward towards the Danube with the twin towers of the church rising above the high walls.

This is perhaps the most important baroque building in Europe. It has been an important religious and artistic centre since AD976 when it was the residence of the Babenburg Dynasty and as such, some say, the birthplace of Austria. Originally a Roman stronghold, the Babenburgs handed the building over to the Benedictine order at the end of the eleventh century. The abbey has a good collection of art work including paintings by Paul Troger, Michael Rottmayer, Antonio Beduzzi and Jorg Pren. There is a summer festival arranged annually in July and August, featuring Biedermeier comedies by leading Viennese actors, as well as choral and organ recitals. There is a tavern in the abbey where you can sample the local wines.

The building as it is today is the work of Jakob Prandtauer, who was paid 300 guilders to rebuild the existing monastery in the early eighteenth century. The abbot Berthold Dietmayr hired Praudtauer who was born in the Tyrol and had been trained as a sculptor before setting up home in St Pölten in 1689. He had already designed several popular buildings, and the foundation stone for the present monastery was laid in 1702, after the original was largely destroyed by fire. There was a delay of several years between the destruction by fire and the beginnings of reconstruction, due to the Turkish wars. Prandtauer died before this, his greatest work, was complete; but his cousin Joseph Munggenast finished it according to his original plans, completing the building in 1738. The colourful history didn't end there though. Napoleon set up his headquarters here from 1805 to 1809. Today Praudtauer's work is in a state of some decay (despite the impression from a distance), but restoration work — which like the building itself has to be done on a massive scale — is underway.

The monastery has always been an educational establishment and currently contains a grammar school run by the monks. It also has one of the most famous libraries in Austria, containing nearly 2,000 manuscripts and 90,000 books, some of which are more than a thousand years old. Both the library and the marble hall are exceptionally beautiful buildings. The latter has ceiling paintings by Troger and the library contains pictures of Praudtauer and the abbey's founder, Leopold III. Other Austrian rulers are framed in the Emperor's Gallery.

The abbey church, with twin towers and a large dome, is one of the finest baroque churches in Europe. It has rich decoration of gold, marble and frescoes with figures mounted on the altar, nave and dome and an ornate, delicately carved pulpit. On the high altar St Peter and St Paul are depicted saying farewell before their martyrdom.

Beneath the abbey the town of Melk has preserved its ancient layout intact. There are numerous burghers' houses dating from the Renaissance period in the Sterngasse, old towers and remains of the town walls are still standing. It has a picturesque square with the Nuremberg Gingerbread House (Lebzelterhaus) from 1657, and an old town hall. The parish church is fifteenth-century Gothic and has an interesting Calvary group.

Leisure activities in Melk are largely centred on the riverside park and include tennis courts, a large swimming pool, minigolf, a rifle range, cycle rental, paddle boats and 32km (20 miles) of marked paths.

Eight kilometres (5 miles) south of Melk is the Schloss Schallaburg. This sixteenth-century building has an attractive two-storeyed arcaded courtyard and an unusual garden. It now houses a Renaissance museum. The route from Melk to the castle passes the Wachberg which is famed for its views of the abbey and the Danube basin.

From Melk, road 1 and the *autobahn* A1/E5 continue to run due east towards Vienna while the Danube makes a steep sweep up towards the north. Road 33 then follows this lead and plunges you back into the steep sided Wachau valley.

The first settlement is **Schönbühel** at an altitude of 232m (750ft). The village is dominated by the fairytale castle of the same name which overlooks the Danube from a rock only 40m (130ft) above the river. There has been a castle here since the 1100s but the present building is early nineteenth century. The village also contains a Servite convent built in 1674.

A few more miles along the river you reach the picturesque village of **Aggsbach Dorf**, across the river from sister-village Aggsbach-Markt which is reached by a ferry. Two roads go up into the hills from here. The first takes you back south towards the motorway/main road at Loosdorf. The other heads north-east to Maria Langegg, a Servite monastery. This contains a beautiful library and the church, which was rebuilt in the baroque style in 1773, contains some interesting frescoes. If you continue along the hill road it takes a reasonably straight path to Krems. Alternatively you can turn right shortly before reaching the monastery and follow the road through the hills south-east to Weyersdorf and on to St Pölten.

This region, which fills the triangle between Krems, St Pölten and Melk, is the Dunkelsteinerwald, an area of high hills with some steep roads linking relaxed villages. This is perhaps the last oasis before the Viennese suburbia begins in the east, with a good many Austrians commuting to the nearby towns and cities.

Back on the riverside road you soon pass the imposing ruins of the castle of Aggstein, former home of the infamous 'Robber Barons' and looking especially imposing perched on top of a 1,000ft cliff. It housed the *Kuenrings* (robber barons) in the thirteenth century but was destroyed by Duke Albrecht I, rebuilt by other robber barons and then largely wrecked by the Turks. The dungeons have survived to the present day and these and other surviving parts are used as a youth hostel in the summer.

Next comes the village of Mitterarnsdorf and then as the river bends before entering Krems the small attractive town of Rossatz.

Mautern is linked to Stein/Krems by a road bridge. It is the older town and has several major historical connections with the Romans. There is a museum in the marketplace, which also contains Celtic items. There is also the residence of St Severinus and the town appears in the 'Nibelungenlied' legend. The remains of the Roman town walls along with a tower and a road are still visible. The Gothic parish church contains pictures by Kremsner Schmidt.

There is a motorway (S33) from Krems to St Pölten, but the main road that goes first through **Göttweig** takes a straighter route. The huge Benedictine abbey at Göttweig, founded in 1074 by Bishop Altmann of Passau, is one of Austria's most impressive. It stands on a wooded hill, apparently unreachable, but in fact quickly reached by a short road.

The site pre-dates even Bishop Altmann's initiative, as the Romans had a watch tower here, and before then there was a Bronze Age village. The current building was begun in 1719 after a second serious fire and continued for 74 years though it was not completed to plan. The present building was designed by baroque architect Lukas von Hildebrandt. Inside, the church appears rather grim, but much of the architectural design is extremely impressive and includes the 'Kaiserstiege', one of the finest surviving baroque staircases. Above it is a ceiling painting by Paul Troger dating from 1739. The church, with baroque twin towers, dates from 1765. It contains elaborately carved choir stalls and more paintings by the prolific Kremser Schmidt. In the crypt there's a stone statue of the founding abbot, created in 1570. The library contains many notable manuscripts and artwork by German and Dutch painters; stucco decoration is the work of Franz Amon.

There are excellent views from Göttweig, best enjoyed whilst drinking some of the monastery's own wine. From here it is possible to see another monastery to the south-east at **Herzogenburg,** founded in the thirteenth century but rebuilt by Praudtauer and Munggenast according to a design by Fischer von Erlach. Though this monastery is not as popular as Göttweig, a visit here might be more worthwhile.

The church is baroque, mainly pale green with white and gold decoration. The organ is richly decorated in the rococo style. There is also a monastery museum which contains a collection of German panel paintings of the fourteenth and fifteenth centuries, including four by Jorg Breu. There is also some fourteenth-century stained glass and a carved *Death of the Virgin* from the fifteenth century. From here it's only a few more miles south to the regional capital.

The major argument in favour of **St Pölten** seems to be that, though it looks a rather average industrialised small city, the impression is apparently superficial one. In fact you are in the capital of Lower Austria and you will be surprised by the charm of the old baroque buildings.

For people who have come direct from the peace, beauty and cleanliness of the Wachau via Krems, the rather shabby, if originally beautiful, architecture of St Pölten has little chance of impressing. But if you dig more deeply you will find much of great interest. Also, if you don't insist on viewing the city on the same level as the places just mentioned, you may be pleasantly impressed by the excellent shopping facilities in a largely pedestrianised town centre, which should not be sniffed at as part of a complete Austrian holiday experience.

The history is there to be discovered for those prepared to give the place a chance. There is a cathedral, five churches and two squares. Most of the streets are narrow affairs, full of modern shops. Probably the best known area is the Rathaus Platz. The Rathaus from which it gets its name is composed of two fourteenth-century houses, remodelled from Renaissance to baroque. It has an octagonal clock tower.

At the north end of the square is the rococo Franciscan church (1757) with four altarpieces by Kremser Schmidt. It is similar in terms of frontage to the church of the Carmelites just off the square to the right of the Rathaus. The latter was built by baroque architect Jakob Praudtauer who is one in a long list of past masters who worked in the town. Others include Munggenast and Altomonte. The convent buildings next to Praudtauer's church and on the street named after him now house a history museum.

The cathedral stands rather detached in an often quiet square, shielded by the backs of shops and offices from the busy centre. Dating to the twelfth century it was originally Romanesque, but was remodelled in baroque by Praudtauer in the first half of the eighteenth century. The Bishop's Palace is to the north of the square.

Between the station and the cathedral runs the Klostergasse which contains Praudtauer's house, now a museum. Another building worth a closer look is on the Linzerstrasse, running south behind the Rathaus. This is the ornate 'Institute of the English Ladies' and housed an order of nuns founded by Mary Ward in 1609. It is a fine example of eighteenth-century baroque.

Cultural events are given a high priority with one festival running into another as various events are crammed into the summer months. They include days of international sacred music, art and history exhibitions, bandstand concerts and concerts in the castle.

For the hyper-active there are the usual selection of sporting facilities (indoor and outdoor pools, hiking, tennis and riding). Once you escape the industrial and commercial areas of the town you will be surprised to find substantial parks, woods and gardens. So you may find that the apparent effort involved in staying a few days here (after the simplicity of village life) is well worth the effort after all.

Road 20 runs due south out of St Pölten towards Lilienfeld and on towards Steiermark. An old railway line also makes the journey which follows the river Traisen (another Danube tributary) upstream.

On leaving 'suburbia' the first town of any real interest you come to is Wilhelmsburg. The town is dominated by its old Gothic church in the main square. On top of the church tower you can see the 'Herzogshut' or Duke's Hat — a medieval symbol; there is also some early fifteenth-century glass and a sixteenth-century wooden Madonna. There are two old castles, Ochsenburg and Kreisbach nearby.

The town also has a summer sports complex including four pools with diving pools, tennis courts, curling area and camping nearby. All standards of walker are catered for as gentle hills become gradually steeper as the mountains come closer.

A few kilometres higher up the valley is **Traisen**, where the old 'Johanneskirche' dates to the twelfth century. The town is best known for it's steel industry, the largest in the region. There are again good sports and leisure facilities including a BMX cycle track.

The river Golsen flows west into the Traisen at this point and a road follows it upstream and eventually on to Vienna. **St Veit** is set in the gentler rolling hills and meadows of the Golsen valley. There is an old Gothic church from 1257 here, though this is rather spoilt by the surprising decision to build a very ugly concrete block across the road from it. Sports facilities include downhill skiing and ski hiking in the winter, or tennis cycling and bowling in the summer. The Gasthof Hinterhofer with more than 100 beds is one of the largest hotels in the region.

Back on route 20, a couple of kilometres (just over a mile) south of Traisen lies **Lilienfeld**, a good place to base yourself for a while before returning to Vienna. If you do not have time to stay then it is also a good winter or summer destination for a day trip from St Pölten, or an en route stop.

The reasons for this interest are the peacefulness of what is an ancient village, coupled with lively, cosy, friendly and good value bars and restaurants plus a beautiful monastery for the summer and the very original alpine ski resort for the winter. For Lilienfeld was the home of Mathias Zdarsky (1855-1940), for most of his life at least, a rather remarkable man and widely acknowledged as the father of alpine skiing. Certainly it was he who developed the modern alpine ski, the earliest of which is in the town's museum. He also invented the modern method of downhill skiing, the first ski brake and the first slalom course, all at the turn of the last century. Development of alpine skiing in countries as far away as Japan has been traced back to Zdarsky's (free) teaching and now Lilienfeld has a sister town in that country as a result.

For the non-skier Zdarsky should still be of interest. He was Czech born, probably regarded as an eccentric in his day, and was a philosopher and artist, as well as an inventor of other things besides ski paraphernalia. In the museum there is a hot and cold wash hand-basin he put together, and he also invented the cement mixer and solar powered swimming pools. Back up the mountains he invented a survival tent which is credited for saving the lives of thousands of Austrian soldiers in World War I. It was not all success however; in his early years he was a poor man, and when in the Austrian army's avalanche rescue team in northern Italy in World War I he was directed into the path of an avalanche by mistaken planning and ended up with seventy-seven broken bones.

The museum also houses other artifacts from the region's history and is situated in the old watch tower by the bridge over the river.

Zdarsky's popularity is such that the main street and a little park are both named after him, with a monument to him in the latter. But Lilienfeld's other great attraction is the Cistercian abbey, the original buildings of which now form much of the old part of the town.

The abbey was founded in 1202 by Duke Leopold Babenberg and first consecrated in 1230. From that year to 1260 the largest cloister in Austria was constructed here. It contains stained glass from the fourteenth century. From 1730 to 1746 the church, the largest in Lower Austria, was given a baroque interior using black marble from Traisen. The picture in the high altar represents the assumption and was painted by Daniel Gran in 1746.

Lilienfeld, which was designated a market-town in 1973, has its history tied up closely with the monastery. It also has a more eventful past than is suggested by the present peace and quiet. In 1683 the town defended itself successfully from a Turkish invasion and in 1810 a fire devastated the monastery.

Also within the abbey there is a fantastic baroque library containing 25,000 volumes, including some 300 especially valuable manuscripts. The most famous of these is the *Concordantiae caritatis* written and illuminated by the abbot Ulrich between 1345 and 1351. It is possible to look inside the door of the library, but it is mainly screened off to visitors. Apparently when the Russians occupied the area after World War II the monastery was about to be ransacked, but the Russian commander found a Russian Bible in the library and was so impressed that he ordered that no one could touch the building or its contents. There are now many bullet holes that bear witness to the fighting in that war, which devastated much of the abbey. Rebuilding and renovation was carried out from 1957 to 1962.

The abbey also contains the only remaining medieval sleeping hall for lay-brothers and medieval monastery door in Austria. Outside there's an early example of fish farming, with a pond full of trout. The monastery buildings are reached easily from the town itself and as such are perhaps not so quite as dominating and spectacular from without as others previously mentioned.

It is worth having a quick review of the town's restaurants for a change, because it has a number that are historically interesting, and today very pleasant places to spend an evening. Perhaps the best place to start is the monastery, which has its own inn, selling exclusive wines from its vineyards in the north-west corner of Lower Austria, not far from Zwettl. It seems strange to stop for a drink in a monastery and yet the place has as much of a feel of history about it as the monastery itself and the wines are exceptionally good (and reasonably priced!).

Built into the old walls is the Gasthaus Steg, also with a good selection of wine. The original building is twelfth century — a century older than the monastery — and contains an old prison cell. Gasthaus Zum Weissen Hahn is owned by the Kurz family and was founded in 1758 (the date is carved above the door). It is now a modern hotel with restaurant serving a wide selection of excellent food.

Finally the Gasthof zum Schutzen, situated near to the small railway station, is a cosy inn with friendly staff and management and is particularly popular with the locals. It has a 'Zdarsky Room' and modern bedroom suites are in a block across the road from the bar/restaurant.

Also in Lilienfeld there's a statue which was built into the river around 1695 (though this was away being renovated at the time of research) and also Mount Calvary — one of Austria's best with more than twenty statues.

Winter recreation includes five ski lifts for downhill, curling and cross-country skiing. In the summer there are hiking trails, swimming, fishing, tennis, sacred music festivals in the monastery and folklore evenings.

This journey south officially ends here, but it is worth continuing on to the northern borders of Styria for those wishing to go on in this direction. The mountain scenery is beautiful and there are more attractive little villages, many with good skiing facilities.

St Aegyd 27km (17 miles) to the south of Lilienfeld, is one example, dominated by two mountains — The Gippel (1,697m, 5,475ft) and the Goller (1,796m, 5,794ft). It's popular both in summer (holidays on a farm are available, and wood carving courses) and winter. For the first time, in 1989, it was the scene of the Austrian National Cross Country ski championships in early February. This was a snow-free year and lorry loads of the cold white stuff had to be carried down to the village circuit at about 600m (1,968ft) above sea level. The competition went off without hitch. There are also a number of ski tows, a major ski jump and further cross-country trails in the mountains above the village, as well as the usual selection of summer sports. St Aegyd has the densest woodland in the Lilienfeld region.

St Aegyd also contains a factory which is not much to look at, but manufactures the cables used in ski lifts around Europe. So next time you're hanging in the air on a flimsy looking chair, you can at least say you've been to the place where the cables were made!

Further Information
— The Danube from the Traisen to the Enns —

Places of Interest in the Area

Altenmarkt im Yspertal
Museum
Open: Saturdays and Sundays, 9-11am or by prior arrangement.
☎ Hans Wick (07415) 492

Amstetten
Castle Museum
Open: every 2nd Saturday and 4th Sunday in the month, 2-5pm.

Farming Museum
Open: mid-May to end October, 9am-6pm.
☎ (07413) 8302

Artstetten
First Duke Franz Ferdinand Museum

Open: beginning April to beginning November daily 9am-6pm; early November to end March, visits for groups in excess of fifteen by arrangement.
☎ (07413) 8302

Ardagger
Militaria Museum
Admission charge.
For information on opening
☎ (07479) 239

Klam Schloss (including museum)
Near Grein
Open: daily beginning May to end October (closed at lunch time).
Special guided tours by appointment.
☎ (07269) 36117

Göttweig
Abbey
Open: May to October, Tuesdays,
Fridays-Sundays and holidays,
9.30am-12noon and 1.30-5.30pm.
☎ (02732) 5582

Grein
Schloss Greinburg with Shipping
Museum
Open: daily, beginning May to
beginning November, 9am-12noon
and 2-5pm.

Hafnerbach
Museum
Open: Saturdays 2-4pm, Sundays
10am-12noon and 2-4pm.
☎ (02749) 2278

Kottes
Franz Kitzler Private Collection
Open: by arrangement.
☎ (02873) 310

Mineral exhibition
Open: daily (except Mondays)
☎ (02873) 254

Krems
History Museum
Open: mid-April to end October,
Tuesdays-Saturdays 9am-12noon
and 2-5pm. Sundays and holidays,
9am-12noon.
☎ (02732) 2511 ext 338 or 339; or
4927.
It is possible to visit during closed
periods by prior arrangement.

Wine Making Museum
Opening times and contact number
as for History Museum above.

Radio Museum
Open: by arrangement.

Krems - Egelsee
Motoring Museum
Open: Wednesday-Sunday and
holidays, 9am-5pm.
☎ (02732) 731013

Beethoven House — Memorial
Rooms
Open: by arrangement
☎ (02732) 68075

Lilienfeld
Zdarsky/Town Museum
Open: Sunday 9.30-11.30am;
Thursday 5-7.30pm; Saturday
3-5pm. Admission charge.
☎ (02762) 221217

Abbey
Open: weekdays, 9am-11am and
2-5pm. Sunday and Festivals
10-11am and 2-3pm.
☎ (02762) 2204

Maria Laach
Natural History Exhibition
Open: by arrangement.
☎ (02713) 474

Maria Taferl
Treasure chamber of the pilgrim-
age church.
Open: usually daily, May to
October.
☎ (07413) 278

Mautern an der Donau
Chapel and Museum
Open: Saturdays 10am-12noon and
2-4pm, Sundays and Festival days
10am-12noon.
☎ (02732) 3151

Melk
Abbey
Open: daily 9am-4pm

(5pm in summer).
Guided tours in various languages
take 1 hour.
☎ (02752) 2312

Mühldorf
Schloss Oberranng
Open: May to October, weekends
and holidays, by prior arrangement with guide.
☎ (02713) 8221

Neuhofen an der Ybbs
Austrian Commemorative Site —
documentation of the first naming
of Austria.
Open: late March to end November, Tuesday-Saturday 10am-
12noon and 2-4pm. Sundays and
Festivals 9am-12noon and 1-4pm.
☎ (07475) 2321 or 2700

Ottenstein
Relaxation Camp — Stauseen
Open: Easter to All Saints Day,
Tuesday-Saturday, visits by prior
arrangement.
☎ (02826) 254

Persenbeug
Local Museum
Open: Monday-Friday 8am-12noon
or by prior arrangement.
☎ (07412) 2206

Pöchlarn
Local Museum
Open: mid-June to mid-September.
Tuesday - Sunday 10am-12noon
and 2-5pm.
☎ (02757) 310

Pöggstall
Museum with Torture Chamber
Open: beginning March to end
November 9am-12noon and

2-4.40pm, with timed guided tours
and in winter by arrangement.
☎ Fr Rotzer (02758) 2397

Old Criminal Law Exhibition
Open: by arrangement.
☎ tourist office for information.

Pottenbrunn
Tin Figures Museum
Open: Tuesday-Sunday, 9am-5pm.
☎ (02785) 2337

St Pölten
History Museum
Open: Tuesday-Saturday 10am-
5pm, Sunday 9am-12noon. April to
November admittance by arrangement.
☎ (02742) 2531

Local Museum
Open: May to October, Tuesday-
Friday 10am-12noon and 2-5pm.
☎ (02742) 2101

Former Synagogue
Open: as museum above
☎ (02742) 67171

St Michael in dem Wachau
Schloss Schallaburg
Open: end April to early November, daily 9am-5pm, Sundays and
holidays 9am-6pm.

Spitz an der Donau
Shipping Museum
Open: beginning April to end
October, daily 10am-12noon and
2-4pm (Sundays until 5pm)
☎ (02713) 246

Stein an der Donau
Monastery
Open: by arrangement
☎ (02732) 73074

Traismauer
Local Museum
Open: beginning April to end
October, Sundays and holidays
10-11.30am or by prior arrangement.
☎ (02630) 8240

Waidhofen an der Ybbs
Local Museum
Open: Easter Sunday to mid-October, Tuesday-Saturday 9.30am-
12noon and 2-5pm, Sunday 9am-
12noon. Closed Mondays.
☎ (07442) 2511 17

Weissenkirchen in der Wachau
Wachau Museum
Open: beginning April to end
October, daily except Mondays,
10am-5pm. Admittance only with
guide.
☎ (02715) 2268

Wölbling
'Wild Animals of the World'
Exhibition
Open: by arrangement
☎ (02786) 2420

Tourist Information Offices

Amstetten
A-3300

Dürnstein
Information on opening of historic
buildings
☎ 02711 219

Falkenstein
A-6873

Gutenbrunn
A-3665

Klosterneuberg
A-3400

Königswiesen
Mr Rammer
Fremdenverkehrsverband
Königswiesen
A-4280

Lilienfeld
Mr Heinz Eppensteiner
Stadtgemeinde Lilienfeld
Lilienfeld
A-3180

Neuhofen an der Ybbs
A-3364

Purgstall an der Erlauf
A-3251

Rechberg
A-4322

St Georgen am Walde
Ms Helene Sengstbratl
Fremdenverkehrsverband
c/o Sengstbratl
Ob St Georgen 9
A-4370 St Georgen am Walde

Tulln
A-3430

Ybbs
A-3370

12 • Lower Austria: The North-Western Corner

T he north-western corner of Lower Austria is also a large part of the Waldviertel which stretches down to the north bank of the Danube. Traditionally this is a green land of hills and dense forests, based on former granite uplands that have been greatly eroded and which become gradually lower as you travel north and away from the alpine forelands. The northern Waldviertel is perhaps not quite so typical of the region's image as a whole as are the parts down by the Danube. Instead the woodland is often less dense forest, more sporadic and broken up by agricultural land. On the very northern boundaries there is an increasing number of natural lakes and streams, many of which run into the Thaya. There are also stretches of moorland which definitely do not fit the Waldviertel image.

Tourism in the northern villages is not so well developed as down by the Danube either, though the small rural hamlets remain pretty much the same. Historically, it is often the same architects and artists from past centuries who are prominent in design, as those who are prolific down around the Danube basin.

There are few large towns in the area for the villagers to commute to so the majority of people work in traditional trades. Austrians are well known for their friendliness of course, their airline uses the image to promote itself; but here with the relaxed, timeless, attitude people are immediately anxious to be friendly and helpful, if only to satisfy their own curiosity.

Horn is perhaps not the best place to start a tour of the region, because in terms of general interest it does not have a great deal going for it. However, as the nearest point to Vienna along the main road, it is not a bad starting point for a clockwise tour of the north-western corner of Niederösterreich. It is possible to see the town in a more enthusiastic light if you are prepared to look closely. There

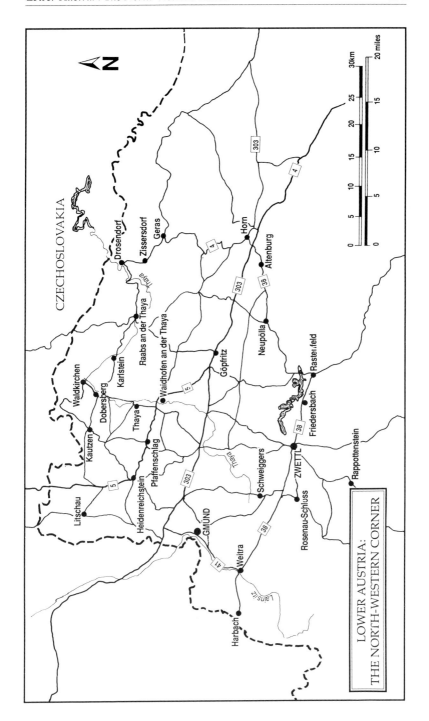

CZECHOSLOVAKIA

Drosendorf
Zissersdorf
Geras
Horn
Altenburg
Thaya
Raabs an der Thaya
Waldkirchen
Karlstein
Dobersberg
Waidhofen an der Thaya
Göpfritz
Neupölla
Rastenfeld
Kautzen
Thaya
Friedersbach
Pfaffenschlag
Heidenreichstein
Schweiggers
ZWETTL
Rappottenstein
Litschau
Thaya
GMÜND
Rosenau-Schloss
Weitra
Lainsitz
Harbach

303
4
4
303
38
5
38
303
5
38
47

30km
25
20
15
10
5
0
20 miles
15
10
5
0

LOWER AUSTRIA:
THE NORTH-WESTERN CORNER

are several churches worth visiting, as well as surviving medieval wall towers and a sixteenth-century castle, plus the odd example of Renaissance housing. However, it would probably be best to use Horn as a route-stop rather than an overnight base.

Soon after leaving the town and taking the Zwettl road (route 38), the village of **Altenburg** is worth a stop. There is a Benedictine abbey here, altered to baroque in the eighteenth century by Joseph Munggenast but founded some 600 years before then. The library which Munggenast designed is particularly impressive with a good deal of intricate decoration. The abbey also includes a cupola fresco designed by Paul Troger, as well as a crypt containing paintings from *The Dance of Death* (not for the squeamish). Further along the road you pass the Renaissance castle of Greillenstein, containing more examples of Troger's work.

Neupölla marks the eastern tip of one of Austria's largest army ranges which touches Zwettl in the south-west and Göpfritz to the north. The road from here borders the range so don't wander off to the north or east too far from the road.

The already bendy route 38 from Neupölla to Zwettl is unable to take a straight course because of the presence of the Ottenstein reservoir, a lake artificially created just over 20 years ago by the damming of the river Kamp, which provided the locals with hydro-electric power and summer water sports. There is a restaurant and boat hire active in the summer months and the ruins of Burg Lichten-fels can be seen. More dramatic is Burg Ottenstein situated upon a wooded hill and in a good state of preservation. This was originally built by Rapoto of Kuenring-Schönberg in the twelfth century and has a huge keep dating back to that period, as well as five courtyards, later additions containing Gothic and Renaissance frescoes.

If you're planning to spend the evening in Zwettl and find you still have time to kill before you arrive, a short detour south to **Rastenfeld** and then back to Friedersbach is worth the excursion. The former has a thirteenth-century parish church and neighbouring castle ruins; whilst **Friedersbach** church has stained glass windows and a beautiful carved wooden crucifix, both created in the fifteenth century. There are also good sports and leisure facilities in the area.

And so to **Zwettl**, the major settlement of the area, although in fact just a medium-sized market town with a population of 13,000. It first appears in records in the early part of the twelfth century. It is also the administrative centre for the western area of Waldviertel. Zwettl is situated on the upper course of the Kamp river, which is here joined by the river tributary after which the town is named, before it

Eggenburg

eventually flows into the Danube a few miles to the east of Krems.

Within the town, visitors should head first to the old town walls of which substantial stretches have survived the ravages of time. Six towers and two gates still stand with them. One of the towers, the Antonturm (thirteenth century), houses the small Anton-Museum which contains general historical objects from the region's past, including weapons, illustrations and practical implements.

Elsewhere there is an interesting 'plague column' (1727) in the town hall. The hall itself, built in 1307 and renovated many times through the centuries is worth a visit. There are a number of Gothic and Romanesque churches within the town, including the 'Propsteikirche' — formerly the private church of the counts of Kuenringen — which dates back to Zwettl's early years.

Zwettl's major attraction, however, lies a few miles to the northeast of the town in a bend of the river Kamp. This is a beautiful Cistercian monastery which can be reached by foot or by following the old road that runs alongside the railway line. Founded in 1138 it was altered in the eighteenth century. Old and very old blend surprisingly well together and it seems that the most beautiful architecture from each era has survived (a rare treat).

The church façade is eighteenth century, of grey granite with white detail. The most spectacular part of the building is within; gold ornamentation is in abundance and there is a particularly impressive altar. The Gothic winged altarpiece features a seated Virgin with Child. St Benedict and St Bernard stand on either side under a golden canopy. The centre of the altar was carved by Gregor Erhart in the year 1500, but the wings on either side were added, perhaps almost immediately, by Jorg Breu. The western part of the nave is baroque, as are the furnishings; however, the eastern part is Gothic and provides the fine narrow pillars. The choir stands out with white and pink colouring, complemented by the dark wood choir stalls and golden figures above them. One side of the chancel contains a richly gilded pulpit, the other side houses the organ. There are also stained glass windows from the fifteenth century and a Romanesque crucifix dating to the abbey's foundation.

The church tower is yet another example of Munggenast's work. Started in 1722, it took 5 years to build, with a gilded figure of Christ topping its near 93m (300ft) height.

The abbey contains a Romanesque canonical house, which is one of the oldest still surviving (1159-1180). It is really a simple building in terms of decoration but the splendid arches and vaulted ceiling emanating from a central granite column are of near perfect construction. The library is very different. It is baroque, and again Troger, with Munggenast, were able to elaborately decorate the vast room. It contains more than 50,000 volumes as well as over 400 original manuscripts and more than 300 incunabula. The abbey's baroque organ (in the church) was built in 1731 and is the largest of its type in Austria. If you are lucky one of the occasional concerts will be held on the day you choose to visit.

Far more than a tourist attraction, though guided tours are available to sufficient numbers, the abbey also contains grammar and choir schools, a museum and a modern day sanctuary or 'house of retreat'.

Zwettl is at the centre of a network of roads which spread out across the hills and plains in all directions. For this route however, the direction is east towards Weitra near the Czech border, with perhaps a short and minor detour to the castle with a Freemason's museum at Schloss Rosenau. The rococo building was restored only 20 years ago, though the current structure dates from the early eighteenth century. It is possible to return to the Weitra road from here, without having to double back. A little further south, and off this route, is Schloss Rappottenstein, parts of which date from the twelfth century and which contains Austria's best preserved torture chamber.

The windmill at Retz

In the centre of the wooded and hilly triangle of countryside between Weitra, Gmünd and Zwettl — typical of the Waldviertel — lies the village of **Schweiggers**, with its twelfth-century church containing fourteenth-century frescoes. It lies in the centre of a web of minor roads and at least seven radiate out in every direction from the outskirts. But following north-west through villages such as

Jagenbach and Wornharts, you rejoin route 119 at Weitra.

Weitra was once fortified and still contains the remains of the walls. Much of the old centre remains, making this a very attractive town that reminds one more of Robin Hood than the 'fairytale' pinnacled buildings and villages found elsewhere in the region. The sixteenth-century castle which dominates the town contains a beautiful old theatre, not dissimilar to that in Grein down by the Danube, although this is slightly larger and more ornate.

Amongst the interesting old buildings in the town are the Rathaus and those around the town square, and there is a fourteenth-century parish church. Steam trains run along the old railway line in the summer. Indoors there's a discothèque, sauna and swimming pool; outdoors there is a boating lake and tennis courts.

Weitra marks a minor border before the official one. It stands on road 41 which runs roughly parallel to the border, however the wooded strip of countryside between the two is remarkably undeveloped. Due west of Weitra is the peat spa of **Moorbad Harbach** situated in a valley between the Mandelstein 899m (2,900ft) and Nebelstein 992m (3,200ft) mountains. Of course it's a relaxing area to stay, but the health spa is the village's major claim to fame. A modern spa centre has been built and for those who feel they don't need the health giving baths, there are plenty of other water-based activities for pure leisure. Even here, right on the north-western Czech border, you are still only 137m (85 miles) from Vienna.

You can continue along minor roads in the rural 'border belt' to Gmünd or you can return to route 41 and follow the main road by the Lainsitz river.

Gmünd, which should not be confused with the more popularly known Carinthian town of the same name, is a major closed border point with Czechoslovakia. This lesser known Gmünd was once walled and the remnants are still to be seen, as are many beautiful Renaissance buildings. The thirteenth-century Rathaus is a very interesting building one of several in the town centre. There is also a glass museum which follows the history of glass making in the region since medieval times. All around this area you can buy glass items.

The main road from Vienna through Horn and on towards Czechoslovakia (303) passes north of Gmünd. Between the roads and the border there is a nature park which contains indiginous wildlife and has interesting geological features. Just past where road 41 meets road 303 you come to the industrial town of Schrems. Following road 30 northwards from there you reach **Heidenreich-**

Rastenfeld

stein. The town is most famous for its huge castle and indeed it was first documented in 1205 because of the castle, which has foundations dating to around 1190 and massive round towers. It is one of Austria's best preserved moated castles and also has a small lake. The original castle was built by the Gars/Eggenburg family and in the 1205 document a descendant is already named, 'Otto of Heidenreichstein'. The present castle dates to the fourteenth century. It has had several owners through the centuries. From the fourteenth to sixteenth century it belonged to the Puchheims, some of whom were renowned soldiers, and killed numerous Turks. In 1648 the castle became the property of the Palffy family who owned it for 300 years until January 1947 when the last Palffy prince, Ladislaus, died. Since then the castle has been owned by the Van Der Staten family.

The castle's protection allowed a town to spring up and by the late fourteenth century already it had been awarded a coat of arms. Through the following centuries up to the Napoleonic invasions Heidenreichstein survived fires and frequent attacks from the Bohemians and others. The Turks did not make it as far as the village although many refugees from the fighting came in 1663. It had an important place on the old imperial road between Prague and Vienna, and in the 1880s textile mills developed alongside the new metalworking industry.

In 1932 Heidenreichstein was granted town status and it now has a population of 5,300. There are a couple of ugly concrete blocks in the town, but the majority of dwellings are traditional and the town retains its olde worlde charm in many quarters. Karl Kiesewetter, the man who invented the match (in Jönköping, Sweden) was born here. There are modern sports facilities which might be welcomed by some and these include a multi-fitness gym and a bowling alley. Riding, cycle hire, tennis and cross-country skiing are available at various times of the year. There is also a large lake nearby used for swimming, boating and windsurfing, and a BMX track for the children.

The Gothic parish church dates from about 1200, but was badly damaged by fire in 1621 and took ten years to rebuild. The church tower was erected in 1755 although one of the five bells it contained dated from 1666. This was taken away in 1942, presumably to help the war effort. New bells were installed in 1952 but there have been 'electric' bells since 1967.

The pillory in the market place is a monument with an interesting history. It was first erected in 1688 and was decorated with the figure of a knight. This did not last long and was replaced by a flag; the story is that the people in the half of the town which faced the knight's back wanted the figure removed. In 1945 a headless, armless figure was discovered; it was decided that this was the old knight and he now stands near the church. At the pillory today there is a 'quarrel stone' which was hung around the neck of troublemakers who had to stand by the pillory wearing it on market days. The symbol of judgement, a sword arm, is placed at the pillory during the 2-week annual fair as it always has been. There is also a bell on the pillory which is rung at 9 o'clock. This is because, in days gone by, the tavern had to close at 9pm in the summertime and 8pm in the winter. That is one tradition the people of Heidenreichstein were happy to forget!

One of the main businesses today is carp fish farming, but generally the town has suffered in employment prospects along with other parts of Austria and the rest of Europe in recent years.

North from Heidenreichstein road 5 heads again for the border. In the hills and meadows that mark the north-west corner of Lower Austria the largest village is **Litschau**. This has several small beautiful lakes around it. The Gothic church of St Michaels is fourteenth century, and the castle nearby dates from the thirteenth century.

Heidenreichstein is surrounded by numerous small lakes, one of which, shortly before Pfaffenschlag on road 5 south-east, begins a tributary into the great Thaya river. The Thaya and its tributaries criss-cross the area of the Waldviertel to the east of Heidenreichstein: you will cross the tributary several times in the few kilometres to Pfaffenschlag. In fact much of the Thaya valley around this area is quite beautiful, densely wooded in places, and unlike other areas of the Waldviertel there can be quite swift changes from forest to agricultural land and back again, depending on which route you take.

As with the Mur in the south-eastern corner of Austria, the Thaya forms a large part of the Austrian/Czechoslovak border, particularly once round the north-eastern corner of Austria when it joins the March before eventually flowing into the Danube by Bratislava. During its brief sorties into Czechoslovakia en route, the river forms several large and often beautiful lakes.

Back in the river's birthplace however, is a region called, naturally enough, the Thayatal. The first town to take its name is **Waidhofen an der Thaya** about 12 miles from Heidenreichstein and a similar distance the Czech border to the north. It should not be confused with the better known Waidhofen near the Danube on the Ybbs river. This is a baroque town, with a beautiful church (constructed 1716-1723), containing interesting frescoes. There is also a sixteenth-century Rathaus. The countryside round about flattens down a great deal and there is more agricultural land, which is not as inspiring as other areas of the Waldviertel, though pleasant enough.

Road 5 bends further south after Waidhofen and soon merges with road 303 to Horn. Road 36 from Ybbs and Zwettl also cuts through Waidhofen's western edge passing the village of **Thaya** on the left. This has a beautiful market square with a renovated town house. The church is Romanesque and there are two Renaissance fountains and a small local museum. At the year end there is a festival here.

If you continue northwards from Dobersberg along road 36 you come to a closed border just past the village of Fratres. However, there is a right turn a few miles before, signposted **Waldkirchen**. This is a peaceful little village surrounded by the Nadelwalder area of woodland which is famed locally for it's beautiful walks. There is a puppet museum in the village's old school.

Dobersberg itself has a nature park containing wild boars and interesting geological features. The twelfth-century market place is surrounded by several attractive buildings. The local castle is sixteenth century. The parish church of St Lambrecht is twelfth century and has a Gothic choir. There is a ski lift here and plenty of organised summer activities.

West of Dobersburg is the quiet little village of **Kautzen**, a good base for those interested in 'back to nature' type holidays.

The road east from Dobersberg quickly brings you through undulating agricultural countryside to **Raabs an der Thaya**. Known as the 'Jewel of the Thaya Valley' (to the Austrian Tourist Board at least!) this is indeed a very attractive town. The eleventh-century castle towers over it and exhibitions and concerts take place each year. The town also has a small museum and the ruins of Kollmitz castle nearby. Recreational facilities are above average: a leisure centre houses indoor and outdoor pools, sauna, solarium, minigolf, huge chess, three tennis courts and curling. Fishing, cycling and boating are also available. Between Dobersburg and Raabs is the village of **Karlstein** which contains Austria's only college for watch makers.

From Raabs you can follow the Thaya to the Czech border, at the top of road 4 which goes straight back to Horn. In fact all roads lead to Horn, eventually, from here, the most direct route taking you past the castle of Wildberg near Messern.

Geras is the closest the route comes to the north-eastern corner of the Waldviertel, though the actual boundary is still some miles off. The countryside is hardly characteristic of the better known Waldviertel areas, being 'bleak' and flat by comparison. However Geras has a lot to offer the visitor who wishes to stay there. One possible 'hotel' is the twelfth-century abbey (founded 1150), rebuilt in the eighteenth century from a design by Munggenast and containing a beautiful baroque pilgrimage church (originally Romanesque).

You can also stay in the Hotel Alter Schuttkasten which was built in 1670 as a granary belonging to the abbey. It towers above the other buildings in the village centre but remains peaceful despite its situation. There is also a public restaurant which has an excellent reputation, game and fish are specialities and there are several special dishes available from the old abbey kitchens. The hotel is also the centre for the art and traditional craft/hobby courses organised in Geras. These include pottery, music, icon painting and woodwork.

For those who prefer life under canvas there's a camp site with cycle hire available and several hiking trails, in the nearby 350 acre nature park and bird sanctuary. Geras is in a sheltered corner of the countryside and is said to have particularly clean air.

Road 4 north of Geras passes through Zissersdorf and then Drosendorf, from where there is a direct (but windy) road back to Raabs, before coming to a stop at Thurnau on the border. **Drosendorf** is an attractive village. The main hotel here, run by one of the

Drosendorf

major local landowners, is the beautiful Schloss Drosendorf.

Further Information
— Lower Austria : The North-Western Corner —

Places of Interest in the Area

Altenburg
Treasure Chamber with various relics and religious artifacts.
Open: Easter to All Saints Day, 9am-12noon and 1-5pm.
☎ (02982) 5451

Breiteneich
Renaissance castle
☎ (02982) 2303

Brunn an der Wilde
Small private museum of local crafts, tools through the centuries.
Open: by prior arrangement.
☎ (02989) 2341

Dobersberg
Scientific Information Centre of Thayatal-Naturpark
Open: beginning May-end October, 9-11am and 1-4pm Saturdays, Sundays and holidays.

Castle Mineral Exhibition
Open: Easter to beginning November, Friday-Sunday, 9-11am and 1-4pm.
☎ (02843) 332

Drosendorf Stadt
Town Museum
Open: by prior arrangement.
☎ (02915) 213 or 321

Geras
Church and buildings
Open: beginning May to end
September at 11am, 2, 3 and 4pm
(except Mondays). Visits only with
a tour guide.

Gmünd
Town Museum
Open: May to September, Monday-
Friday 9am-12noon and 2-5pm.
Saturdays, Sundays and holidays
open 9am-12noon; October to
April open Sundays and holidays.
Closed 24 December to 6 January.
☎ (02852) 2506 18

Glass Museum
Opening times and contact number
as for Town Museum above.

Stone Museum
Opening times and contact number
as for Town Museum above.

Gmünd Eibenstein
Nature Park Information Centre
Open: mid-April to end August.
☎ (02852) 3817

Nature Park Museum
Open: daily.

Greillenstein
Castle Museum
Open: beginning April to end
October at 9am.
☎ (02989) 8321 or 8216

Bad Grosspertholz
Local Technology, History and
Geography Museum
Open: Monday-Friday 7.30am-
12noon and 1-4.30pm.

Nature Park Information Centre
Open: in summer months and in
good weather at 9am.

Grossschönau
Local Museum
Open: daily 8am-12noon and
2-5pm. Sundays 9am-12noon.
☎ (02815) 252

Harbach/Moorbad/Lauterbach
Forestry and Farming Museum
Open: daily 2-4pm or by prior
arrangement.

Heidenreichstein
Town Museum
Open: mid-April to mid-October,
daily except Mondays, 9, 10, 11am
and 2, 3 and 4pm. Visit with tour,
minimum five people. Larger
groups by arrangement only.
☎ (02852) 2268

Heidenreichstein-Kleinpertholz
Town Museum
Open: beginning June to end
September, Sundays and holidays
9am-12noon. Group visits can be
arranged at other times.
☎ (02862) 2336

Local Peat and Moors Museum
Open: details on above number.

Horn
Hobarth Museum
Open: Palm Sunday to All Saints
Day, daily except Monday 9am-
12noon and 2-5pm.
☎ (02982) 2372 or 2656

Mader Museum
(farming and agriculture)
Opening times and contact number
as Hobarth Museum above.

Archive for Forestry Historical
Research
Open: weekends and by prior
arrangement.
☎ (02982) 30612

Litschau
Local Museum of Town History
☎ (02865) 219 for details

Messern
Castle Wildberg
☎ (02985) 382 for details

Neu-Nagelberg
Glass studio and museum
Open: Monday to Friday 8am-
12noon and 1-4pm, Saturday 8am-
12noon. Groups by prior arrangement.
☎ (02859) 237

Raabs an der Thaya
Town Museum
Open: summer, Monday-Friday,
9am-12noon and 1-5pm, Saturdays
9am-12noon.
☎ (02846) 365

Raabs-Oberndorf
Raabs Castle Museum
Open: June to October, Monday-
Thursday 8am-12noon and
1-4.30pm. Fridays 8am-12noon and
1-2pm. Saturdays, Sundays and
holidays 9am-12noon and 1-5pm.
By arrangement and with a guide
between November and May.
☎ (02846) 659

Reingers
Small 'Home' Museum
Open: daily 8am-5pm.

Schloss Rosenau
Austrian Freemasonry Museum
Open: Palm Sunday to mid-
November, daily 9am-5pm.
☎ (02822) 8221 26

Rosenburg
Castle Museum

Open: mid-March to end September, 9am-12noon and 1-6pm;
beginning October to end November, 10am-12noon and 1-4pm.
☎ (02982) 2911

Rudolz
Private Puppet Museum
Open: by prior arrangement.
☎ (02845) 858

Schrems
Museum
Open: under construction at time
of writing.

Thaya
Museum
Open: Sundays 9am-12noon.
Closed in winter from beginning
November to end April. Entry
outside opening hours by prior
arrangement.
☎ (02842) 2665

Thaya-Peigarten
Schloss Peigarten
Open: Monday-Friday by prior
arrangement with gentlemen
below.
Monday to Friday, Dr Wolfer
☎ (0222) 439363
Saturday and Sunday, Josef Fasch-
ling (02842) 2987

Waidhofen an der Thaya
'House' museum
Open: Sundays 9am-12noon. July
and August weekdays 9am-
12noon, only by prior arrangement.
☎ Eduard Fuhrer (02842) 2621 12 or
2823

Museum
Opening hours and contact number as for 'House' museum above.

Family Museum
Open: Monday-Friday, 7am-
12noon and 1-4.15pm.
☎ Leopold Dangl (02842) 2535 13

Waldkirchen
Museum
Open: Easter to mid-October,
Tuesday-Saturday 9.30am-12noon
and 2-5pm. Sundays 9am-12noon.
☎ (07442) 2511 17

Puppet Museum
☎ Voranmeldung, Frau Hanisch
(02843) 858

Weitra-Oberbrühl
Weaving Museum
Open: by arrangement.
☎ (02856) 2451

Zwettl-Dürnhof
Museum of Medicine and
Meteorology
Open: daily except Mondays, end
April to end October 9am-5pm.
☎ (02822) 3180 or (0222) 364453 ext
247 or 206

Abbey Museum
For safety and security reasons it is
only possible to visit certain areas.
Open: Monday-Thursday at 10,
11am, 2, 3 and 4pm. Friday-Sunday at 11am, 2, 3 and 4pm. Beginning October to beginning May by
appointment only.
☎ (02822) 2391 or 2578 or 3181

Town Museum
☎ (02822) 2414 for details.

Zwettl-Grosshaslau
Private collection in Schloss

Grosshaslau.
Open: by prior arrangement.
☎ (02823) 503

Tourist Information Offices

Amaliendorf-Aalfang
A-3872

Heidenreichstein
Hans Pichler Esquire
Stadtgemeinde Heidenreichstein
3860-Heidenreichstein

Liebenau
A-4252

Moorbad Harbach
A-3970

Raabs an der Thaya
A-3820

St Martin-Harmanschlag
A-3971

Waidhofen an der Thaya
Robert Ertl Esquire
Stadtgemeinde Waidhofen an der
Thaya
Hauptplatz 1
Postfach 72
A-3830 Waidhofen an der Thaya

Zwettl
Mr Schrenk
Verkehrsverein der Stadt Zwettl
Gartenstr 3
Zwettl
A-3910

13 • Burgenland

Burgenland is the youngest and smallest of Austria's federal provinces and certainly the least explored. It covers 3,965sq km (1,531sq miles), has a population of about 270,000, and runs in a narrow strip along the eastern borders of Austria, from just south of the Danube in the north to Neuhaus in the south. In the north-east you can look over the heavily guarded frontier into Czechoslovakia, and the hill town of Bratislava. It is separated by barbed wire and floodlit watch towers in the east from Hungary, and in the south it borders Yugoslavia for a short distance. At its narrowest point the province is only 4km (3 miles) wide, and at its widest just 65km (40 miles). Its name gives a clue to its troubled and bloody history: Burgen means 'castles', and as a border province on the extreme eastern part of western Europe, it has seen much fighting and feuding.

Burgenland is noted for its wines and agricultural produce, its castles and its birdlife, especially the roof-top nesting storks. Lake Neusiedl is Europe's only steppe lake, surrounded by massive reed beds, and home to many of Europe's rarest birds and plants. It attracts bird watchers and naturalists from all over the world. In the summer, the sun beats down on the flat, baked landscape and you can often look up and count scores of birds of prey gracefully circling high above as they take advantage of the thermal currents. The lake and its surrounding areas provide some of the best birdwatching countryside in the world. And, after a day out in the field with your binoculars, you can relax in the evening drinking a glass or two of the very good local wine.

Other memorable features of the region are the ancient wells which dot the landscape. Huge poles are pivoted over the well and used to draw up the water.

Burgenland was founded in 1921 from the German-speaking border areas that had formerly belonged to Hungary. The people, however, still retain much of their Hungarian heritage and this is visible from the style of many of the buildings both in the towns and countryside, as well as their cooking and customs. There is still a strong tradition of wearing the 'national' costume on Sunday, and this is more characteristic of central Europe than other Austrian provinces.

The province is divided into districts, the administrative centres of which are: Eisenstadt, Güssing, Jennersdorf, Mattersburg, Neus-iedl-am-See, Oberpullendorf, Oberwart and Rust. It is primarily concerned with agriculture, and its rich black soil is very fertile. The area under vines has increased dramatically in the last decade or so, and now produces about a third of Austria's wine, sweetcorn, vege-tables of all kinds, and fruit. In the spring, it is a delight to drive through the countryside, and it seems as if the whole province is a mass of cherry and almond blossom.

A sort of prosperity has returned to Burgenland in recent years after the hardships caused when the border with Hungary was closed. Many of the small communities had strong links with Hun-gary, and a lot of produce used to be sold across the border. All that came to an end when the barbed-wire topped fencing was erected, as the Iron Curtain spread south. At that time many of the rural commu-nities were poor and the buildings delapidated, but all that has changed, with delightful villages, simple churches and beautiful abbeys to explore. There are the magnificent buildings of Eisenstadt, the provincial capital, famous for its links with the composer Haydn and the fabulously rich Esterházy family.

Because this region has not really been discovered by tourists, the roads and lanes are uncluttered, the small country hotels offer a warm service at a fraction of the prices of the normal tourist haunts, and there is a leisurely pace that is easy to fall into for a totally relaxing get-away-from-it-all holiday.

There are spas at Bad Tatzmannsdorf, famous for treating heart disease and female disorders, and at Sauerbrunn where people go to take the waters. Near Bad Tatzmannsdorf are two castles, the thir-teenth-century Burg Lockenhaus on the Hungarian border, and the fortress Burg Schlaining. The noble families of Hungary and Austria built many castles throughout Burgenland and most were on hilltops commanding spectacular views. Almost all the population is con-cerned with farming, forestry or wine making, although Burgenland does have its own small, but special industry. Around the village of Bernstein is found a kind of yellow jade, and Bernstein in English actually means 'amber'. This kind of stone is only found in Burgen-

The mighty baroque castle of the Esterházy family in Eisenstadt

land and it is exported in jewellery and ornaments all over the world. The thirteenth-century castle in Bernstein has been converted into the local hotel, but has retained the torture chamber — presumably for those reluctant to pay their bills!

About 88 per cent of the population is of German stock, about 10 per cent are of Croatian descent and about 2 per cent of Hungarian heritage. The Croatians settled there in the sixteenth century and the Hungarians are mostly of Magyar descent.

Being at the crossroads of western and eastern Europe, Burgenland has constantly been in the thick of wars, invasions and political intrigues. Over the centuries, the province has been overrun by the Celts, Romans, Huns and Goths. It was then invaded by the Bavarians, followed by the Turks and then the Hungarians. It was a Hungarian territory until after World War I and was ceded to Austria in 1919 as part of the Treaty of St Germain. Two years later, it became a federal province, one of the nine that make up modern-day Austria.

Most visitors who go to Burgenland travel there because of Lake Neusiedl, but there are many more things to see and do and all of them are truly off the beaten track. In the north, the hills gradually descend to the Pannonian Plain, part of the great Hungarian steppe, or *puszta*, and in the centre and south of the province, there are charming rolling hills draped with vineyards. These uplands are an extension of the Styrian hills, on the flanks of the eastern Alps.

Lake Neusiedl dominates the area, both because of its size and its impact on the climate. It is 36km (22 miles) long, up to 16km (10 miles) wide, but rarely more than 2m (7ft) deep. Three-quarters of the lake is in Austria, and one-quarter in Hungary. The border crosses the lake and is patrolled by frontier guards using fast launches. Its total area is 320sq km (124sq miles). The lake is warm and salty from mineral salts brought up by the underground springs. It is surrounded by reeds, one of the largest remaining reed beds in Europe, and is host to many unique plants and birds, because the lake is the meeting point for alpine, Baltic and Pannonian flora and fauna.

The rest of the province consists of wood-covered hills, one of the healthiest natural forest areas in the western world. One third of the province is forested and one quarter protected by nature conservation laws because of its exceptional scientific and environmental interest.

The gentle landscape of Burgenland is matched by its gentle climate. The winters are mild, and the summers long, hot and dry. The number of days of sunshine is well above the average, which explains the growth of its fine, full-bodied wines and lush vegetables and plants. There are natural sparkling mineral water springs and clean, unpolluted air.

It has, therefore, an enormous amount to offer visitors, especially those who like to explore and be in the open air. During the day you can walk in the hills, through the sweet smelling pines, you can fish, swim or birdwatch. There are scores of miles of cycle tracks to follow, lakes to boat on, or trails to pony trek across. In the evening you can relax and enjoy true Burgenland hospitality. The whole province is famous for its Burgenland-Pannonian cooking, particularly the strongly seasoned soups and spiced fish, and after your meal, enjoy the music of the region.

The people of Burgenland love to sing and dance, whether it be traditional, classical Pannonian, or fiery, temperamental Croatian. Burgenland often calls itself the land of music, and it plays host to many music festivals. Franz Liszt was born in the Burgenland town of Raiding in 1811, and even though it was then part of the Hungarian empire, Haydn is considered an adopted son of Burgenland because of his association with the Esterházy family in Eisenstadt. There are still regular concerts in the castles in Eisenstadt, Kittsee, Halbturn and Kobersdorf. There is the musical 'wine summer' in Donnerskirchen, and the candlelight concerts in the Fishermens' church in

Rust. There are special summer chamber music recitals in Lockenhaus, an annual international open-air jazz festival at Wiesen which
lasts for several days and the operetta performances performed on a
floating platform at Mörbisch, with the sun setting on Lake Neusiedl
as its backdrop. And, everywhere, in cafés and village squares, in
churches and restaurants you will find people playing folk or classical music, singing and dancing.

The people of Burgenland are also proud of their brass bands. At
the last count the province had eighty-three, consisting of 3,000
bandsmen and women, of which more than half were under twenty
years old. They can always find an excuse to bring out the band, and
brass band music is played at virtually every function in all towns
and villages. Traditional music is preserved and flourishes. Folk
music and folk dancing go hand in hand and are encouraged, especially in the schools. The *tamburizza*, an instrument which is something between a balalaika and a mandolin, is the traditional Croatian
folk music instrument and there are *tamburizza* groups in nineteen of
Burgenland's villages. Three folk dancing troupes from, Oberwart,
Unterwart and Oberpullendorf perform songs and dances of their
Hungarian forefathers and also keep in touch with the dances of
contemporary Hungary.

The people of Burgenland have survived centuries of trouble and
strife, and it has given them a philosophical outlook. They enjoy the
finest things of life, good food, good wine and good company. Their
hospitality, friendliness and tolerance are renowned, what more
could the visitor want?

A Tour Round Lake Neusiedl

The reed beds encircling the lake cover an area of about 156sq km
(60sq miles) and much of it is inaccessible, which is why the wildlife
abounds. The lake itself is treated with great respect by the local
fishermen. It is considered unpredictable because winds can whip
the water up into violent squalls very quickly, and there are many
myths and legends about demons and monsters who live in its
shallow waters. When fierce winds spring up, the water is pushed
along to one end of the lake, leaving the other end with hardly any
water in at all. As soon as the winds drop, the level evens out again.

The lake is fed by springs and on very rare occasions it dries out
completely. The last such occasion was between 1868 and 1872, and
families still talk about the feuds that developed over ownership of
the newly exposed land. Almost all the water loss is through evapo-

ration during the summer, and the level of the lake at its highwater mark is regulated by the Einserkanal. Salt marshes and beds of reeds, 2m (6¹/₂ft) and more high, surround the lake. More than 250 species of bird can be spotted here, from egrets to spoonbills, bee eaters to great white herons, and glossy ibis to marsh harrier. There are thousands of waders, geese, ducks and marshland birds. Fishing and shooting are both favourite pastimes of the locals, but many areas of the lake are now protected. The number of water birds is so great, that local hunting has little impact.

Being only about 50km (30 miles) from Vienna (Wien), the lake attracts large numbers of visitors during the hot summer weekends. These Viennese come to sail, fish or swim in the warm, salty waters. As the lake is so shallow, it quickly warms up in the summer. Fishermen use special flat bottomed boats and nets to catch the fish. The small circular nets are thrown into the water and almost immediately hauled back in by the fishermen.

The picturesque villages of Rust and Neusiedl make good bases for exploring the area, and bicycles are an excellent way to get around. The flat plains to the north and east of the lake are excellent cycling country, and it is the leisurely way to travel through this wildlife haven. As the Hungarian border passes through the lake, it is impossible to drive or cycle all the way round, but it is possible to catch a boat across from Rust, Podersdorf, Illmitz or Mörbish.

There are many small towns and villages where you can stop to admire the buildings, or enjoy a rustic lunch and the local wine. There are also many wine cellars to visit and most have tasting facilities as well. Many of the villages around the lake have strong Magyar traditions, and you can enjoy their spicy Hungarian cuisine. If you are cycling or driving through the area in June be sure to stop and enjoy the magnificent local strawberries, those grown in the Rosalia region are especially famous.

The village of **Rust** stands high above the lake half way down its west bank, surrounded by vineyards and orchards growing on terraces carved out of the hillside. The whole of the old town is preserved and in 1975 was declared a model town by the European Council. Many of the houses, especially in the town centre, have well preserved Renaissance or baroque façades. It is a typical wine producing village. Many of the houses lie behind tall ornately-carved wooden gates and stone walls which enclose cool, shady courtyards. Nobody is quite sure why the walls and gates are so imposing — whether this is to protect the wine stored inside, or is a remnant from the region's troubled past and the constant threat of attack. It has been producing wine for centuries and such was its fame that in the seventeenth century it received the royal warrant. Ever since, the winemakers have been able to decorate the vats in their cellars with the coat of arms of Rust.

The village square is the focal point for the community and an excellent place to try the local Ruster Ausbruch wines. There are many cafés and wine shops, as well as the uniquely Austrian *heurigen*, pubs owned by winemakers and only allowed to serve their own wines which must be less than one year old. This young wine, or *heuriger* is usually served in large jugs and gulped down rather than sipped. They are often drawn straight from the barrel without filtration, so are cloudy, but they can be deliciously refreshing when chilled and served with local delicacies. Two words of warning, however. The owners often serve free of charge highly salted snacks to accompany the wine to encourage a thirst so you will drink more; and this young wine can have an amazing laxative effect on some people.

Apart from its excellent wines, Rust is famous for two things: It claims to be the warmest place in central Europe, and is the home for scores of storks every summer. The magnificent white birds start to arrive in April and they stay until August. Many of the houses have platforms built on their roofs and chimneys so that the birds can nest there. It is considered very good luck to have a stork nesting on your home, and there is an old saying that disaster will strike the village and its occupants if the storks fail to return.

Rust is also well known for its basketwork and the reeds provide the raw materials for this, and for other local crafts industries. It is also noted for its many Hungarian restaurants and in the evening you can dine to the accompaniment of gypsy music.

There is a thirteenth-century sailors' church here, surrounded by a churchyard and defence wall. The church was once Catholic but is now Protestant. It has frescoes in the choir, transept and Marienkapelle, and the stone pulpit is decorated with floral paintings.

Tourists stay in Rust, but take the causeway on the east of the town to the lake with its beaches and bathing huts. A charge is made for use of the lakeside car park and for access to the beach. From here it is possible to take boats for a cruise of the lake, to swim, fish or dine in the lakeside restaurants.

Just to the west of Rust on the B52 is **St Margarethen**, where a Roman quarry provided stone for *Carnuntum*, and which is now used to display modern sculptures. It is also noted for its Passion Plays. If you have children you could also visit the 'Fairy tale' forest.

This has walks created especially for children, with sculptures and models hidden among the trees.

Mörbisch is the neighbouring village to Rust, lying 3 miles south. It too is noted for its storks, white wines, its Hungarian restaurants and especially its lake festival. Every summer thousands of people gather to listen to musicals and operettas performed on a floating stage. The village has a very popular lakeside beach, for which there is a small admission charge, and a sailing school. From Mörbisch it is less than a mile to the Hungarian border, and this is the last village on the western side of the lake before the frontier. The approach to the border is blocked by barbed wire and ditches, and the strip of no-man's land is guarded by armed Hungarian border troops in one of the watchtowers which dot the imposing Iron Curtain.

It is a charming village, strongly Hungarian in tradition with its typical Magyar-style houses bunched together and separated only by narrow alleys. The whitewashed homes have pretty outside staircases covered by porches, and doors and windows are usually brightly painted. As in many of the villages, you will see bunches of maize hanging up to dry, but in Mörbisch this has almost become an art form, with the corn cobs hanging decorously in clusters together with bunches of flowers beside the shutters.

To the west of the village lies Forchtenstein castle, an old fortress set on a cliff and looking out over the Hungarian plain. The castle is noted for its fine collection of arms and armour dating from the sixteenth to nineteenth centuries. Built in the fourteenth century by the counts of Mattersdorf, the castle was extended by the Hungarian Esterházy family in the early seventeenth century and was in the firing line of the Turkish sieges of 1529 and 1683. It is open all the year round, and there are escorted tours available. Today the castle is surrounded by firs, chestnut and cherry trees, and during the summer months is the venue for a season of light hearted plays.

There is a charming road northwards out of Rust which takes you along the western shores of the lake to the village of Neusiedl-am-See. With reed beds on your right and vineyards on your left, the road runs through **Oggau**, where you can camp, swim or relax on the lakeside beach, past the See Hotel at Seehof, where it joins the B50. Follow the route through Donnerskirchen and Purback, both of which have camp sites and good beach facilities and are wine towns. **Donnerskirchen** is an ancient market town with a baroque church and stocks, and **Purbach** is noted for its *Türkenkeller*. You then follow the road to **Neusiedl-am-See**. This village is an essential stop if you are interested in history, wine or the natural history of the region. It has prehistoric, Roman and Celtic remains, there are wine tasting cellars and a very good flora and fauna museum. It also has restaurants and hotels.

Take the B51 out of Neusiedl-am-See to explore the eastern side of the lake. About 5km (3 miles) out of Neusiedl, and about 1km (just over half a mile) beyond the village of Weiden, turn right on the unnumbered road to **Podersdorf** to find a camp site, good swimming beach, and facilities for water sports. You can also take cruises around the lake from here. As you approach the village look out for the decorated, single-storey building on the right. South of Podersdorf, the area becomes much wetter, and there are scores of reed-encircled lakes.

If you continue south about 10km (6 miles), you will come to the village of **Illmitz**, in the heart of a vast, natural wildlife sanctuary whose desolate marshes are noted throughout Europe for their flora and fauna. The village, which has a population of 2,500, is also noted because it is the lowest in Austria. There is a 5km (3 mile) causeway running down to the beach, where there are reed huts and brightly coloured horse-drawn caravans for hire. The road continues south through the small village of Apetlon, down to Pamhagen, almost on the Hungarian border, where it ends.

To the east of Apetlon is the nature reserve covering the Lange Lacke, administered by the World Wide Fund for Nature (formerly the World Wildlife Fund), and at **Pamhagen** there is a zoo featuring the native animals of the Hungarian steppes, such as wolves, wild boar, eagles and other birds of prey. This area is also the centre for wine making on the east shore of the lake and the main centres are at Illmitz, Apetlon, Gols, Podersdorf, Mönchhof and Halbturn.

Return by taking the B51 northwards from Pamhagen, through Wallern and St Andrä, both of which have swimming facilities, to **Frauenkirchen**, which has a very famous pilgrimage church. Originally built in 1335 it was constantly attacked and damaged by the Turks during the sixteenth and seventeenth centuries. The present structure was designed and built by Italian architect Francesco Martielli in 1702 after being commissioned by Prince Paul Esterházy. The twin towers with their double domes are the most striking outside feature and dominate the landscape. Inside, the church is decorated in magnificent baroque style. The frescoes and stucco decorations are by Luca Antonio Columba and Petro Antonio Conti. On the high altar there is a framed painting of the *Madonna and Child*, and above it a thirteenth-century linden wood statue of Maria with the infant Jesus dressed in an embroidered mantle. There are eight

*Harvesting grapes for Burgen-
land's* spätlese *wine*

spectacular and brilliantly decorated side altars, and the choirstalls with their painted panels, and the pulpit, are masterpieces of baroque art. Although well off the beaten track, this is considered to be one of the finest churches in Austria.

After Frauenkirchen, follow the B51 north to Mönchhof and then back to Neusiedl-am-See and Rust, or take either of the smaller roads at the crossroads in Mönchhof to explore the north and east of the region. The minor road off to the right takes you to **Halbturn** with its parish church built to the plans of J. Emanuel Fischer von Erlach, and the castle of Leopold von Hildebrandt, and then south to the villages of Andau and Tadten, and you can either retrace your route or return via St Andrä and Frauenkirchen. If you take the minor road straight over the Mönchhof crossroads, after about 13km (8½ miles) you will reach a T junction. The left fork, on the B10, will take you to Nickelsdorf and then down to the border crossing at Hegyeshalom, while a left turn on to the B10 will take you to Zurndorf and Gattendorf before the road swings round to take you back to Parndorf and Neusiedl.

If you are staying in Eisenstadt and want to drive around the lake, the route through Rust, Neusiedl, Podersdorf, Illmitz, Pamhagen, Frauenkirchen, and then back through Neusiedl and Schützen to Eisenstadt will cover about 160km (100 miles). It is possible to do it in a day but you will not be doing it justice. It is much better to base yourself in Rust for a day or two to explore the west side of the lake, and then to move to Neusiedl to concentrate on the eastern shore.

In Search of the Wildlife of Burgenland

Lake Neusiedl

The waters and reedbeds make this one of the richest wildlife habitats in the world, and one of the most important in Europe. More than 250 species of birds live or breed in and around the lake. Reeds only grow in shallow waters so they thrive on the fringes of the lake, as do the birds, animals and insects which have adapted specially to marshland habitats. Several jetties and piers have been built out into the huge expanse of reeds and these make good observation platforms, but the best way to watch the wildlife is to stroll along the embankment which runs parallel to the eastern shore of the lake.

Both Rust and Neusiedl-am-See make ideal bases for a bird watching holiday and from either you can quickly travel to all the best sites, both east and west of the lake. If you plan to cover large distances, a car is essential for getting about, but bicycles can be hired in Eisenstadt, Rust and Neusiedl and are the ideal form of transport. They are silent and give you the extra height to spot birds lurking in the reeds or on the other side of the hedges.

The region supports so many species of birds because there is such a wide variety of habitats. To the west of the lake and north of **Eisenstadt** there is the Tiergarten, with its woodland walks. South of **Mattersburg**, about 20km (12¹/₂ miles) to the east of the lake, the hills start to grow in stature and are pine-clad.

To the south-east of the main lake, there are scores of little ponds and lakes, many of them close to the Hungarian border. To the north-east of the lake is Parndorfer Heide, the flat plains over which the birds of prey soar in the summer. Around **St Andrä**, there are more plains, usually planted with crops, and here you can find one of Europe's most majestic land birds, the great bustard, which, alas, is also one of the most endangered species. This large grey and white feathered turkey-like bird was hunted to extinction in England more than a century ago and birds taken from around Neusiedl were released on to Salisbury Plain a few years back to try to re-establish the great bustard in the UK. The experiment failed, but you can still see these great birds on the plains around the lake. They are very shy and will always try to run away from trouble but if they do take to the air, they fly low over the ground on their huge wings.

There are many other striking birds which inhabit the region.

There are the large glossy ibis which fly low over the reed beds and plunge into the shallow waters in search of food. There are the white storks nesting on the rooftops of the village houses and foraging over a wide area for food to feed their young. Other exciting birds to watch include the great white heron, grey heron and purple heron — which is actually brown. There are spoonbills, white storks and other long-legged waders, and cranes, if you are lucky enough to spot them. In the spring you can hear the booming call of the bitterns as they seek mates or protect territories, while overhead you are likely to spot one of the largest collections of birds of prey in Europe. There are many species of eagle, harrier and buzzard. It is possible to spot more than thirty birds of prey enjoying the thermals, including honey buzzard, buzzard, hen harrier, marsh harrier, golden eagle, imperial eagle, sparrow hawk, kestrel, peregrine and black kite. You can watch the spectacular aerobatic displays of the marsh buzzard, a slender winged bird of prey whose mating ritual consists of eccentric aerobatics performed above the sedimentation zone at the water's edge. This buzzard only builds its nest in the reeds, and several dozen pairs breed around the lake. There is probably no other place in Europe so rich in birds of prey.

Among the reed birds there are rare warblers and other small, secretive birds. There are also colonies of great reed warblers and you can hear more often than see Savi's warbler and the shy grasshopper warbler. Other rare members of this reed- and scrub-loving family to be seen are icterine, Dartford and melodious warblers.

Almost all members of the tit family are represented including the more unusual long-tailed, bearded, marsh, willow, penduline and crested tits. There are colonies of the exotic and beautiful bee eaters and rollers, and you can easily spot hoopoes and water kingfisher.

Geese and water fowl abound both on the lakes and in the surrounding marshes. There are Canada, Barnacle, Brent, Grey lag and white fronted geese, shelduck, mallard, teal, gadwall, garganey, pintail, shoveler, pochard, tufted, goldeneye and mandarin ducks. There is also the rare ferruginous duck. Find a suitable vantage point overlooking the marshes and you can spot hundreds of waders during migration periods, and crakes and rails all the year round.

There are all the common species of woodpecker, as well as the rare wryneck, grey headed and Syrian woodpecker. You can see crested larks, most of the wagtails and pipits, shrikes, flycatchers, chats and thrushes, including the beautiful bluethroats.

Hidden in the reeds you will also spot brown frogs and red-bellied toads which do a head dive into the water when danger approaches. If you are patient you can see deer and red squirrels in the wooded hills, stoat, weasel and hare on the plains, and musk rats in the marshes. On the plains you should also be able to see many types of lizzards and snakes, mostly smooth and grass varieties. As the hills merge with the Alps you can see marmots diving for cover as you approach.

The best time for a walk by the lake is at daybreak or dusk, but there is always something to see. At dusk, however, the atmosphere is heightened by the wind in the reeds, the incessant noise of the frogs and toads, and the calls of literally tens of thousands of birds.

Lange Lacke

To the east of Lake Neusiedl lies Lange Lacke bird sanctuary, in an area known as the Seewinkel, which extends into Hungary. It is considered one of the three most important sanctuaries for aquatic birds in Europe along with the Camargue in the south of France, and the Coto Donana on Spain's Atlantic coast. It is open to the public all year round and there is a small admission charge.

Every autumn evening up to 30,000 wild geese arrive here to break their southward migration journey. They appear on the horizon in their immaculate V-formations — a flight pattern now known to save energy — and at the end of their approach over the lake, they run over the water on their webbed feet before gliding to a halt. Only when the lake freezes over do they continue their migration to warmer climates in the south.

Güssing Game Park

The game park, which is within the grounds of Güssing palace, covers just over a square mile, and is located just under 1km (just over half a mile) north-east of Güssing in the far south of Burgenland. There are also open enclosures in the palace grounds which offer an opportunity to watch the animals in near-natural surroundings and at very close quarters from specially built observation posts. Both areas of the park are used for zoological experiments.

The enclosures contain aurochs, wild horses, red deer, Hungarian steppe cattle, black water buffalo, Korean stags, fallow deer, mountain goats, wild pigs, Macedonian dwarf monkeys, moufflons, wild boar, Balkan sheep and zebus. The park is open all year and evening visits are specially recommended. There is a charge for admission.

The palace was a medieval fortress which was enlarged in the sixteenth and seventeenth centuries. It has a fine baronial hall, an art gallery and an arms collection.

The black cat which sits on top of the best barrel of wine

Discovering the Wines of Burgenland

The shorelands of Europe's most mysterious lake provide some of the world's most exotic and unusual wines, most of which are available in Britain and the United States and all of which can be tasted locally. Despite its relatively small size, Burgenland is Austria's second largest wine producer, contributing a third of total production — about 125 million litres out of 370 million litres. Although it became part of Austria in 1921 its climate and geography is totally different to any other part of the country. It has been producing fine wine for many centuries helped by the very hot dry summers and cold winters, more typical of central than western Europe.

There are two main wine growing areas. In the south there is **Eisenberg**, where both red and white wines are produced, and around **Lake Neusiedl** in the north, where many fine wines are to be had. The main red grape variety and a typical speciality is the Blaufraenkisch, or Blue Franconian, although other red varieties now used include St Laurent, Blauer Portugieser and Blauer Burgunder (Pinot Noir). White grapes include Grüner Veltliner, Rheinriesling, Wälschriesling, Müller-Thurgau, Muscat Ottonel, Neuberger,

Traminer and Weissburgunder.

The larger wine growing area is around Lake Neusiedl and centres on Rust. The lake has a profound influence on local wine making. Because of its shallowness, the lake heats quickly in the summer, and it retains this heat through the autumn, thus keeping the surrounding area humid and permitting late harvests in the vineyards. These are essential conditions for producing the highest quality wines.

Wine making in the Rust-Neusiedl area may even date back to Roman times. It is certain that in 1639, the people of Rust petitioned Leopold I to grant them a royal licence because 'the only way to make money is wine growing'. In 1681, Rust was made a free city, part of the annual payment for the privilege being to supply 30,000 litres of fine wines to the royal court in Vienna.

Vines grow east, north and west of the lake and are protected both by it and the Leitha mountain. In the sandy soils of the Seewinkel, ungrafted vines still produce grapes. The sand prevented the spread of phylloxera which devastated most of the vineyards in Europe, and this is one of the few remaining that can still grow vines on its original rootstock, rather than having to graft them on to phylloxera rootstock imported from the United States.

White wines are produced from Wälschriesling and Muscat Ottonel, and good reds from Blaufränkische. At the end of long hot summers, the grapes are picked late so they are crammed with sugar to produce the famous Ruster Ausbruch wine. The main wine centres are Oggau, Mörbisch, St Margarethen and Rust. On the eastern shore the principal centre is Gols. The vineyards are close to the lakes and planted in sandy soils to produce *sandweine*. Places to visit include Gross-Höflein, Klein-Höflein, St Georgen, Podersdorf, Illmitz and Apetlon.

In the foothills of the Rosalien mountains is the Mattersburg wine producing district. The vineyards produce mainly red wines. Places to visit include Pöttelsdorf, Trauersdorf, Neckenmarkt, Deutsch-Kreutz and Lutzmannsburg.

The final wine producing area is in south Burgenland around Eisenberg and Rechnitz, which specialises in very drinkable, soft red wines. Following the Magyar battles in the twelfth century, the dukes of Güssing earned themselves a great deal of money by recultivating the vineyards. In later years, however, it was the Cistercian monks who took over the vineyards and kept the fine wine making traditions alive. **Rechnitz** is a small wine town lying at the foot of the Geschriebenstein. The Rechnitz river actually divides the town's

A Klapotetz, a noise-making machine to scare off birds from vineyards

market, so there is a German market on one side, and a Hungarian market on the other. The well fortified castle town of **Güssing**, and **Heiligenbrunn**, about 8km (5 miles) to the south-east, with its picturesque thatched, white-painted wine cellars, are both well worth making a detour for.

Burgenland is best known for its production of vintage wines. These are very strictly defined by the Austrian Government into the following categories: *spätlese* — a quality wine which must be made from completely ripe grapes, picked after the main harvest; *auslese* which is a *spätlese* made from hand picked grapes; *beerenauslese* which is an *auslese* wine made from overripe grapes; and *trockenbeerenauslese* which is made from overripe grapes that have been allowed to dry out totally on the vine until they have shrivelled to resemble raisins. The grapes are then hand picked, and the resulting wine is heavy with natural sugar and golden yellow in colour.

The other categories of wine worth looking out for are *ausbruch* which is special to Austria, and *eiswein*. *Ausbruch* is a wine made exclusively from overripe grapes which have started to dry naturally on the vines. It is full of natural sugar. *Eiswein* is made from grapes left on the vines until after a hard frost. They are then picked early in the day and pressed while still frozen.

At the end of September, Burgenland celebrates the grape harvest and there are lots of street processions led by brass bands and fireworks. On 11 November there are goose fairs to celebrate Martinmas. This date is also important for another reason: after 11 November the wine from the last vintage becomes *alter wein* (old wine) and can no longer be sold in the *heurigen*.

Exploring Eisenstadt

Eisenstadt lies at an altitude of 180m (about 590ft) among the warm southern slopes of the Leithagebirge hills, surrounded by forests, vineyards and orchards. The town has a population of about 11,000 and has been the capital of the province since 1924.

Although the administrative centre of the region and an important wine making town, Eisenstadt's growth has been stunted because of its proximity to Vienna, and it is still little more than a large village with a single main street. At the top of the street is the Esterházy Palace, and near the other end is the lane leading to the house where Haydn lived when he was in their service.

The town owes its fame to these two great names: the Hungarian Esterházy family, and Josef Haydn, one of the world's greatest composers. The Esterházy family claimed their descent from Attila the Hun and were in great part responsible for the success of the Hapsburgs reign in Hungaria, although they were always fiercely independent. In 1809 the Prince risked the wrath of Napoleon I by rejecting the offer of the Hungarian Crown. They established themselves in the town in 1296 and quickly became champions, defending many minority groups including the Jews who settled in the area under their protection. Even before this, however, there had been a synagogue in the town.

The prince's castle, Schloss Esterházy took 10 years to build and was completed in 1673 by the Italian architect Carlo Antonio Carlone, on the site of a medieval fortress. The original palace was surrounded by four huge walls around a central courtyard, a court of honour, and each of the four corner towers was capped by a massive dome. Early in the eighteenth century the castle's architecture was modified by the French architect Moreau, as the original building was considered a little too ornate with its great domes. Although the Esterházy family had many magnificent palaces, this was considered their favourite.

Behind the garden frontage and impressive façade decorated by the busts of ancestors of the Esterházy family, Kings of Hungary and generals, there is a simple courtyard. The rooms are elegantly furnished including some early nineteenth-century Chinese wallcoverings and baroque furniture. As you enter the courtyard, take the staircase on the right to get to the Haydn Room.

Josef Haydn (1732-1809) was in the service of Prince Esterházy for thirty years, although some of this time was spent at the family's other palaces in Hungary. He was invited to become assistant conductor in 1761 and his tasks were numerous, from conducting the orchestra and choir and writing music to looking after all the musical instruments. In 1766 at the age of 34 he was appointed musical director although he still had to combine this with his duties of musical librarian and administrator. He found time, however, to compose, and having his own orchestra and choir, and a theatre for them to perform in, his fame steadily grew throughout Europe. He became a friend of Mozart and his greatest inspiration. Haydn died in Vienna in 1809 but his body was brought back to Eisenstadt by Prince Nikolaus Esterházy in 1820. Haydn's head had been stolen by an admirer but this was finally traced in 1895 and put on display under a glass case in the museum of the Society of Friends of Music in Vienna. Body and head were finally re-united in 1932 when Haydn was laid to rest in 1932 in a mausoleum built by Prince Paul Esterházy in the Kalvarienbergkirche, the hilltop Calvary church in Eisenstad.

His house, at 21 Haydngasse, where he lived between 1766 and 1778, is now a museum containing the memorabilia of his work and lifestyle. It contains many of Haydn's manuscripts, including that of the *Creation*, written in his own hand. It is a small house and you get to it by going through a covered passage into a charming courtyard, usually full of flowers. It is open between Easter and October. Since 1982 Eistenstadt has held an annual Haydn festival.

The Haydn Room is on the first floor of the *Schloss* and it is open all year round. During Haydn's time it was the grand state hall, and scene of some of the composer's finest concerts. There are guided tours in English. The room is still decorated in its lavish eighteenth-century style, with frescoes and a magnificent ceiling painted by Carpoforo Tencala. It is still used today for recitals.

Behind the *Schloss* there is a park with two small lakes, an orangery, temple and some delightful walks through the trees, and opposite is the town hall with its colonnaded façade. The Haupstrasse is the centre of the town and has a fountain, the Florianibrunnen, and a trinity column.

The Bergkirche and Mount Calvary are to the west of the town, on the road to Vienna. The Mount Calvary is unusual because it is wholly artificially constructed. Along the stairs of the Way of the Passion are caves and chapels, and twenty-four stations leading up to the Chapel of the Cross. In 1960 the parish church of St Martin in Pfarrgasse, was raised to the status of a cathedral. Parts date back to the twelfth century but the fortifications in the massive tower indicate that the present building was designed to repulse the Turks in the fifteenth century. Inside there have been many alterations. The pulpit and organ are baroque, there are two portraits by Dorfmeister (1777), and a number of medieval tombstones. Until 1938 there was a Jewish community in the lower town and the cemetery has survived as well as three houses which are now part of the Burgenland museum in Museumgasse.

The museum is very comprehensive and covers every aspect of the history of the province, and especially the development of the vineyards. There is a superb mosaic floor from a Roman villa, and 'moon idols' found in the excavation of a neolithic settlement at Loretto, about 12km (8 miles) north of Eisenstadt on the Leithagebirge.

The road east out of Eisenstadt, towards Lake Neusiedl, is called the Weinstrasse and is lined with cellars and stalls selling wine and local produce like corn dollies, plants and fruit.

The town of **Neckenmarkt**, 32km (20 miles) south of Eisenstadt upholds the centuries old ceremony of banner waving. This dates back to the Thirty Years War when the soldiers of the town commandeered fourteen enemy standards in 1620. To commemorate the event the town still holds a procession in which the banners are paraded on the eve of the first Sunday after Corpus Christi.

The village of **Raiding** is 46km (29 miles) south of Eisenstadt and the birthplace of Franz Liszt. Take route 50 out of Eisenstadt, and just after Weppersdorf turn left on the B62 to Horitshon, and then right the 3km (2 miles) to Raiding.

It is a small village with a population of about 2,100 and proud of its Liszt museum, Liszt-Geburtshaus, which is where the composer was born. Liszt's father was employed by the Esterházy family as bailiff to the estate and the house went with the job. The museum is open from Easter to the end of October, and contains many of Liszt's documents and the old church organ on which he used to play.

If you leave Eisenstadt on the Ruster Strasse (route 59a) to go to Rust, you will go past the Liszt statue on your right.

It is worth visiting the baroque pilgrimage church of **Loretto** to the north of Eisenstadt. A Roman settlement has been found nearby as well as Bronze Age graves and Illyrian burial mounds.

A Tour Through Burgenland

There are many small country roads to drive along if you want to explore the province south of Eisenstadt. At one stage at about 6km (3¹/₂ miles) south of Forchtenstein, the province narrows into a bottle neck only 6km (3¹/₂ miles) wide before spreading out again into the mountains. There is no need to rush in Burgenland, so no need to take the main roads. There is a delightful drive from Eisenstadt which takes you down through the centre of the province to Güssing, and you can spend a few days here exploring and walking, or continue your journey through Austria, by travelling on to Graz, for instance. The route takes you through the mountains and past many of the castles for which the region is famous. Many of these castles have now been converted to hotels and make excellent atmospheric places to stay.

From Eisenstadt take either the route 50 or S31 south down to **Mattersburg,** a small market town famous for its strawberries in early summer. It has an early fifteenth century church in a fortified cemetery, and 3km (2 miles) to the south-west is Forchtenau, dominated by its castle which crowns a spur below the Rosaliengebirge, which rises to 748m (2,453ft). A winding road climbs up to Schloss Forchtenstein, which is approached by a bridge across a dry moat cut into the rock. The castle was built in the fourteenth century, and the bastions were added in the seventeenth century. It became the property of the Esterházy family in 1622 and portraits of members of the family still hang in the picture gallery. There is also a fine collection of arms and armour. If you make your way back to the main roads south they start to climb higher into the mountains passing through what is known as the 'waist' of Burgenland, with the Ödenburger Gebirge (606m, 1,988ft) to the east. The crest of the mountain marks the border with Hungary. To the south-west rises the hilly Bucklige Welt, and to the south-east, the vineyards of the red Blaufränkischer, which extend as far as the border.

The S31 and route 50 continue to run parallel to each other down to Weppersdorf with its castle, Schloss Kobersdorf. Building started in the twelfth century and continued off and on for 500 years. There are a couple of comfortable guesthouses in the village, which makes a convenient base if you want to explore the area. About 11km (7 miles) to the east along the B62 is Raiding, already referred to as the birthplace of Liszt. Further along the B62 and almost on the border is the village of **Deutschkreutz.** The Esterházys rebuilt the old castle here in 1625 and in recent times it was the home of the artist Anton

Lehmden. South of Weppersdorf there is a camp site and this whole area is a photographer's paradise. In the winter it resounds to the calls of skiers. To the west is the small village of **Landsee**, famous for its now ruined thirteenth-century keep, while about 8km (5 miles) south on the B61 there is **Stoob**, a village of potters.

The road continues round **Oberpullendorf**, which has a seventeenth-century castle, and the B61 swings round in a loop touching the Hungarian border at Rattersdorf where there is a customs post, before travelling westwards to rejoin the route 50 just beyond Lockenhaus.

It is worth stopping in **Lockenhaus** because it has a marvellous church, dating from the middle of the seventeenth century and richly decorated. Above it stands the *Burg* (castle) built in 1254 with a fine Gothic hall. Dominating the view to the south is the Günser Gebirge, a range of hills which stretch across the border into Hungary. If you take route 56 south from Lockenhaus, after about 10km (6 miles) you will spot the castle of Geschriebenstein towering above you on the left hand side of the road. If you take route 50 south you will come to **Bernstein** which has a thirteenth-century fortress, almost completely rebuilt in the seventeenth century. It is now a hotel.

Follow the road to **Mariasdorf** with its striking late Gothic church. Just out of town there is a minor road on the left which will take you to **Stadtschlaining**, with its fifteenth-century walls and Gothic and baroque church containing a classical high altar. The thirteenth-century *Schloss*, now a hotel, stands on the rocks above, and dominates the village. The *Schloss* was rebuilt in the fifteenth century by Andreas Baumkircher, who was later one of the ringleaders of a revolt against Friedrich III. The revolt failed, he was captured and beheaded at Graz. Some of the rooms still contain stucco work dating back to the end of the seventeenth century.

Back on the main road again, the route bypasses the village of Jormannsdorf with a seventeenth-century *Schloss*. A little further south and there is a turning on the left to the small spa town of **Bad Tatzmannsdorf**, where a typical Burgenland village has been reconstructed. Continuing south you come to **Oberwart**, a town famous for its wines and surrounded by vineyards. It lies in the fertile valley of the river Pinka. After sampling the wine, and then taking a good long walk along the river banks through the vineyards, take the B57 south through the Strembach valley to **Stegersbach**, which has a very interesting little local museum. At St Michael in Burgenland you can make another detour by travelling east to Kohfidisch. There are a number of treasures to be visited in this area. At **Kohfidisch** there is a fine eighteenth-century *Schloss* just north of the crossroads, and at **Eberau**, about 12km (7¹/₂ miles) south-east, and again almost on the Hungarian border, there is a fine moated castle. Following the road south for about 3km (2 miles), still hugging the border, and you come to **Gaas**, and nearby, its pilgrimage church of Maria Weinberg. It was built in 1524 but was later dramatically altered under the influence of the baroque style. Follow the B56 to **Güssing** and the end of the journey. The church, Pfarrkirche, has the famous Batthyány crypt, built in 1648, in which lies the lead coffin of Prince Karl Batthyány (1697-1772). The Batthyány Schloss dominates the town and contains a fine collection of paintings, many of members of the noble family. Old Masters hanging there include Dürer, Brueghel and Cranach. There is also a fine collection of Hungarian and Turkish armour used at the Battle of Mohács in 1526. There are a number of other collections on view, including a very early organ.

Further Information
— Burgenland —

Activities

Andau
Horse riding, fishing, tennis, cycle trails, swimming.

Apetlon
Horse riding, fishing, tennis, cycle hire, cycle trails and fishing.

Bad Tatzmannsdorf
Fishing, tennis, cycle hire and cycle trails, indoor and outdoor swimming facilities.

Bernstein
Swimming

Breitenbrunn
Fishing, tennis, cycle hire and cycle trails, swimming, yachting and surf boarding.

Deutschkreutz
Tennis and swimming

Deutsch Schützen-Eisenberg
Swimming

Donnerskirchen
Swimming, tennis, cycle trails.

Drassburg-Baumgarten
Horse riding, swimming.

Drassmarkt
Tennis and swimming.

Eisenstadt
Cycle hire, cycle trails, indoor and outdoor swimming.

Eltendorf
Fishing, Tennis

Frankenau-Unterpullendorf
Horse riding.

Frauenkirchen
Horse riding, fishing, tennis, swimming.

Gattendorf-Neudorf
Fishing, tennis, swimming.

Gerersdorf-Sulz
Tennis.

Gols
Swimming, tennis

Grafenschachen
Fishing, tennis, swimming.

Grosspetersdorf
Tennis, swimming

Grosswarasdorf
Fishing

Güssing
Game park, fishing, tennis, cycle hire, cycle trails and swimming.

Halbturn
Fishing, tennis

Heiligenbrunn
Horse riding, swimming, fishing, tennis, cycle trails.

Heiligenkreuz
Horse riding, fishing, tennis, swimming, cycling.

Horitschon
Horse riding, fishing tennis.

Hornstein
Tennis.

Illmitz
Horse riding, fishing, tennis, cycle hire, cycle trails, swimming, yachting, surf-boarding.

Jennersdorf
Fishing, tennis, swimming, cycle trails.

Kaisersdorf
Tennis, swimming.

Kittsee
Tennis.

Klingenbach
Tennis.

Kobersdorf
Tennis, cycle trails.

Kohfidisch
Swimming.

Kukmirn
Fishing, tennis.

Lackenbach
Swimming.

Leithaprodersdorf
Tennis.

Litzelsdorf
Fishing.

Lockenhaus
Tennis, swimming.

Loipersbach
Fishing, swimming.

Mannersdorf
Swimming, tennis.

Mariasdorf
Swimming.

Markt Allhau
Fishing, swimming.

Mattersburg
Tennis, swimming.

Minihof-Liebau
Tennis.

Mönchhof
Tennis.

Mörbisch am See
Horse riding, fishing, tennis, cycle hire, cycle trails, swimming, yachting and surf boarding.

Mogersdorf
Fishing, tennis.

Neuberg
Tennis.

Neudörfl
Tennis, swimming.

Neufeld
Horse riding, tennis, swimming, yachting, surf boarding.

Neuhaus
Cycle trails, swimming.

Neusiedl am See
Horse riding, fishing, tennis, indoor and outdoor swimming, yachting, surf boarding.

Neutal
Tennis, swimming.

Nickelsdorf
Tennis.

Nikitsch
Tennis.

Oberpullendorf
Tennis, swimming.

Oberschützen
Horse riding, cycle trails, swimming.

Oberwart
Tennis, swimming, cycle trails.

Oggau
Fishing, swimming, cycling.

Pamhagen
Horse riding, fishing, tennis, cycle trails, swimming.

Pinkafeld
Tennis, indoor and outdoor swimming.

Piringsdorf-Unterrabnitz
Tennis.

Podersdorf am See
Horse riding, fishing, tennis, cycle hire and cycle trails, swimming, yachting, surf boarding.

Pöttsching
Horse riding, swimming, tennis.

Purbach
Horse riding, fishing, tennis, cycle trails, swimming, yachting and surf boarding.

Rechnitz
Fishing, swimming, tennis, cycle trails.

Ritzing
Swimming, tennis.

Rohrbach
Tennis.

Rudersdorf
Tennis, fishing.

Rust
Fishing, tennis, cycle hire and cycle trails, swimming, yachting, surf boarding.

St Andrä
Horse riding, fishing, tennis, swimming.

St Margarethen
Horse riding, tennis, swimming.

St Martin
Tennis.

St Michael
Fishing, tennis, swimming, yachting, surf boarding.

Sauerbrunn
Swimming, tennis.

Schattendorf
Tennis, swimming.

Siegendorf
Horse riding, fishing, tennis, swimming.

Sieggraben
Tennis.

Sigless
Swimming.

Stadtschlaining
Tennis.

Stegersbach
Horse riding, tennis, cycle trails.

Steinbrunn-Zillingtal
Tennis, swimming.

Stinatz
Tennis.

Stoob
Tennis.

Tadten
Fishing, tennis.

Tobaj
Tennis.

Trausdorf
Tennis.

Wallern
Cycle trails, swimming.

Weiden am See
Fishing, tennis, cycle trails, swimming, yachting, surf boarding.

Wiesen
Tennis.

Winden am See
Fishing.

Wolfau
Fishing, swimming.

Wulkaprodersdorf
Tennis.

Places to Visit in the Area

Bad Tatzmannsdorf
Open-Air Museum
☎ (03354) 284
Open: all year round, dawn to dusk.

Bernstein
Castle
☎ (03354) 220
Open: all year round 8am-12noon and 1-5pm.

Museum
☎ (03354) 320
Open: all year round, 9am-12noon and 1.30-5pm.

Breitenbrunn
Museum
☎ (02683) 5213
Open: all year round, 9am-12noon and 1-5pm.

Deutschkreutz
Museum
☎ (02613) 203
Open: all year round, 8am-4pm.

Eberau
Moated castle
Open: all year round.

Eisenstadt
Castle and Haydn Room
☎ (02682) 3384
Open: June to September 9am-5pm; October to May 10am-4pm. English guided tours every half hour July to September, every hour October to May, and June.

Haydn's House
☎ (02682) 2652
Open: Easter to October 9am-12noon and 1-5pm.

Museums
☎ (02682) 5040
Open: all year round, 10am-5pm; Saturday and Sunday 10am-4pm.

Monastery
Open: all year round.

Forchtenstein
Castle
☎ (02626) 8212
Open: all year round, 8am-12noon and 1-4pm.

Gattendorf-Neudorf
Museum
Open: all year round.

Güssing
Pfarrkirche
Open: all year round.

Castle
☎ (03322) 24 91
Open: all year round, 9-11am and 1-5pm.

Palace and Game Park
Open: all year round.
Evening visits recommended.

Monastery
Open: all year round.

Halbturn
Baroque Palace
☎ (02172) 2237 or 8577
Open: all year round.

Heiligenbrunn
Museum
Open: all year round.

Illmitz
Museum
☎ (02175) 2015
Open: all year round, 8am-12noon and 3-9pm.

Jormannsdorf
Castle
Open: all year round.

Kittsee
Palace
☎ (02143) 2304
Open: all year round, 10am-4pm.

Kobersdorf
Palace
☎ (02618) 8200
Open: all year round, 10am-4pm.

Museum
Open: all year round.

Kohfidisch
Castle
Open: all year round.

Landsee
Fortress
Largest in Burgenland.
Open: all year round.

Litzelsdorf
Museum
Open: all year round.

Lockenhaus
Castle
☎ (02616) 2394
Open: all year round, 8am-5pm.

Museum
Open: all year round.

Loretto
Seventeenth-century monastery
Open: all year round.

Lutzmannsburg
Museum
Open: all year round, 8am-6pm.

Mattersburg
Museum
Open: all year round, 10am-12noon
and 2-4pm.

Mörbisch am See
Museum
Open: all year round.

Mogersdorf
Museum
☎ (03325) 8217
Open: all year round, 10am-6pm.

Neuhaus
Museum
Open: all year round.

Neusiedl am See
Museum
☎ (02167) 84493
Open: April to October, 2.30-
6.30pm.

Nikitsch
Museum
☎ (02614) 8314
Open: all year round 9am-8pm.

Oberpullendorf
Castle
☎ (02612) 2207
Open: all year round, 8am-4pm.

Museum
Open: all year round.

Oberschützen
Museum
☎ (03353) 6357
Open: all year round, 8am-12noon
and 2-6pm.

Pilgersdorf
Museum
Open: all year round.

Pinkafeld
Museum
☎ (03357) 2351
Open: all year round, 8am-12noon
and 1-4pm

Podersdorf am See
Museum
☎ (02177) 2345
Open: all year round, 10am-
12.30pm and 3.30-7pm.

Raiding
Museum
☎ (02619) 7220
Open: all year round.

Rust
Museum
☎ (02685) 468
Open: all year round, 9am-12noon
and 1-6pm.

St Margarethen
'Fairy tale' Forest
Open: all year round.

Museum
Open: all year round.

Siegendorf
Museum
☎ (02687) 8261
Open: all year round.

Stadtschlaining
Castle
Open: all year round.

Museum
Open: all year round.

Stegersbach
Museum
☎ (03326) 2577
Open: all year round, 9am-12noon
and 1-5pm.

Steinberg-Dörfl
Museum
Open: all year round.

Stinatz
Museum
Open: all year round

Stoob
Museum
☎ (02612) 22436
Open: all year round.

Weppersdorf
Castle
Open: all year round.

Wiesen
Museum
Open: all year round.

Winden am See
Museum
Open: all year round.

Tourist Information Office

Burgenland Information Office
Schloss Esterházy
A-7000
Eistenstadt
☎ (2682) 3384

Index